Adrian Van Eck

Your Guide To Personal Wealth

Presented By
The Financial Research Center, Inc.

Drawings by Rick Keene.
Most charts produced by Thomas Myles, overall art production director.

Adrian Van Eck

DEDICATION
To George Danforth

Back in the "Eisenhower 1950's" I had the privilege of serving a multi-year apprenticeship in Massachusetts under a man whom I regard as the greatest economic forecaster who ever lived. His name was George Danforth. At a time when many others (including a famous Harvard professor) were predicting the imminent return of the Great Depression, George Danforth was writing extremely well-researched forecasts predicting a new boom and bull market. George Danforth said (and taught me to believe) that the Full Employment Act of 1946 (see dotted vertical line on facing chart) had made depressions obsolete in America. For the first time, the Federal Government had committed itself to managing and regulating the economy. George Danforth was certain that growth would continue along a planned, acceptable course - with both booms and recessions kept to moderate limits. He has been proven correct by time over the past thirty years as you can see. Unfortunately, the fame that might have been his was eclipsed by the presence *next door to us* of the great Roger Babson - the man who had correctly predicted the stock market crash of 1929. This guide is meant to honor and continue George Danforth's pioneer work in the field of economic forecasting.

ADRIAN VAN ECK.

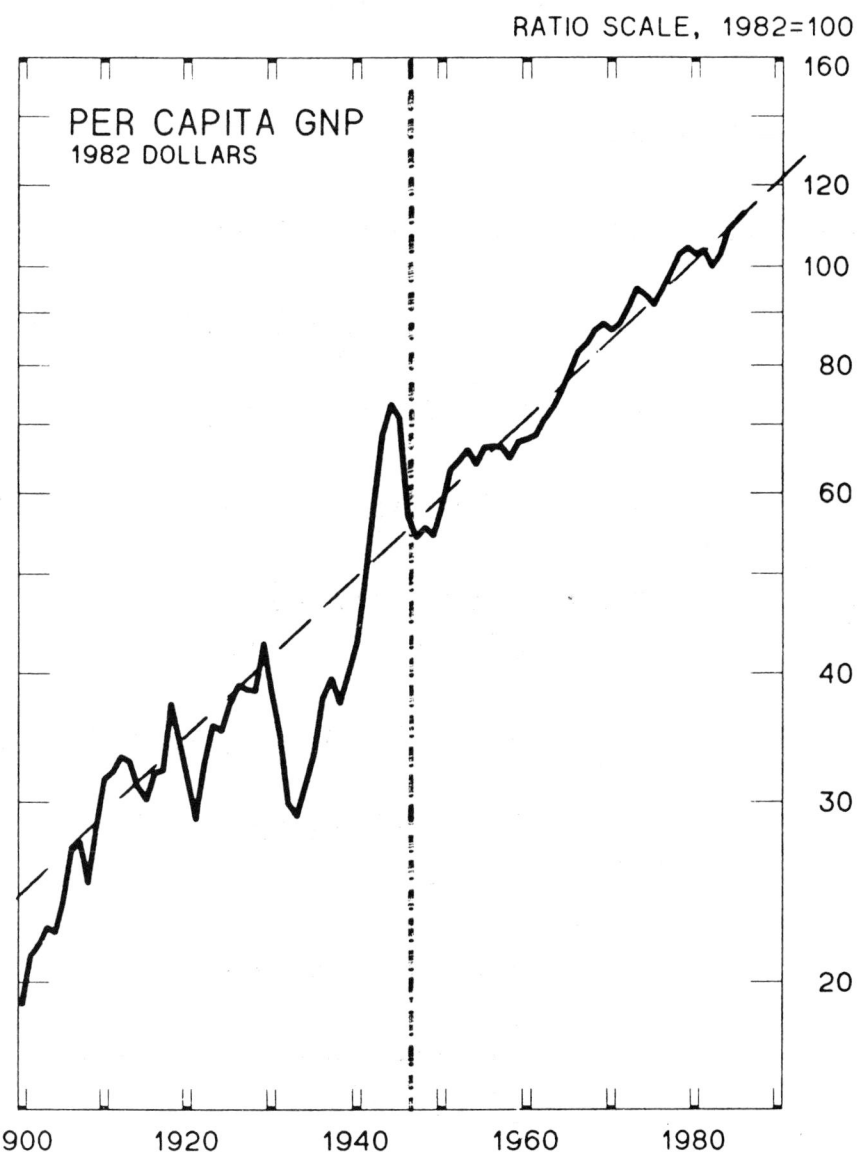

RATIO SCALE, 1982=100

PER CAPITA GNP
1982 DOLLARS

Adrian Van Eck

Table of Contents

Foreword

Boom With Deflation!

BOOM WITH DEFLATION. IT'S COMING FOR SURE! IT'S THE ONE THING NO ONE EXPECTS. I SEE NEW FORECASTS OF A BOOM WITH INFLATION... OF A RECESSION WITH INFLA-TION... AND OF A RECESSION WITH DEFLATION. BUT NO ONE - AT LEAST NO ONE I CAN FIND - IS TALKING ABOUT *A BOOM WITH DEFLATION.* YOUR CLEAREST PROOF SUCH A RARE PHENOMINON IS COMING IS THE HOWLING AND SCREAMING, HAIR TEARING AND BREAST BEATING, THE CRYING AND FINGER POINTING GOING ON ALL AROUND YOU SINCE OCTOBER 19, 1987.

From the time I began writing my own forecasting Letter, I had in mind an elite audience. I made it a rule - which I have never broken - never to agree to appear on television or radio... never to address a convention or a business group and *never, never to tailor my messages just to seek short-term popularity.* It was always my intent, and remains my plan today, to find people who are intelligent enough, open-minded enough, alert enough, sensitive enough and *self-confident enough to appreciate the truth about Money and People. For it is Money and People that make markets go. The rest comes afterward!*

As I see it *999 out of every 1000 Americans and Canadians would not believe my Letters.* Most people are locked into a set of mistaken and false beliefs about the world... and they go through their entire lives being *surprised* again and again by events that they later say "could not have been foreseen by anybody!" You must have heard that expression a hundred times of late, have you not? But it does not have to be that way. I heard from a subscriber - an American - who had just had a *most remarkable experience in the British West Indies.* He had struck up a poolside conversation with a gentleman from Canada. In the space of a few casual questions and answers they found that they shared, in common, *an intense awareness and understanding of current economic, political and financial events. Suddenly, in a flash of insight, the American leaned closer and said: "By any chance, have you ever heard of Adrian Van Eck?" The American who told us this story said his new Canadian friend just smiled.*

I loved that story when I heard it. I still do.

Permit me to share with you another Letter I have

received. The mail brought this message from the Vice President of a major brokerage firm.

"Dear Mr. Van Eck,

"In addition to your Forecast Letter I subscribe to several other services, I sit on a number of investment commitees advised by the most prestigious banks in New York City and I have access to the best technical and fundamental analysts in the investment industry.

"You were the only advisory service in August and September, 1987, to put up the red flag. It is only now that analysts are talking about the drop in housing starts and lower automobile production. Your Letter in September 1987 rang the warning bell loud and clear and I congratulate you on your foresight and financial wisdom. I have always read your Forecast Letter with great care but from now on I will read it with greater care."

OKAY. *I CONFESS THAT MADE MY DAY... NO NEED TO DENY THAT.*

A long and deep study of history has persuaded me that people do not sit idly by and let their fate overwhelm them. This is the real reason I simply have to doubt the panic stories... the scare stories... the hysterical stories that so many advisory Letters are now conjuring up for 1989 and 1990. *If you were to believe these folks, you* *might just as well throw in the towel now... because bad times are coming... we are all doomed... gold is going to $5,000 an ounce because the Fed will print so much money they will have to call in all of America's savings and replace it with new funny money... play money worth only 10¢ on the dollar. And there is nothing anyone can do to save us!*

RUBBISH! What is wrong with America that we even listen to that kind of junk? That is just *not* the way it is here. (Or in Canada either!) You know, a few years ago I saw a television special on problems in a Cairo, Egypt slum. The people in this slum were just sitting there... waiting. *And there were flies everywhere...* on their eyelids and their noses and even on their lips. And the interviewer said something like: "Why don't you brush the flies away... and maybe get a sticky fly-catcher to hang up... then find out where they are hatching and kill them, *before they give you and your children some kind of sickness?"* And the discouraged, fatalistic man sitting there replied: "It is Allah's will that the flies are here. If Allah did not want the flies to be here, he would not put them here!" As I recall, the interviewer turned away to hide his own feelings. But I could guess what those feelings must be. *"That's not the way we think in America... not the way we do things!"* WE DO NOT SURRENDER TO FATE! WE GRAB HOLD OF IT AND WE SHAKE IT UNTIL IT GIVES US WHAT WE WANT! That is the way it was in 1620... in 1776... in 1861. *That is the way it was during the thirty-year-long period of change and expansion after the Civil War, as America developed the West!*

It is the way America was in 1917. Europe was exhausted from three years of war. The Marines *landed* and moved up towards the sound of shooting. On the way they came upon thousands of French troops on their way back from the front. A French officer held up his hand and told the Leathernecks "STOP! The Germans have mounted a major offensive. We have been ordered to retreat. *You must turn around and retreat too!"*

THE AMERICAN OFFICER STUCK HIS CHIN OUT AND SAID: *"RETREAT, HELL! WE JUST GOT HERE!"* He waved at his men and said: "Follow me!" The Marines moved right through the lines of the tired, straggling French soldiers. *And at the crack of dawn the next day they fixed bayonets, charged out of their trenches and stormed the German lines. The Germans fought fiercely and then broke and ran. Later the German High Command demanded to know of an officer why his battle-hardened combat troops had yielded like this. He saluted crisply and then snapped: "THESE AMERICANS ARE NOT HUMAN. I SWEAR TO YOU THEY ARE DEVIL-DOGS!"* (The Marines heard of this and adopted the nickname.) But, you see, that is the way we Americans have always been. And that is the way we always *will* be.

Yes, there are problems in the economy. But now

America is standing up to these problems. *That is all it takes. Stand up to them. We are not fatalists in America. We do what has to be done. And we make things better than they were before the problems appeared!*

NOT A LITTLE BETTER. A LOT BETTER! I agree wholeheartedly with John Templeton, the founder of 8 Templeton Funds based in St. Petersburg, Florida. Mr. Templeton, a self-made multi-millionaire *cut from the mold of the giants who built America,* says: "Better trained managers and continued research will lead to *higher-quality and lower-cost goods and services, and will likely double the standard of living over the next thirty years."* He added: *"We think you can deal with the future more clearly if you don't focus on the next week or the next year."* (End quote.)

I COULD NOT POSSIBLY AGREE MORE! I found myself thinking along similar lines a some months ago when the television mini-series "Napoleon and Josephine" was on. I noticed, as you probably did, that *the series played fast and loose with history.* Napoleon's early career, for example, was changed drastically. He was shown as being put in jail for refusing to serve the tyrant, when as a matter of fact he was jailed precisely because people had feared that he was a close and loyal ally of the tyrant. He was shown as being very important *before* meeting Josephine, the widow of a general beheaded in the revolution. The fact is that he met her *early*... and *she used her considerable influence with her friends to advance his career at a lightning pace.* And of course there were the ladies' necklines. Television censors forced the show's producer to cut them higher than they really were after the French Revolution... or the series would have been banned from network television. BUT DESPITE THESE SMALL "REVISIONS" OF HISTORY *THERE WAS SOMETHING ACCURATE ABOUT THE SERIES THAT CAUGHT MY EYE AGAIN AND AGAIN AND AGAIN! It was this: Napoleon and his wife, even when he was Emperor of France, lived a life that was not as comfortable or luxurious as that enjoyed by hundreds of thousands... perhaps even a million or more... upper-middle income American families of today!*

So much progress has been made in building and construction, in heating and air conditioning, in electricity and electronics, in telephones and automobiles and in trains, not to mention airplanes and cruise ships, that Emperor Napoleon and Josephine lived in a manner that many people in America today would regard as a STEP DOWN!

What has happened since Napoleon, of course, *is a general improvement in the standard of living of the entire population, greater than the world had even suspected as being possible before the reign of Queen Victoria (1837 to 1901).* It seems so unfair today that Victoria, and the Victorian Age which took its name from her, is looked upon as being a bit "stuffy." Nothing could possibly be further from the truth.   First in England and then in America - *it was a time of growing wealth that changed the way people lived and thought* - Victoria built a mighty Navy, which kept peace in the world and protected the interests of both Britain and the United States. *Then she told her business people: "Go forth and make money!"*

New inventions and innovations cut costs and let a mass market develop. Competition kept the new ideas coming, and *forced their adoption even if companies found constant change inconvenient!* America cashed in on the New Age. Our imperative... westward, ever westward... drove us to the shores of the Pacific Ocean... *and then across an ocean to trade with China... and to force open a closed Japanese society. It was, Americans said, our Manifest Destiny. "Go West Young Man And Seek Your Fortune."* The growth of America was so great that we imported capital from that rich island nation: Great Britain! And we invested that capital! As a matter of fact, J. Pierpont Morgan the Elder made an annual trip to London each summer in his yacht. He visited the homes and offices of the very rich (old money) and the rich (new money). *He brought back to America each year the investment funds that permited twelve more months of modernization, expansion and relocation by U.S. industry. Morgan became a sort of bridge, across which the surplus funds of London moved to America.*

I KNOW WHAT YOU WANT TO SAY NOW. I CAN PICTURE YOU, SMILING, SAYING YES YOU CAN

SEE WHAT I AM LEADING UP TO... THE ENORMOUS *TRANSFER OF WEALTH* TAKING PLACE TODAY... THE LOANS AND INVESTMENTS BY JAPANESE INSURANCE COMPANIES, BANKS, INDUSTRIAL CONCERNS, CONSTRUCTION OUT-FITS AND PRIVATE INVESTORS TO AMERICAN CORPORATIONS. You are right *but you are ahead of me.* Give me a moment to make one more point:

After the Civil War, America looked like a good bet for a general depression. In fact, *it was widely expected that America would come crashing down from its inflationary "high" late in the war. After all, the Federal Government had borrowed so much money to finance the war that its debt equalled one full year of America's GNP - the Gross National Product.* But the gloomy Gus types were wrong. The new growth and expansion lasted eight full years before the first time of contraction. Then there was another big wave of investment and growth. And another time of contraction. And finally a third leg of new growth. *NOT UNTIL THE ENTIRE THIRTY-YEAR PERIOD WAS OVER IN 1895 COULD ANYONE REALLY GAIN THE PERSPECTIVE TO SEE THAT IT HAD REALLY ALL BEEN JUST ONE LONG ERA. BY THE TIME IT WAS OVER, AMERICA HAD INCREASED ITS REAL GNP FIVE-FOLD! And when I say real growth, remember that prices were edging downward at an average of 1% each year... a total drop of 30% in thirty years.* That is how long America took to "work off" the inflation of the 1860's! Think of this and tell it to anyone in the future who tries to tell you that inflation is the NORM in America... or that once prices have gone up they can *never* go back down again!

People who say that today resembles 1929 do not really have any idea what they are talking about. You can pick and choose facts from almost any year... any age... and *stretch them* to show that they look like another period of time. But there is more to it than that. *Each age has a beating heart, a living soul, a distinctive personality! It is not that easy to find one period that really resembles another.* When you do find one, it is likely that few will see the similarity. Let me make that plainer. Nature, in the form of *inherited genes,* can play tricks. A little child can be so much like a grandfather or grandmother when they were young that it is eerie. To anyone who recalls the grandparent as a child (an older sister or brother or an active great-grandparent) *such a similarity can make shivers run down the spine.* You may have had such an experience... seeing a little girl walk and run and talk and laugh and hug in a way so distinctively similar to her grandmother that it brings tears to your eyes. *I SAY THAT TODAY'S ECONOMY REMINDS ME OF THE POST CIVIL WAR PERIOD IN AMERICA IN JUST SUCH A WAY! Think about it!*

In those long-ago days, America had unmet needs everywhere. *But the Federal Government was in no position to do anything about them. It was borrowed up to the hilt... choking on debt. And besides, the President, who had turned out to be a loveable and much-loved man, was distracted often when scandals - one after another - rocked his Administration! It was up to MONEY to run things... to allocate capital... to plan and push investments! Luckily there was strong leadership in the Western World... England had a Lady in charge who took no nonsense from anyone and knew exactly what she was doing! And there was CAPITAL... lots of capital... coming in from an island nation making more money than it wanted or needed to spend... money it saved and invested.* See what I mean. THAT IS LIKE TODAY!

I have heard it said by many sources since the middle of October, 1987, that American industry would now pull in its horns, cut back on investment and begin to shrink. I believe Wall Street is looking in a mirror, seeing itself and thinking it is seeing America at large! *I knew such negative thinking was far wide of the mark on November 29, 1987. That was the day it was announced that machine tool orders in October had leaped upward 48% from year earlier levels!*

I saw a comment by Richard T. Lindren, President and CEO of Cross & Trecker Corporation that warmed my heart. "Since the stock market crash," he said, *"orders are going like a house afire.* Our order picture is pretty good, and we're very optimistic about the outlook for the machine tool industry."

AND WHAT REALLY BRIGHTENED THE PICTURE

WAS THE FACT THAT THE 46% GAIN OVER SEPTEMBER IN ORDERS FOR MACHINES THAT SHAPE METAL PARTS WAS FOR MACHINES BUILT IN THE UNITED STATES... NOT FOR UNITS IMPORTED FROM FOREIGN NATIONS! For too long much of the business that did show up was being grabbed mostly by imports! One industry spokesman said: "Buyers are coming out of the woodwork that we were not aware were in the market for machines. Suppliers of parts to the auto and truck industry are in the market buying." An even more promising item: *Export sales are now starting to Boom.* China was in with a one million dollar order for machinery to make oil field pumps. There were even orders coming in from South Korea... a nation that has a big trade surplus with America.

I have been saying for several months now that the United States is heading into a genuine Boom. *You are finally going to see a SUPPLY-SIDE BOOM. This will be the real thing. The United States of America is about to greatly expand its capacity to produce industrial goods.* It will do so in modern state of the art factories. I believe many of these factories will be located in rural areas, rather than in old industrial cities. It is my further conviction that they will recruit people with a positive attitude about disciplined high-quality work... rather than just hire out-of-work employees laid off by plants that were shut down and in many cases torn down earlier. You are going to see *a rebirth of the work ethic* that made America the envy of the world in the 1950's and earlier!

Mergers and acquisitions will lose much of their appeal for this basic reason: *THE HIGH DEBT LOAD THEY CARRY WILL PUT THEM AT A TREMENDOUS DISADVANTAGE IN COMPETING WITH PLANTS BUILT WITH LOW BORROWING,* OFTEN BY CASH-RICH JAPANESE FIRMS SEEKING AMERICAN MANUFACTURING LOCATIONS! *ONCE AGAIN, OPERATING PROFIT WILL BE THE GOAL!*

The real reason most American big business executives tell forecasters that *they expect higher inflation in 1989 is simply because they are looking ahead to raising their own prices. Boy, are they in for a big surprise. This falling dollar business is greatly over-rated as an inflation producer.* Oh, yes, it is true that for the past two years American business executives have been ignoring the chance to grab bigger chunks of the U.S. market as foreign companies have raised prices. Instead, U.S. firms, by and large, have chosen to *charge as much as they could get away with. The goal was short-term profit, and let the future be damned.*

Sometimes I have the feeling that companies in the U.S. have forgotten what it means to really compete, because the essence of competition is *price competition.* It is not in advertising tiny or even imagined product differences.

As the dollar has fallen, U.S. companies have too often seen it as *a buffer or a shield against REAL price competition. And so they raised prices.*

But if American managers and executives think the falling dollar will let them raise prices again in 1989, *they have another think coming! 1989 is going to be a year of brutal competition. Ruthless competition. Even life or death competition inside America! The new plants I am talking about are not going to be put up because people want to put them up. Proof of that comes in the Soviet Union.* Communist planners and communist plant managers there are *quite* satisfied with old factories whose costs are far out of line with plants in Japan, France, West Germany, England or America. I have yet to be convinced that so-called "reformers" in the U.S.S.R. can overcome this *built in sloth and inertia* just by making a few speeches. Human nature being what it is, *only war can make people do things differently. And as businessmen in Victoria's day were fond of quoting: "Competitive capitalistic business is the closest substitute for war that mankind has ever found!"*

Japan Inc. is perfectly aware of the fact that Congress will eventually pass restrictive, protectionist laws to keep out Japanese products, unless something is done about the Japanese trade imbalance with America. *So the instinct of self-preservation is forcing the Japanese to invest in brand new plants inside America... plants that are just as effective as those in Japan. (And that is the biggest surprise to come out of this wave of Japanese investment in America.) Honda is planning to build a parts factory in Ohio to supply its auto assembly plant, also in Ohio. And Toyota will put up a $300,000,000 engine plant near its*

MAJOR COMPONENTS OF GROSS NATIONAL PRODUCT

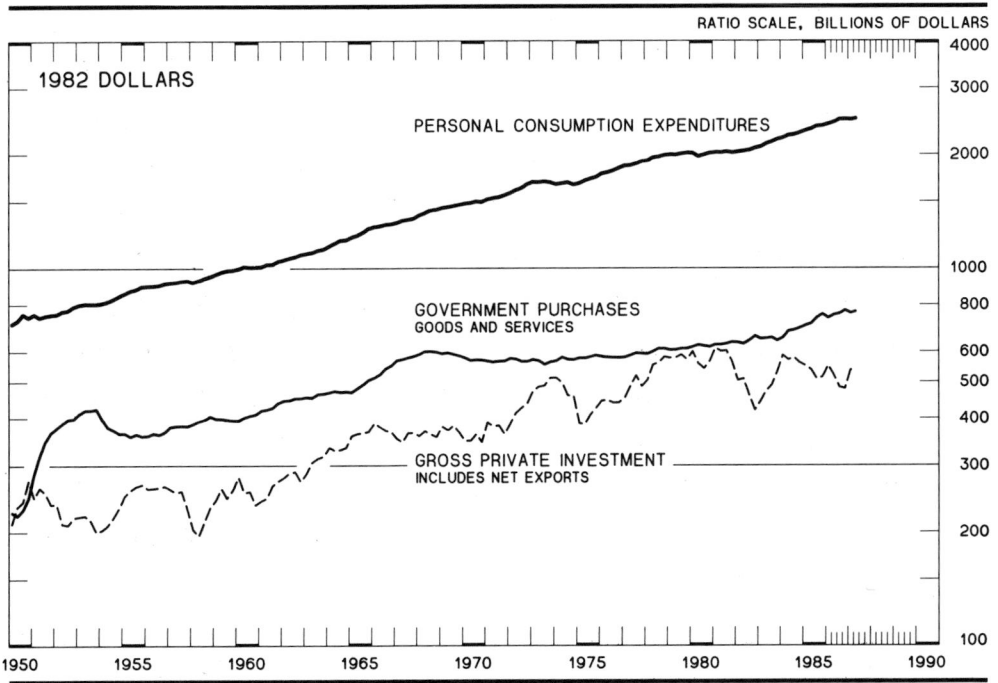

You can see that gross private investment in America has been flat since 1980. The easy way out has been to "source" goods overseas. Now the lower dollar has made America cheaper than foreign sources. *It is an awkward moment for management caught looking outward when changing times dictate that they move aggressively inward!*

new $800,000,000 auto assembly plant in Kentucky. The new Toyota parts plant will produce 75% of the parts Toyota needs for its U.S. assembly factory. You can bet your last nickel that Honda and Toyota plan to go *toe-to-toe on pricing in the U.S. with Chrysler, Ford and GM* - like hefty wrestlers in a ring. And what you are seeing in autos is now being duplicated in other industries. *The invasion of America by Japanese manufacturers is the best thing to happen here in many years. It forces Americans to do what we do best: COMPETE TO WIN!* A by-product will be steady prices and maybe even a slight bias towards DEFLATION. One percent a year deflation is the best prod to gains in productivity. It is flies in the face of conventional postwar wisdom in America. It has long been thought that a little INFLATION is the best stimulant to prosperity. America has since found out that a little bit of inflation is like a little bit of pregnancy! It grows and grows and grows!

When you have 1% a year DEFLATION, as America did from 1865 to '95, companies are always on the edge of losing money if they choose to just stand pat. A few years of losing money can put all but the richest companies into insolvency... and bankruptcy. The only companies to survive in the 1990's will be those that invest in modern plants and equipment. The new numbers show that *this race for survival may have begun on the 19th of October, 1987.* To that extent, I see the market crash as a positive, healthy event!

Competition tends to create gluts. And gluts are notorious for pushing prices down. Usually when prices fall, producers try to restrict output to raise prices. *But such efforts always end in failure. One or more producers blessed with natural advantages of location, etc. will increase output... defying the others. Prices collapse... and fall to a natural level. Weak producers are eliminated. That is real supply-side economics at work. You will now see it working!*

One place I think it will be allowed to work is in farming. America cannot afford to contribute 50¢ of each dollar in farm earnings. *One out of four farmers will be driven off the land as the farm subsidies are phased out.* But this will not mean a depression in farm country. Quite the opposite. The cheap land will attract U.S. and foreign manufacturers who want to locate factories in America... as a way of placing output *in the middle of a national and international distribution system. Farmers are prized as potential workers. They are used to working around big machines... expect them... understand them... relate to them... learn fast how to use, operate and maintain them! Also farmers are widely appreciated as hard workers... people who have been getting up before dawn and working until sundown... the opposite of the shirkers, clock-watchers and malingerers who gave U.S. industry a bad name in the 1960's and 1970's.* (Sometimes as many as 20% of workers at some U.S. factories have "missed" work on Mondays, causing severe dislocations in production schedules. A plant in farm country usually has a much different attitude in its work force!)

The brutal competition resulting from new plants will be joined by other deflationary factors. To begin with, the Federal Reserve Board is now strongly committed to *preserving the hard-won gains of the Volcker era. So loose money is not in the cards.* Secondly, the Federal deficit is heading downward. As the Boom unfolds - producing surprisingly high income tax flows - the downward trend in the budget deficit will *accelerate.* Also, it grows clearer with every passing month that *the deadbeat nations of the world... meaning most of Latin America, Africa and a now-growing portion of the communist bloc... are never going to pay off their bank loans.* For years it was believed by bankers, Third World Goverments and gold promoters that the U.S. Treasury would pay off the loans "someday." *Not very likely!* That is the new awareness. So all over the world nations are cutting back on interest payments and demanding that at least *half of their loan principal be written off. The banks do not want to do that. But in 1987 you saw a beginning of just that process, with American banks increasing reserves for bad debts by billions of dollars. This is deflationary. It wipes out large chunks of money.*

Another source of DEFLATION will be the real estate price declines I expect in America - *at least in those over-heated, overpriced markets such as Southern California, New York, Northern New Jersey, Southern Connecticut and Greater Boston.* The Secretary of Defense has told his Joint Chiefs of Staff to slash the fiscal-1989 defense budget by tens of billions of dollars... as a part of the new drive to lower the Federal deficit. *It will not take long for property owners in the "hot" areas listed above - plus the Greater Washington D.C. area - to learn how much of the housing price inflation in such communities has stemmed from the tripling in recent years of the defense budget, from $100 billion to $300 billion. They will also learn that prices will go down as well as up.* AND SPEAKING OF DEFLATION... did you know that we are now exporting it, just like back in our inflationary 1970's when we exported inflation?

The price of oil (calculated in dollars but then converted to marks, yen, pounds, etc.) has been in a *steep decline* in much of the world. AS YOU KNOW, RISING OIL PRICES CAUSED MUCH OF THE INFLATION IN THE WORLD IN THE 1970's. Now oil is causing deflation. *Japan in particular is in the grips of deflation.* I think that is one reason why it has suddenly sprung into life in a new domestic-oriented Boom. *Deflation is good for business. It forces companies to cut costs and become lean and efficient. It demands that they modernize even when sales are weak.* It is likely that the U.S. generated deflationary pressure on West Germany will also force that nation into new *cost-cutting investments soon.* (They are now taking steps to follow Japan in stimulating their domestic economy.) One result may be that we export less than Washington contemplates in its dreams. The other will be that *we also import less... force-feeding a*

Boom in America and slashing our trade deficit faster than most observers now think likely. The man who wins the White House in 1988 will be lucky indeed. He is probably thinking of ways to save America from a depression. He will not have to. He will get credit for a Boom now being born!

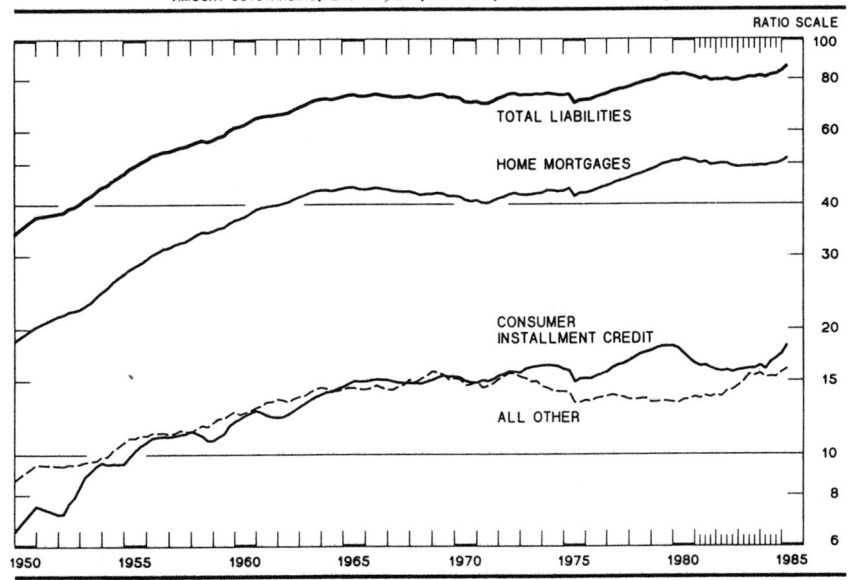

HOUSEHOLD DEBT OUTSTANDING
PERCENT OF DISPOSABLE PERSONAL INCOME
AMOUNT OUTSTANDING; END OF YEAR, 1950-51; SEASONALLY ADJUSTED, END OF QUARTER, 1952-

One reason doom and gloom folks give for expecting a new depression in America is what *they perceive to be a debt overload being carried by American households.* And you can see that debt is up. But you can't look at debt *in isolation.* You must see it as part of a balanced view.

Adrian Van Eck

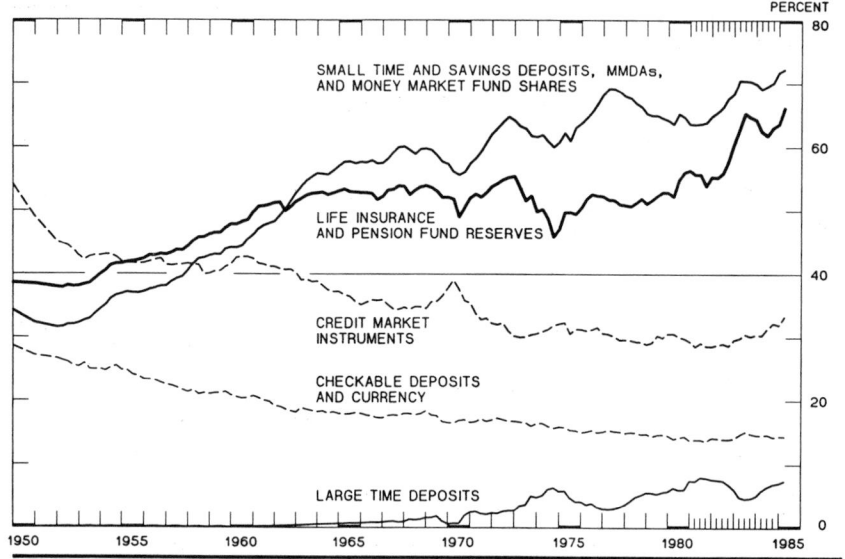

FINANCIAL ASSETS HELD BY HOUSEHOLDS
PERCENT OF DISPOSABLE PERSONAL INCOME
AMOUNT OUTSTANDING; END OF YEAR, 1950-51; SEASONALLY ADJUSTED, END OF QUARTER, 1952-

See the enormous increase in financial assets owned by U.S. households: money-market fund shares, savings accounts, life insurance cash value and pension fund reserves. *And this chart doesn't even include equity in homes and small businesses or common stocks. Put everything together and you get a sounder economy than worry-warts want you to have.*

- 28 -

FEDERAL BUDGET
NIA BASIS
SEASONALLY ADJUSTED ANNUAL RATES, QUARTERLY

BILLIONS OF DOLLARS

The federal government has finally begun to get spending under control, as the top line (expenditures) shows. Revenues are rising and as the coming boom hits the U.S. they should rise faster, even with the new lower tax rates. We still expect to see a compromise on revenues.

Adrian Van Eck

COMPREHENSIVE PRICE MEASURES

CHANGE AT ANNUAL RATES, SEASONALLY ADJUSTED, QUARTERLY

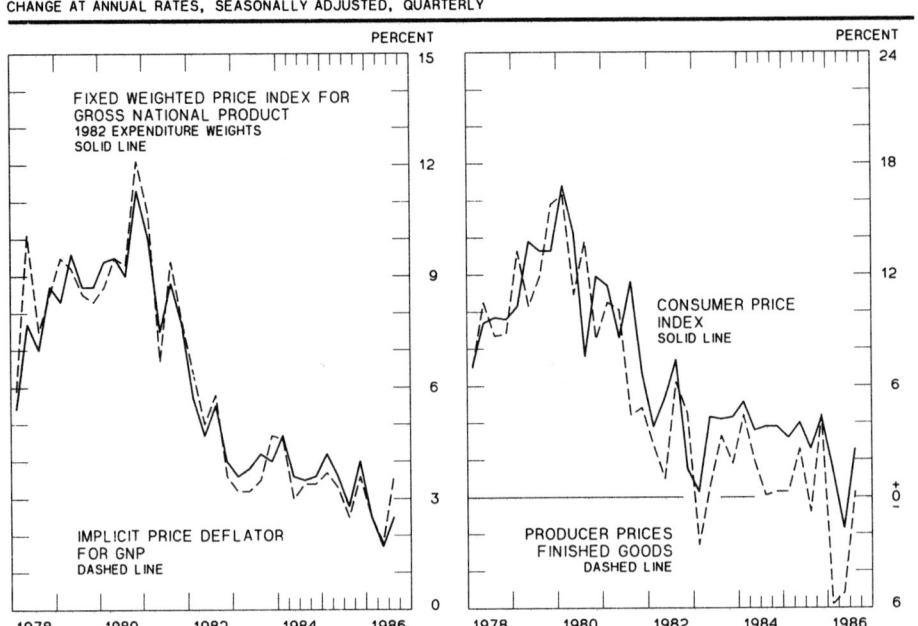

Many investors and businessmen think that once we push Japan out of our markets they can raise prices. That is why you still here lots of inflation talk. But such idle gossip ignores reality. The real price competition is coming from new modern plants here in the U.S., such as the mini steel mills, which can produce steel cheaper than imports, and are grabbing a bigger share of the market!

An Introduction: How The World Sees Us.

The dollar did not fall. The yen went up. The West German mark went up. The Swiss franc went up. That is the way things look to the rest of the world.

If you were an oil producer in Arabia selling oil to the West Germans or the Swiss or the Japanese you would be - by trade custom - pricing your oil in dollars. (And that is bad enough, you would think. Because the dollar price of your crude has tumbled, slipped and slid from $22.50 a barrel in August, 1987 to $16 a barrel in recent trading.) But to make the situation even worse from you point of view, here comes the buyers from Japan... waving yen in your face... pointing out to you that their yen have gone up in value 100% from the level of early 1985. They are demanding, and you have to give them, twice as many barrels just to compensate for the decline in the price of oil in dollars - down from a 1985 high of $32 a barrel. Then you have to double that again a second time to make up for the value of the yen having doubled. So the Japanese traders are now able to buy four barrels of crude oil in Arabia today for the same number of yen they spent to buy just a single barrel of oil in 1985. That, dear reader, is what you call deflation with a vengance. What it means is that Japanese chemical companies use only one-fourth as many yen now to buy their raw material in Arabia as they did in 1985. And yet American economists, politicians and Wall Street pundits are still waiting in vain for Japanese chemical companies to double their American sales prices. *That is why gold has not yet collapsed $100 an ounce.* It is why many American factories keep raising prices in a deflationary age, hoping that what they see as a "falling dollar" will give them windfall profits. It is why the White House talks of stabilizing the dollar but *really hopes it will fall to 100 yen* and whisk the Republican candidate into the White House.

It is - and this is most important of all - why I am very close to being alone among economic forecasters in predicting 1% a year deflation in the U.S. for the next seven years! American wholesale prices went up 2% in 1987, matching a decline of 2% the year before. In two years, U.S. wholesale prices have stayed at flat zero. But even more important, as I see it, is a definite deflationary trend. The whole basis for high interest rates in America - and we now have the highest REAL interest rates in history, after subtracting out the inflation rate, so far as I can tell - is the persistent false expectation on Wall Street that the "falling dollar" is going to bring inflation to the U.S. NONSENSE. HORSEFEATHERS. BALDER-DASH!

What America sees as a falling dollar is, as I said, seen as a rising yen, a rising West German mark and a rising Swiss franc. The rest of the world is enjoying sharply lower prices for commodities and American products. But to a degree that simply is not penetrating skulls on Wall Street, in Washington and in a host of American universities, *this DEFLATION is not being passed along to the consumers of the world.* The Japanese cost of living is now falling... but only at a rate of 1% to 2% a year.

In nations such as West Germany and Holland, prices are being artificially held at just about the zero-gain level... *in terms of their own money.* Americans are foolishly waiting for our exports to other nations to simply *explode* because of a "falling dollar." Take a trip to one of them. Go to the stores. *Do you find American goods selling at bargain-basement prices because of a "falling dollar."* THAT IS SOMETHING PEOPLE IN FOREIGN COUNTRIES HEAR ABOUT ON TELEVISION. BUT THEY SEE LITTLE EVIDENCE OF THE FACT IN THEIR OWN EVERYDAY LIVES. WE DOUBT IF ONE PERSON IN 100 IN A COUNTRY WHOSE MONEY IS RISING AGAINST THE DOLLAR COULD

EXPLAIN TO YOU HOW THE MARKET IS *SUPPOSED TO MAKE AMERICAN GOODS CHEAPER IN THEIR COUNTRY,* WHILE MAKING THEIR GOODS EXPENSIVE OVER HERE IN AMERICA.

And I will tell you something else too. In the United States of America the SHOE MANUFACTURERS are fighting tooth and nail to *prevent prices of foreign-made shoes from moving up in U.S. wholesale and retail distribution channels.* That is because most of them have shut down most of their U.S. shoe factories and they have no desire to, nor intention of, re-opening such U.S. manufacturing plants... and that goes for the dollar at 130 yen... or 120 yen or even if (should some of the leaders in the Administration in Washington get their way) the dollar should fall to 100 yen. THEY MAKE THEIR SHOES AT FACTORIES OVERSEAS... IN PLACES LIKE ITALY AND BRAZIL. They intend to go on making their shoes there, whether Wall Street likes it or even understands what is now going on or not. That is a fact of life - or so they think! If Japan chooses to make its own consumers pay too much for products in order to generate profits that subsidize exports to the United States, you will not find Sears or Radio Shack complaining... because they now import a tremendous volume of manufactured goods from Japanese factories... and stick their own brand names on them. You will hear a lot of noise from American auto manufacturers who complain loudly about Japanese cars being sold here.

(They say "cars made in Japan" but if you notice they are more and more directing verbal blasts at Japanese cars in general... including and I suspect especially including Japanese-owned auto plants here in the U.S.) American-owned auto companies have *doubled* their imports in four years. And U.S. truck manufacturers have tripled their imports of parts and trucks. But the Japanese companies building cars in America have announced right up front that they intend to buy all their parts in the United States... and if they cannot do so they are prepared to sink their own money into building factories here in America to make their car parts.

I THINK ONE OF THE REASONS WALL STREET AND WASHINGTON ARE SO "OUT TO LUNCH" ON UNDERSTANDING THE TRADE SITUATION... AND THUS FAR ARE SO MIXED UP ON THE EXPECTATIONS FOR INFLATION AND HIGHER INTEREST RATES... IS THAT THEY CANNOT SEEM TO GET IT STRAIGHT IN THEIR OWN HEADS JUST WHAT MAKES AN IMPORT AND AN EXPORT.

For example, I watched and listened in absolute shock... horror... then laughter as one American politician tried to explain on television why American exports are really understated. What he was saying was that he regards the output of IBM's factories in Japan - using Japanese labor in Japanese factories and selling to the Japanese marketplace - as really being a part of America's exports... although not recorded as such. I cannot wait to see what he is going to call Honda automobiles made in Ohio from American parts, using American labor and sold in the U.S. Will these be regarded as Japanese exports to America? They should be, under his formula for counting IBM's Japanese output as U.S. exports. Will the politicians keep two sets of books... counting U.S.-made products imported from U.S. factories overseas as "domestic production" - while at the same time taking credit for Japanese-made cars built and sold entirely in the U.S., or cars made in Japanese-owned U.S. plants but sold in France, England or West Germany? Can the U.S. eliminate its trade deficit by simply changing labels signifying what is an import and what is an export? I do not think so! And the quicker the politicians, the professors and the Wall Street pundits understand this, the quicker you will see bonds go up sharply and gold plunge.

Trading on Wall Street the day the new trade figures for November, 1987, came out was bigger than on any day since the October 19th crash. That is even more remarkable when you consider that this day was a "getaway day" before the long three-day weekend, at least in thirty-eight states. Normally, on the day before a long weekend, trading is slow as many people get an early jump.

Common stocks broke from the gate right from the opening bell and bonds took off like a rocket. For the first time since October 19th, investors got busy signals again and again when they tried to get through to their brokers. (Only this time the investors were frustrated because they could not get through to BUY orders. I did warn people that when the blast-off began in bonds they would not be able to get into the market.)

However, it is my sad duty to report to you that both stocks and bonds rose this day for reasons that are unreliable.

TAKE BONDS FIRST. They went up because inventory figures rose. Wall Street assumed this was bullish for bonds. Wall Street, you see, operates on the theory that bad economic news is bullish for bonds and good economic news is bearish for bonds. In this case, *the reasoning is that U.S. factories will have to shut down some operations and lay off some workers to trim those inventories. The Federal Reserve Board will then feel free to pump money into the banking system and that will lower interest rates.* A fascinating theory - if one chooses to ignore or forget the past eight years! The trouble with this theory is that it assumes retail sales are still the measure of growth in the U.S. economy. And it assumes that if these sales are cooling down, it will be American factories that have to shut down to bring inventories in line. BUT LOTS OF OTHER U.S. COMPANIES THINK DIFFERENTLY. FACTORY CONSTRUCTION HAS JUMPED SHARPLY. AMERICAN PRODUCTION IS GOING TO GO UP. IF U.S. RETAIL SALES FALL, IT WILL LIKELY BE THE IMPORTERS WHO SUFFER! This U.S. production expansion will largely be self-financed, either through plowed-back earnings or through new equity. Smart managers realize that with DEFLATION at hand debt is dangerous, even destructive. Companies that load up on debt to acquire other firms are in grave danger of not surviving. In the viciously competitive environment ahead, smaller companies with entrepreneur-type managers and very low debt will be in positions to thrive and profit. The Blue Chip stocks so favored in the recent bull market may have to tread water for a few years.

Do not get the idea because of headlines about a decline in trade deficit numbers that the trade problem has been solved. *Those numbers mean very little.* They are not seasonally adjusted. Every year, imports surge in late autumn as U.S. stores stock up for Christmas... then fall in November and December. A lot of that was present in the November numbers. It is too soon for us to know whether trade has now turned! Much depends on how fast new plants are built in the U.S. Korea's $5,500 Hyundai is becoming what the VW Beetle was in the 1960's. It now forces auto makers to keep prices down, even if they hate it. THE JAPANESE ARE BUYING LOTS MORE CARS AT HOME NOW. I expect them to trim their exports to America by a half-million cars. But they will not give up their share of the U.S. auto market. They will build the extra half-million cars here in the U.S. These will be American cars and will be so counted in the import / export numbers. THAT IS NOT ALL. Japan Inc. does not think like American big business. The U.S.

"Big Three" auto manufacturers for example, no longer think of themselves as American companies. They are *international* in their outlook. They will build a car in Brazil and use parts from Taiwan, Mexico, Spain or Korea... then they will import that car to the U.S. and sell it here *as an American car!*

BUT JAPANESE COMPANIES ARE NATIONAL-ISTIC. When they are in Japan, they think of themselves quite naturally, as Japanese. But when they are in the United States *they think of themselves as American.* That may take some getting used to. But if you live in any of the forty states now trying to attract Japanese factories, you will soon have a chance to meet them first hand (if you have not already). You will discover that they bring their nationalistic ideas with them. They will begin thinking of manufacturing in America - and exporting overseas. IT IS ENTIRELY POSSIBLE THAT FOR THE FIRST TIME THE FREIGHTERS AND CARGO PLANES RUNNING TO AND FROM THE UNITED STATES WILL NOW CARRY LOADS BOTH WAYS, INSTEAD OF COMING TO AMERICA FULL AND GOING BACK ON THE RETURN LEG EMPTY. You may start seeing American-owned factories overseas sending their products to America... while Japanese-owned U.S. plants ship their goods to foreign customers... even to Japan itself. Don't laugh. It is already being done with television sets and soon it will happen with other products as well. Since the rising yen, pound, mark and franc now help make American labor the cheapest in the *developed* free world, on a relative basis, I expect that the new state of the art Japanese-owned factories here will keep prices so low in America that exports from U.S. plants overseas will have trouble competing. The next step, as yet unforeseen by Washington or Wall Street, will be for American "international" companies to build *new plants* in the U.S. These plants, like those being built for Japan Inc., will be "state of the art." *Low-cost... highly efficient... very high-quality... thanks to computer-assisted manufacturing and management!*

WHAT OF OVERSEAS PLANTS OWNED BY AMERICANS? Am I suggesting that they must be written off by their American owners, creating a drag on company profits. *Not very likely!*

Unemployment in Western Europe runs around 10% and has stayed near that level for years. They have a great fear of inflation. When they see that a *remarkable investment Boom* is taking place in the United States and a full-scale consumer Boom is roaring along in Japan - *all with DEFLATION and all with very low interest rates* - they will try the same concepts themselves. Indeed, there is already a modest trend in that direction starting to show up. It will simply accelerate.

I expect to see at least half of the Third World debt written off during the next seven years. And I anticipate a cne-third reduction in interest rates. The combination of a 50% write-off and a 33% drop in interest rates would reduce the cost of carrying debt by a full two-thirds, allowing a revival of growth in affected economies. The best news is that international lending institutions, both public and private, are coming to see that lending money to Governments promotes socialism, and that is terribly ineffective. The new trend in Latin America and Africa is already revealing itself. The age of the entrepreneur is about to roll across these nations. A trend like this feeds on itself. The profits become seed capital for other new ventures and executives break loose to start their own companies. The age of jealousy, which prompted the growth of Marxism in the Third World, is giving way to the age of the self-made man and woman! If there is anything that capitalism proved in the Nineteenth Century it is that it can, when unleashed, end inflation. Without inflation, interest rates fall fast and stay down. Hardly anyone on Wall Street today can even imagine such a coming economy. Nor can they visualize a stock market where the Dow Jones Average trades in a fairly narrow range, even while corporate profits move up sharply.

WALL STREET HAS NO REAL MEMORY ANY MORE. IT IS AS IF WALL STREET HAS HAD A COLLECTIVE LOBOTOMY. I am willing to wager that you could go in off the street at almost any Wall Street firm and find *no winners* when you offer a $1,000 prize to any person who can tell you within fifteen seconds *the three years when the American economy moved along in a powerful Boom, with earnings strong...* when new homes were put up at low prices on formerly rural land, when the U.S. Government firmly attacked its budget deficit with shocking ferocity. (The years were 1946, 1947 and 1948.)

The interesting thing about those years is that the Dow Jones stocks did not participate in the Boom. It was as though businessmen had *so many opportunities to make so much money that they did not have time to think about trading in Blue Chip stocks.* I happen to believe that the next year or two could resemble those poorly remembered postwar Boom years in a number of ways.

OF COURSE, WHAT CAME AFTER 1948 WAS THE START OF A STRONG BULL MARKET LEG. I EXPECT THE NEXT LEG OF THE BULL MARKET TO BE JUST AS STRONG AS THE LAST ONE. IN OTHER WORDS, *I ANTICIPATE STOCKS CLIMBING FROM TODAY'S LEVEL... TO 4,000 BY 1995. But if I am correct the Fed will tamp down speculative urges for the next couple of years... making SPECIAL SITUATIONS your most likely vehicles for profit.*

CHAPTER ONE

Where Are We Going?

The really exciting days of the bull market still lie ahead. What you have seen so far is nothing but *preparation for a growth period that will take the Dow up to at least 4,000... by 1995 at the latest!* The constant talk that the "crash of October 19, 1987" marked the start of "Another 1929" was just that: *Talk!*

I got so darned angry in early 1988 as the business press filled up with bad talk about "Another 1929." *They do not know their history!*

As my long-term subscribers know, I have little or no patience with folks who have pumped data about the last week... the last month... the last year... even the last decade into their computers, and then asked the computers to tell them what is coming next in America and the Western World.

These people suffer from a simple common problem: Namely *GROUPTHINK.* They think of history as running back only a year or two or even three. Anything back beyond 1980 is seen as *ancient history.* They cannot believe anything that happened prior to 1976 could have anything to say to us today about the *future.* So in many cases, they scrub this "PRE-HISTORY" from their computer memory banks. What a shame. Because in order to understand what has been going on these past eight years... what is going on now... and what is likely to happen during 1989 to '95, you have to go back and dig very deeply into what actually did go on in the decade we know as *THE ROARING TWENTIES... then look at the 1950's and the 1960's... then look at the late 1800's.*

Lacking this conceptual framework for the 1980's, Wall Streeters in general have been caught by surprise time and time again in recent years. Most of them are suprised anew each waking day. They have no idea *what* is coming tomorrow, no matter what they tell you. If you want to prepare yourself and your money for the coming years - and the opportunity to build your wealth - *then you really have to take full responsibility yourself for what happens to you.* Maybe you will be lucky and your broker and banker will be aware of the message in this book. In that case, do not hesitate to talk about what you are going to do with this person in advance. It helps to get your own goals clearly defined. But if you are not lucky enough to

You can make a mistake early in a climbing market and recover. But, later on, make a mistake and the bear will get you!

have such a financial advisor, it will be up to you and you alone to grasp what you read on the following pages... and use it to set goals for yourself. These goals should include both *Dollar amounts you hope to achieve and Dates that you promise to use as checkpoints along the way.* Always keep these Dollars and Dates in mind!

THERE ARE TWO BASIC FACTS YOU SHOULD KEEP IN MIND ABOUT THE BOOM YOU WILL SEE IN 1989 AND THE EARLY 1990's! One is that during the early part of this next decade you can make a mistake in timing, even quite a serious error - *and still have things work out to your advantage!* By that I mean that you can decide to buy a stock or a mutual fund right at the very top of a short-term move, only to see it fall away in one of those inevitable sinking spells that brokers like to call "corrections." (So who do you know that ever likes to be "corrected" for goodness sake?) But if you hold on tightly and close your eyes and keep real quiet, why almost before you know it the "correction" will be over and your stock or mutual fund will be moving up again... first to the price you paid and then, golly-gee, to a price high enough so that you can, if you so desire, sell it out for a handsome profit. *You do this once... twice... three times and you will be feeling so good about yourself you will want to tell all your friends and relatives about your good fortune.*

If they show an interest in your investing, tell them how you read a fascinating guide... *this one*. And tell them

where you got your copy. Period! Do not loan them your copy. (If they read their own copy and become a fellow believer, *that is another matter.* Comparing notes can be fun and helpful to you both.) *Having money, just quietly having it, gives you security, status, the comforts of life and peace of mind. On a scale from 1 to 100 these four rank up there at 96 or 97... maybe 98... even 99!*

The popular game in town in early 1988 was to guess how much Federal Reserve Board Chairman Alan Greenspan would loosen up money in 1988 to please the White House in this Presidential election year. It was accepted without question that this would be seen by the Fed chairman as his main, if not his only, "assignment" for 1988 to '91. I did not buy that widely-anticipated, commonly-shared image of the new Fed chairman... and recognized him as a quiet man who was already determining America's 1989, 1990 and 1991 economic / financial future!

Had you run into Alan Greenspan then, whether at an airport waiting lounge or at a meeting where he was the honored guest speaker, you might have tried this question on him: "Mr. Greenspan, does it matter to you that 1988 is an election year - and that since President Reagan cannot run for a third term, we will of necessity pick a new man?"

I am willing to bet that he would have smiled his controlled little smile at you... his diplomatic smile that says nothing. (He and Henry Kissinger went to the same high school and I wonder if they both learned that same smile there.) Then he would have looked right through you... as if you had not asked him any question at all. You could have taken that as his answer. It would have told you everything you need to know. He would have said it all! Very few people really understand Alan Greenspan. He remains a man of mystery, even to those who have worked with him intimately for years and who long ago thought they did know him. If you wish to stay ahead of events in the next three years, you must of necessity see into the interior of this man... into the secret places of his very soul! FOR ALAN GREENSPAN WILL COME TO DOMINATE THE WORLD ECONOMY IN 1989 TO '91 JUST AS SURELY AND AS FULLY AS PAUL VOLCKER DOMINATED IT IN 1979 TO LATE-1987.

If you will study Alan Greenspan... not his mere biographical data but rather those tell-tale clues and hints that surface now and then, allowing you *quick glimpses through a window* into his inner-being (before he pulls the drapes closed and shuts his INNER-ESSENCE from your view)... if you will do this, you will soon discover that *you can read him just as simply and clearly* as I trust you came to read PAUL VOLCKER, before he departed from the Fed.

SEPTEMBER 10, 1987
A WINDOW INTO GREENSPAN'S SOUL!

On this date, shortly after Labor Day, 1987, in my

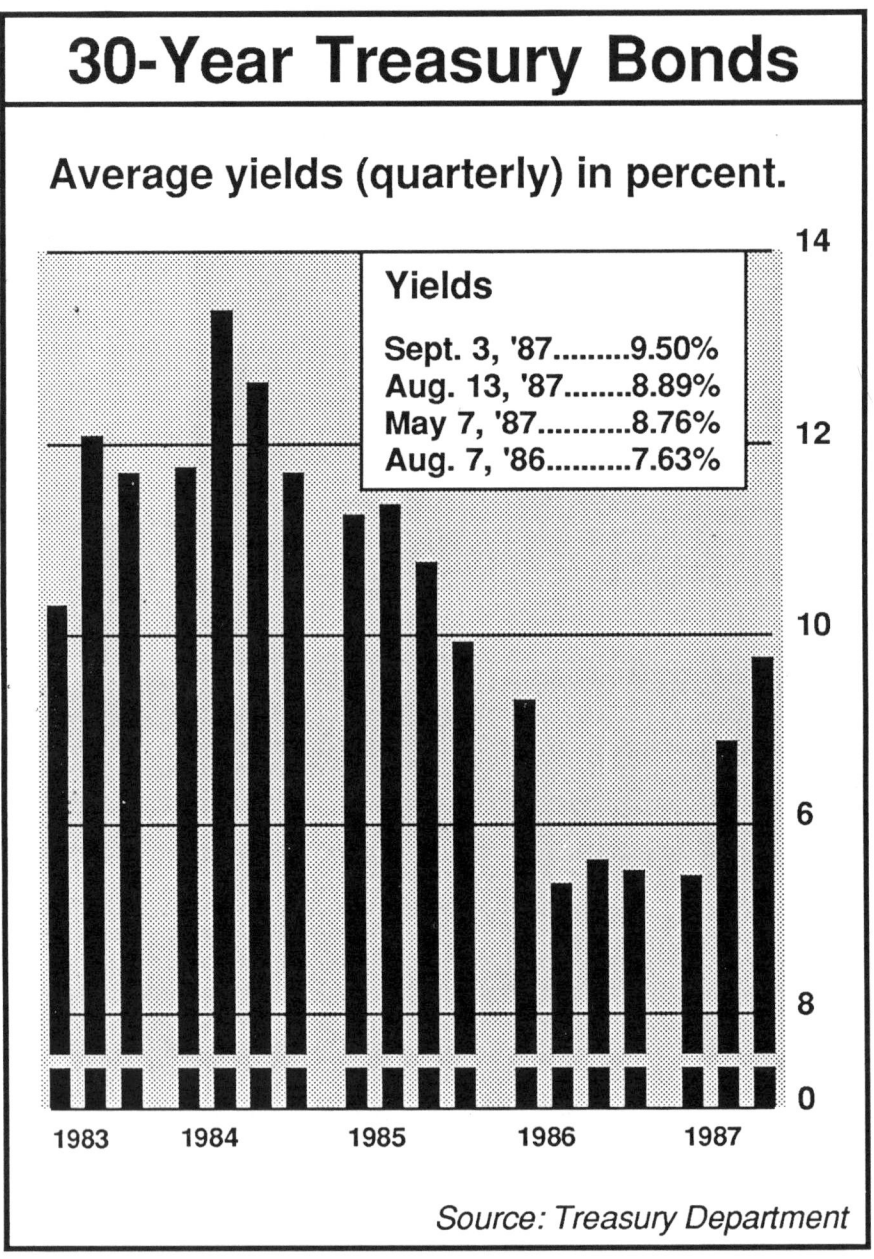

30-Year Treasury Bonds

Average yields (quarterly) in percent.

Yields

Sept. 3, '87..........9.50%
Aug. 13, '87........8.89%
May 7, '87............8.76%
Aug. 7, '86..........7.63%

1983   1984   1985   1986   1987

Source: Treasury Department

October Financial Research Center Forecast Letter I said (page 24):

"If you should part company with us on this matter of where long-term interest rates will end up, we believe you will fall victim to the many false prophets shouting at you from The Tower of Babel on Wall Street. *Study carefully this chart on average yields of 30-year Government T-Bonds.* It may take you a few moments. But do it. We don't care how busy you are. Take the time to study this chart. And that is an order from Adrain Van Eck!" (Note: to save you time, so you will not have to look for your October Letter, *I am now reproducing that yield chart here.)*

And now back to my quote from the October Letter - released September 10, 1987: "Notice how rates went up in late 1983 and early 1984. People on Wall Street were *surprised* by such rate boosts. Indeed, experts there had predicted *falling* rates for late-1983 and early-1984. These folks were saying however, that inflation would explode in mid-1984, forcing Volcker to push rates way up in a big hurry right after the 1984 election. Our own view in late 1983 was that tight money would crush... wipe out... destroy popular delusions about inflation... and that without such inflation expectations, rates would begin a major decline no later then the middle of the year. (We were off by one or two days, as we recall.) Rates for long-term T-Bonds went up a few points as the Fed kept squeezing hard against money growth. But in the interest rate collapse that naturally followed T-Bond yields fell to a level some three points lower than when tight money began to impact the market.

"So first the Fed let rates go up to kill inflation hopes... and then the subdued free market sent rates plunging downward month after month. That is exactly what we see happening again now!" (Note: I want to mention again that *this material was released September 10, 1987 - right after Labor Day* - so that you see it in its proper time context. Now back to that Letter.)

"Wall Street tested Greenspan by building up new fears of inflation. He rose to the challenge when the Fed raised the discount rate. Now investors knew he would risk even a recession to cool inflation down... as Greenspan showed Wall Street that he would match Volcker's grim war on inflation no matter what the short-term cost to the U.S. economy. Bond investors breathed a sigh of relief. We cannot say yet whether the Fed has made its point or whether falling interest rates on thirty-year bonds must await a wider awareness of just how weak key elements of the U.S. economy have become. What we do know for sure is that Greenspan has made his first serious move... it was to stop inflation fears... and that yields on thirty-year T-Bonds are positively, definitely going to fall to 6% or even 5% in the coming major rate decline! Timing? We are dealing here with popular psychology. When the emotional egg-shell cracks, interest rates will fall out with a plop! We insist that Alan Greenspan and his new

personal consultant (Paul Volcker) are restoring credibility to America's money market. The result will be lower interest rates... *YOU WILL SEE INFLATION COLLAPSE."* (End quote from Letter mailed September 10, 1987.)

Four weeks later I continued to outline Alan Greenspan's war on inflation. My November Letter would have reached you nine days prior to the October 19th collapse on Wall Street. In this Letter I said: "Slowly but surely tight money is doing the job it is supposed to do. It has already cooled inflation way down, as the Fed intended... it has forced President Ronald Reagan to accept a revised Gramm-Rudman Act... the only major problem left that the Fed set out to cure is the U.S. trade deficit... when a man or a woman is raised up to a position of trust such as the Fed Chairmanship, they grow into that job. We were sure Alan Greenspan would do so. He has. He is now working to change the outlook for American industry. He will succeed in that too. The recession that America is either about to enter or has already entered will be mild and short. A glancing blow! The Fed will use it to gain the reforms it needs to turn America into an efficient exporting machine. Then it will unleash a mighty new Boom! So first trouble. Then growth and riches!... From the start we have seen this as a man-made recession. It is being deliberately forced on the United States by the Federal Reserve Board... The Fed has squeezed its thumbs hard against the windpipe of money, leaving the economy gasping for air... All of this took place against a backdrop of near-hysteria about a comeback for inflation... If there is one thing we have learned in thirty-two years of observing and forecasting money and inflation in America, it is that a slow and gradual tightening of total checkable deposits is far and away the deadliest form of stopping inflation... you let prices rise, while holding money flat. In a while, people sense there is not enough money around to buy everything at the prices being asked. At first they go deeper into debt to keep buying. *Then the pain gets more intense. They slow down their buying. Goods pile up... unsold.* Now the merchants are feeling the pain. They cut back orders to manufacturers and to importers. Now goods pile up in the pipeline all the way to the U.S. manufacturers or to the docks where imports pile up. *Suddenly warehouses bulge to the point of bursting.* Corporations have to borrow money to carry these inventories. They may also have to borrow money to pay for payroll... *simply because their goods are not moving as they had anticipated.*

"HERE IS WHERE MANUFACTURERS AND MERCHANTS COME FACE TO FACE - MAYBE FOR THE FIRST TIME - *WITH THE REALITY OF TIGHT MONEY*. When the need arises to borrow that money, the banks treat them suspiciously... even rudely. You see, the banks are hurting too. The old days of easy money, careless loans, sloppy accounting and inflationary bailouts are now *gone*. In their place bankers are coming to work each morning to face a desk piled high with bad loans, foreclosures, bankruptcies, strict and severe auditing by aggresive bank examiners... all with the rather new risk of being fired and kicked out onto the street by the FDIC... and possibly (as has already happened to a number of bankers) charged with criminal malfeasance... convicted... sentenced to fines and even jail terms. No fun in all those downside risks. So the bankers are now getting tough... mean... flinty-eyed... hard to deal with. (All of this was foreseen and predicted in our Forecast Letters!)

"The natural consequence of the above series of events - and in a minute we will show you that we are talking fact here, not theory - is as it must be, a temporary jump in interest rates. (We stress temporary because that is all it is. Do not get alarmed.) Events are now rushing towards the goal the Fed has in mind: Low interest rates, low inflation and high growth.

"What always amazes us about a stuation such as America is in today is that each time it happens *most people in the market say 'This time, things are different.'* This time very tight money cannot and will not stop inflation. And nothing can make interest rates go down. Usually at the very crest of interest rates... *the unsustainable peak of interest rates...* lots of professionals who ought to know better are predicting that rates will go still higher... and then stay up! *The answer, of course, is that they are wrong.* MONEY WINS EVERY TIME! You can have raging mobs in the trading pits. You can have sensible investors losing their heads to the surging emotion of the

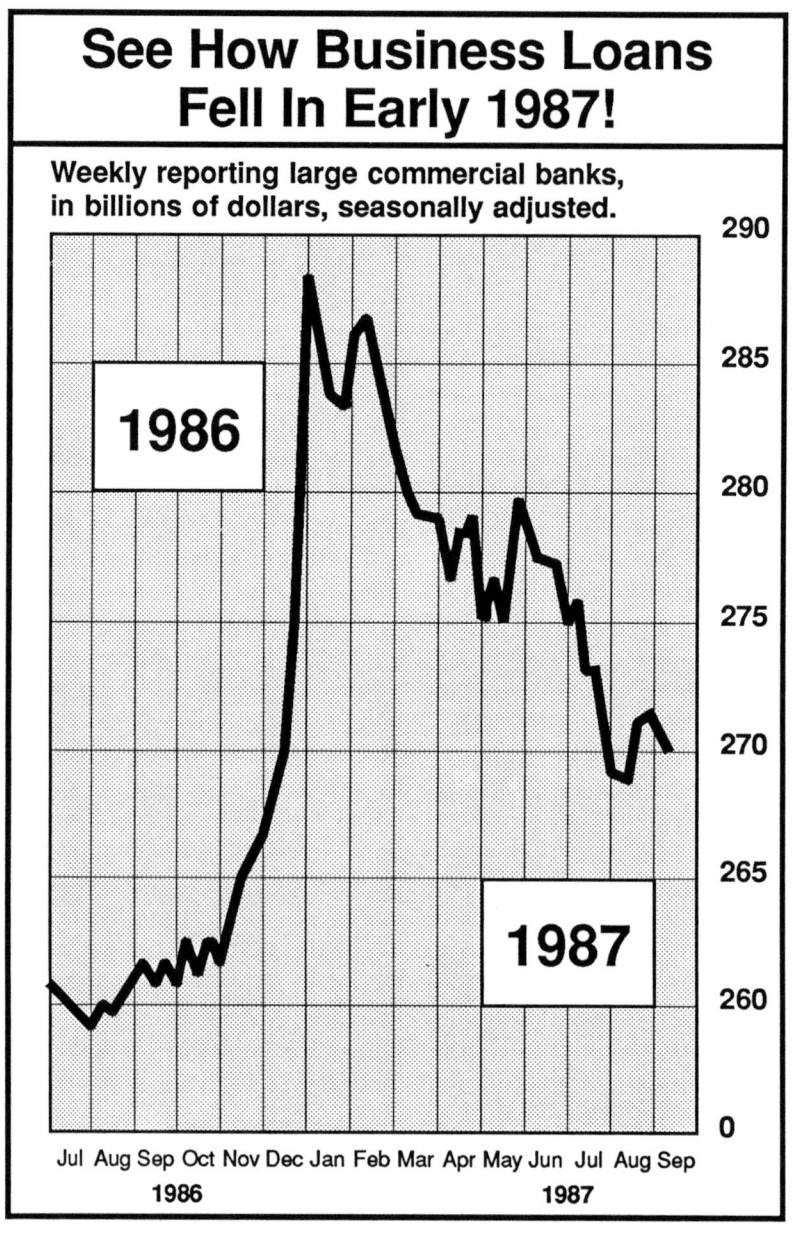

See How Business Loans Fell In Early 1987!

Weekly reporting large commercial banks, in billions of dollars, seasonally adjusted.

1986

1987

Jul Aug Sep Oct Nov Dec Jan Feb Mar Apr May Jun Jul Aug Sep
1986   1987

That Kept Checkable Deposits From Growing!

Averages of daily figures, in billions of dollars, seasonally adjusted.

Jul Aug Sep Oct Nov Dec Jan Feb Mar Apr May Jun Jul Aug Sep

1986　　　　　　　　　　　　　**1987**

To the average of four weeks ending:	Compounded annual rates of change, average of 4 wks. ending:						
	9/8/86	12/8/86	2/9/87	3/9/87	4/6/87	5/4/87	6/8/87	7/6/87
2/9/87	16.1							
3/9/87	16.7	12.8						
4/6/87	14.8	10.4	6.0					
5/4/87	16.2	13.4	12.7	14.4				
6/8/87	13.9	10.6	8.6	8.4	10.9			
7/6/87	10.9	6.9	3.8	2.5	2.4	-7.0		
8/10/87	10.0	6.3	3.5	2.5	2.5	-3.7	-5.4	
9/7/87	9.1	5.4	2.9	1.9	1.7	-3.2	-4.2	0.7

Higher Interest Rates Collided Head-First With This Inflation!

The Commodity Research Bureau's raw industrials spot price index, 1967 = 100.

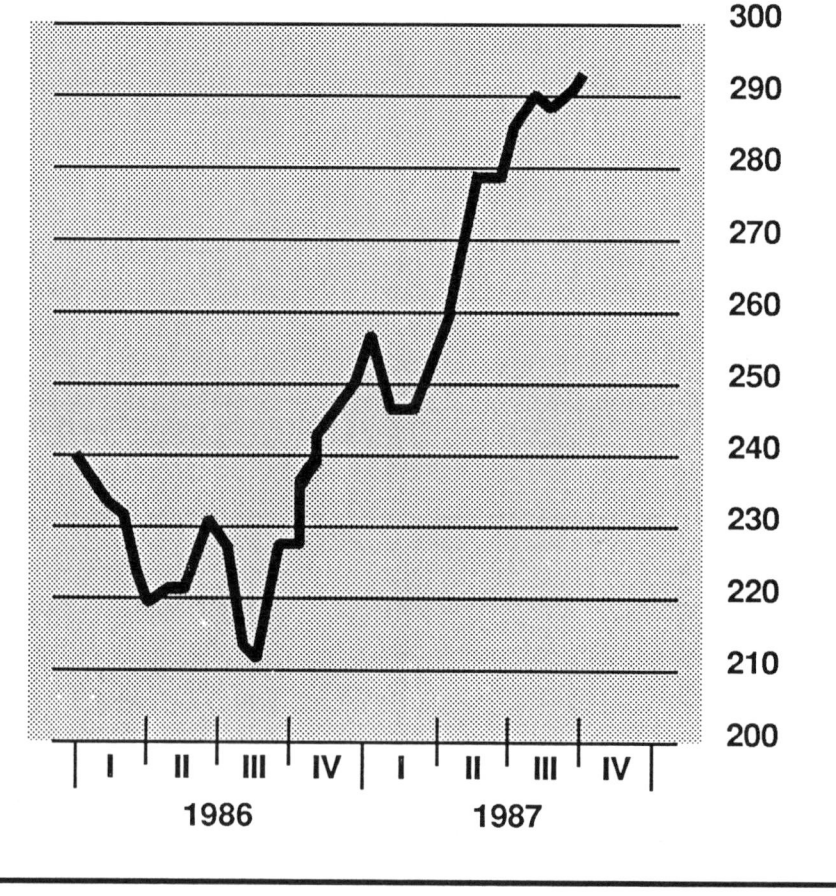

And, Just As The Fed Expected Commodities Stopped Rising!

Once higher interest rates have finished off inflation, you will see rates collapse!

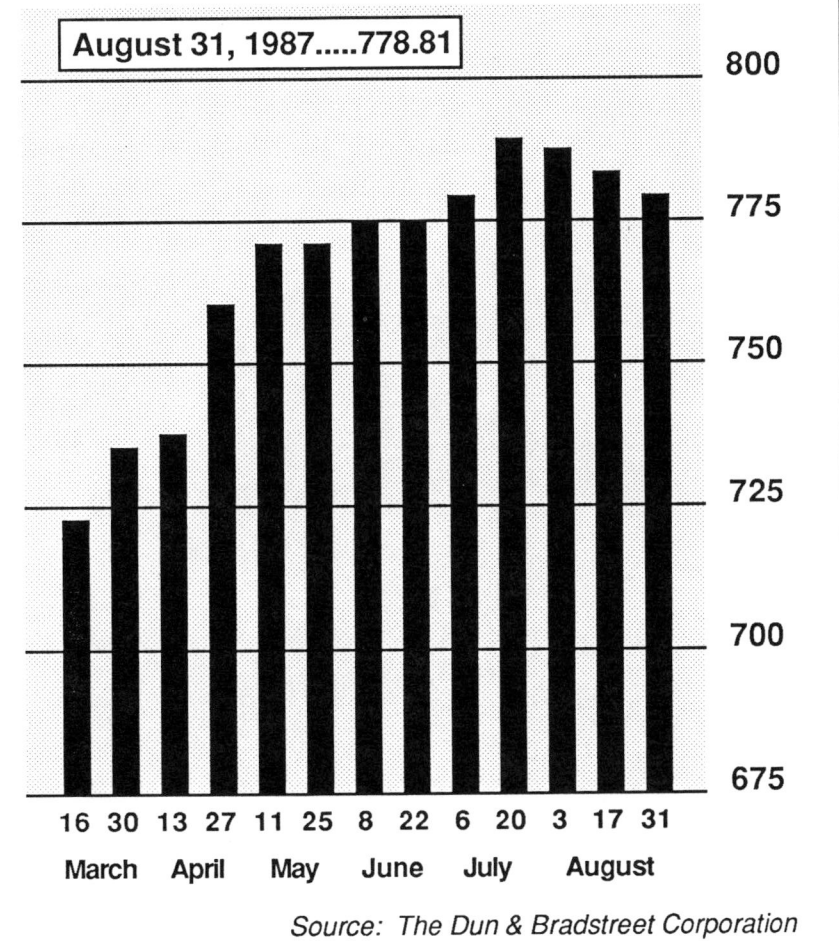

August 31, 1987.....778.81

Source: *The Dun & Bradstreet Corporation*

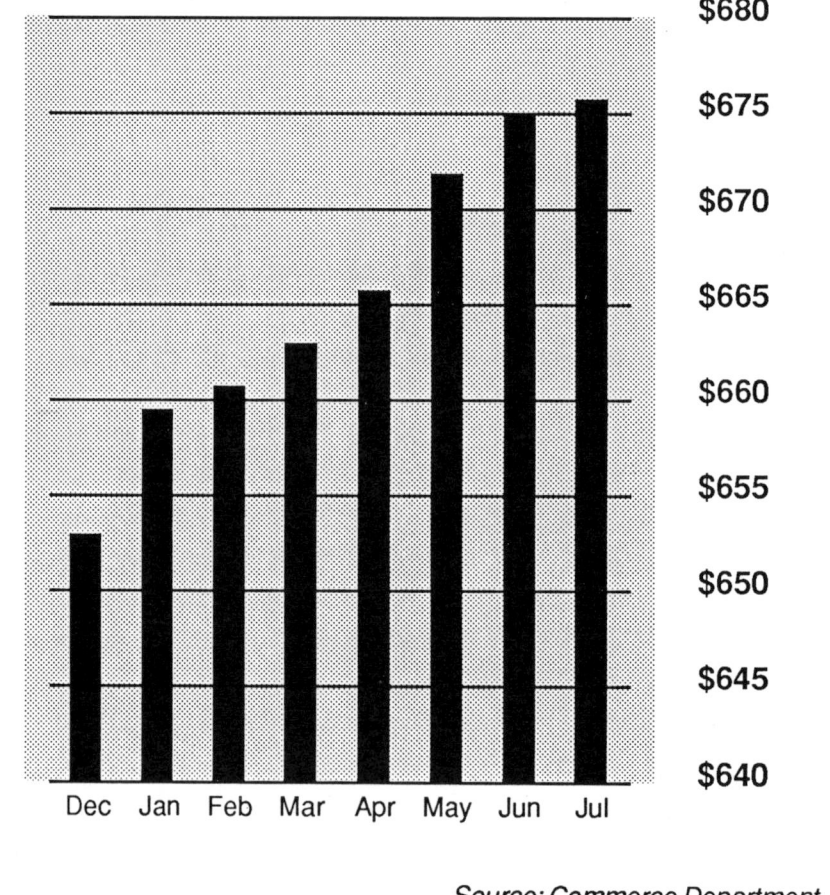

U.S. Manufacturing And Trade Inventories Piled Up!

Inventories of manufacturing, wholesale and retail firms in billions of dollars, seasonally adjusted.

Source: Commerce Department

Surprise! Unsold Goods Caused Cutbacks In Orders!

Manufacturers' total new orders for durable goods, in billions of dollars, seasonally adjusted.

Change From Previous Month

August.................-3.1%
July......................0.0%
June..................+2.0%

S O N D — J F M A M J J A
1986 — 1987

Source: Commerce Department

Adrian Van Eck

And Falling Orders Pressed Down On U.S. Wholesale Prices!

Percent change in Producer Price Index, adjusted for seasonal change, indicating cost changes for finished goods

1987

Monthly change	August
Consumer foods	-1.3%
Gasoline	+4.2%
Intermediate goods	+0.4%
Crude goods	+0.4%

day. And you can have all the experts going on ABC's Moneyline on CNN or being interviewed by the folks who put quotes under the stock market charts in The Wall Street Journal. None of the above matters a damn as compared to the power of money itself. And right now the money power in America says inflation must stop, the U.S. must balance both its Federal budget and its trade accounts. And then interest rates must collapse under their own weight to save Western Civilization...

"People write and call constantly to ask when they will see evidence proving that we are going to be right... again. That evidence is now popping up all around you. *But you must pick it out of the background noise* about the higher inflation and the higher interest rates so many folks are now predicting! Just look at the raw materials commodity prices you see in the chart. Wow! No wonder so many people thought inflation was out of control. But hold on. Will you look at the chart showing what has happened to commodity prices since the Fed turned the screws in late April! First the rise slowed down. Then it turned flat. There was a tiny blip in late July. Then they began to round over and actually decline. Note the word you just read... decline! *Prices can go down as well as up.* We expect to see a correction in that late-1986, early-1987 upswing of raw materials commodities prices.

"Tight money has forced up interest rates for the time being. This is a perfectly natural short term event. Do not let anyone scare you with talk of constantly-rising interest rates. That cannot happen. The reason it cannot happen is that with inflation not only coming to a screeching halt but actually starting to turn back down... into DEFLATION... real interest rates are getting to be so high as to cause corporate and personal financial nosebleeds! Back in the 1950's, when inflation was also down around zero to 1% a year, market rates were a great deal lower that they are today. So the real cost of money (interest charged minus inflation rate) was remarkably low. That is the norm. Call it the natural level of interest rates if you will. We hear a lot of talk about, 'But investors now demand a higher rate of return.' So let them make all the demands they want. But remember this: The new Gramm-Rudman Act requires a steady reduction in Federal new borrowing! It is our firm belief that even a mild recession will be blamed by everyone on this deficit. And politicains will panic and move faster towards a balanced budget. This will leave a lot of money looking for new bonds to buy. *Competition will drive interest rates down!... Anyone who now thinks this will not happen is heading for a rude shock.* So far as we are concerned, it is all so *predictable* that anyone with an open mind should see it just as clearly as we do. Maybe even more clearly than we do.

"WE HAVE IN MIND WHEN WE SAY THAT, THE HOST OF *STOCK BROKERS* - GOD BLESS THEM - WHO ARE NOW PRIVATELY READING THESE LETTERS AND WHO CONTACT US TO SAY THAT

THEY AGREE WITH US, *EVEN IF THIS MEANS THEY ARE OUT OF SYNCH WITH THEIR OWN BROKERAGE FIRMS. It is such letters and calls that make us believers in keeping a "full service" broker as a personal investment advisor... even if it costs you a bit more money getting in and getting out!* After all, the only numbers that really count are these: What you start with and what you *end with.* Details such as commisions and what your investments are listed at in the newspapers on any given day while you still hold them and wait out temporary events such as the recent rise in interest rates... these do not equal what you end with when it comes to relative importance. Remember that!

"In this Letter, we concentrate on money and what it is doing to the economy. Everything else depends on money and flows from money. Keep your eye on what money is doing and be patient... and you will never, never be surprised by unfolding events in the economy." (End quote from November, 1987 Forecast Letter - mailed October 8, 1987.) To illustrate these quotes, I have added seven charts. These charts originally appeared in the midst of the quoted material... and I think compliment it perfectly.

I have taken the time to go back to September / October, 1987, with you for one simple reason: To show you how completely rational events have been in the past five months. The stock market correction was no accident, as so many believe. It was not a surprise, as some would try to convince you. It was planned, coordinated and even forced by the Board of Governors of the Federal Reserve System, Chairman Alan Greenspan presiding. He did it to save the American economy, not to ultimately harm it. *The reason I turned bullish as soon as the events of October 19th scared America was that I believed then (as I do now) that the Fed had acted in time. Greenspan (and Paul Volcker before him) had aborted the runaway enthusiasm of summer and autumn, 1987. Common sense returned to the American enonomic / financial scene.* There was, by sometime in November, no reason to fear a depression any longer. Because depressions are a result of and an aftermath to prolonged periods of wild financial excesses. Since the Fed stopped such a time of excesses in its early stages... and re-directed America's energy onto more traditional growth paths... there is simply no reason to anticipate either a long or a deep adjustment.

What of the popular book predicting a depression in 1990? The book should be listed as a work of fiction, instead of non-fiction. The author says he has made an amazing discovery... a sixty-year cycle in American business affairs. *He says that the only way to save America is to have the Government confiscate a third of the wealth in the nation and distribute this wealth to those who have failed to earn or save money on their own.* Wall Streeters stood in line to buy 300,000 copies of this book, which in effect would propose that we wipe out America's capitalistic system. But I am not here to defend capitalism. I need only point out that if this mysterious cycle is of real value, it must clearly extend backwards in time as well as forwards. If 1930 is the operative year, as he says, then sixty years earlier (1870) is another depression starter. And so is the sixtieth year prior to 1870 (1810). Did depressions start in 1870 and 1810? The heck they did! American industry developed fast starting in 1810. We were then a nation of seven million, mostly strung out from Maine to Georgia on the Atlantic Coast. The U.S. started to make products it had previously imported from Europe, and after the war ended in 1815 the new American industries reached out for a big role in world markets. Our internal commerce developed, thanks to the application of steam as a power source. In one single year (1816) U.S. exports grew more than sevenfold, to $53 million. Ironically, the Government's debt during the war had grown from $80 million to $127 million... and yet our credit in the world was greatly improved. So prosperous was America that the people called this The Era of Good Feeling. Material prosperity spread throughout the Union. If that is supposed to be a decade of depression - according to the every-sixty-years-a-depression theory now given so much credence in America - it was one heck of a "depression." I say it tosses the theory into the wastebasket, where it rightfully belongs!

And if you think the Boom in that alleged "depression" decade was red hot, wait until you hear about the Boom in the decade that started sixty years later... 1870. (That was two full "cycles" ago!)

1870 was the start of the greatest surge of industrial growth and modernization America or the world had ever seen before or has seen since. In this year - *sixty years prior to 1930* - America was coming out of a time that now looks shabby... but was regarded as reasonably prosperous by those in the nation at the time. In 1869, only nine new banks were formed. Their total capital was only $1,500,000. In the same year, seventeen banks failed. Their total capital was $3,372,000. *Remember - this was sixty years prior to 1929.* This should be the end of a Boom, according to current fears. But in 1870 the number of new banks doubled to twenty-two. In 1871, as the Boom really picked up speed, some 170 new banks were started and not a single bank went broke in all of America. 1872 was even better. A total of 175 new banks opened for business... the mark of an economy making real money! So much for the theory that frightens so many now. And I will let you in on something simple and basic that just has to affect the way you feel about the American economy in the remaining months of 1988 and in the next year... even the next seven years. It is clear that forces now gaining control over the American economy are much closer in kind to those of 1808 and 1868... years just before Booms got under way in America... than they are to those of 1928 or 1929 or 1930... years that you are being wrongly told are similar to the current year! And then I urge you to add one more ingredient to this picture: Fed Chairman Greenspan is a professional economist. He probably knows more about the 1810 and 1870 Boom periods than I do. And he knows that the only way America can now avoid such a Boom is if he and others on the Fed heed the whining and begging from behind the scenes in Washington. If they try to stimulate an artificial Boom in this election year, they will abort the natural Boom now rumbling and stirring in the depths of the economy. Greenspan will not do that.

He knows that an artificial Boom would burn out a few months from now... right after the election. But a natural Boom will transform American industry into the leanest, meanest export machine in the entire world. A natural Boom will pile up so many dollars in profits here in the United States that our debt worries will slowly evaporate, like a morning mist early on a hot summer day!

And speaking of debt: On all sides of you people who have no idea what they are talking about now attempt to frighten you with wild stories of debt burdens so great that the Federal Republic itself is doomed to collapse within a decade. Smile and lean back in your seat. It is not so. Total debt and GNP run along side-by-side like a pair of railroad tracks for the entire Twentieth Century. The Federal debt is not as scary as "they" want you to believe. I worry more about MERGER LOANS, which push up non-Federal debt. *(Firms with large debt loads will suffer negative leverage in the absence of inflation. That is why I prefer smaller growth companies - Special Situations - in the early years of the emerging Boom.)*

I am not alone in believing that mergeritis is a disease that can have unpleasant long-term side effects. In fact, it is my belief that the October stock market massacre was engineered partly to bring about the end of such activities. I think the Fed is pressing and pushing U.S. companies to go back to old-fashioned notions of growth... namely investing in plants and machines. I never did think that Fed Chairman Volcker made any effort to hide what he was doing, and I said so.

In my September, 1987 Letter I said: "We have taken the Yellow Flag off the flag pole so we can wave it as vigorously as we can... If you have not yet taken our warning seriously, we urge you to do so at once. Get your personal, business and investment affairs in the tightest grip possible as fast as you can."

I admitted in that Letter the reason for my stern warning was Paul Volcker and the Fed. I asked: "QUESTION OF THE DAY - WHY WAS PAUL VOLCKER SMILING THE DAY HE STEPPED DOWN FROM POWER AS THE CHAIRMAN OF THE FED'S BOARD OF GOVERNORS? It is our opinion that the usually sour-faced central banker was flashing wide grins simply because he knew something almost no one else knew on his last day in office. *He knew that he was getting out of the Fed while the getting was good...* the market celebrated by going up twenty-five points the day before he left and twenty-five more points on the day he actually gave up his awesome, terrifying power at the Fed. He, as we said, laughed at them. It was a private laugh, at his own deadly private joke. For he knew that the U.S. economy was already one month and one week past the point at which a recession usually begins and DEFLATION - or at least sharp and severe DISINFLATION - starts to crush and destroy the careless and the unwary!" I continued in that August, 1987, Letter (as the market was topping out):

"Now we are going to tell you something that is a top secret in America. Volcker knew it when he left. In fact, he hid it very well. It is a fact that we can prove and have proven many times in the last eight years: Volcker is one of the few men in the Federal Government who has mastered the art of keeping a secret in Washington D.C. HE DID SO AGAIN WITH THE SECRET HE TOOK OUT OF THE FED WITH HIM. That 'secret' - as he told newspaper reporters, senators, congressmen, bankers, brokers and White House officials - is that the Fed had tightened money in recent months. Naturally, when you tell the truth in Washington D.C. no one believes you. It is assumed that you are covering something up... usually the opposite of whatever you say. And so the so-called 'smart money' has been betting on renewed inflation. They look at the money numbers and figure that Volcker must have found a way to disguise the real growth of money. They do not know how or when or where he hid the M1 and M2 and M3 money that does not show up on any tables or charts. But they shrug and say that 'it must be in there somewhere.' THAT SOUNDS STRANGE,

WE KNOW. IT IS HARD TO BELIEVE THAT AFTER EIGHT YEARS OF DEALING WITH PAUL VOLCKER HE WAS ABLE TO GO OUT OF OFFICE FOOLING PEOPLE AS EASILY AS HE DID WHEN HE CAME IN! But he did it. Son of a gun. He did it! Just as he did in early 1981 and just as he did in 1983. Each time we spotted it early and told you that he was about to spoil some politician's election year plans for the following year. Each time the market refused to believe the facts staring right at it...

"By late 1983... the word was out everywhere that Volcker would certainly give the White House what it wanted: A Boom in the year Ronald Reagan ran for a second term. We saw a couple of big-name economists predict that inflation would be out of control by October, 1984... and that Reagan would have to slap on price and wage controls the day after the election. They all agreed that interest rates would drop fast during the first half of 1984. The only fear was that inflation might get out of hand too early in election year 1984, forcing the Fed to tighten a notch or two at mid-year.

"It was expected that this would cause interest rates to drift upward in September and October of 1984. We were looking right at money charts that told us plain and simple the whole country was dead wrong. You know us when we have uncovered the proof that we are right. We stood right up and said: They are all wrong. Everyone. Wall Street. Congress. The college and banking and big business economists. And the White House. Especially the White House! Volcker, we said, would destroy inflation in the first half of 1984... and then at mid-year, interest rates would fall sharply on their own, without him doing it artificially. Oh joy of joys, we saw it all happen just as we had predicted. The money numbers had told us true. Our readers protected themselves, then made truly big profits. Everyone else was befuddled, confused and in many cases darn near wiped out. (It was about then that a staffer brought us a sign we cherish. It said: 'We love it when we're right.') In 1984, as in 1982, Volcker saw it as his duty to resist inflation in an election year. And he did so.

"In 1986, America avoided a recession. But the deflation on the Farm Belt and near-depression conditions in 'Oil Country' and the Industrial Belt combined to cost the Republicans eight seats in the Senate. They lost control of it! *The feeling in the White House was that Volcker had done them in again...* (actually) by very late 1986 the M1 money supply was growing very fast again. By the end of 1986 it was moving up at an annual rate of 20.5%. *That convinced a lot of people that hyper-inflation was coming back.* That is why gold and silver turned up. And some other commodities. And as Wall Street saw what it believed to be the signs of reborn inflation, long-term interest rates turned up sharply. Bonds tumbled as a result in the spring of 1987. The irony is that just about the time that the whole country - plus a lot of foreign investors - got it in their head that inflation was coming back, we saw 'Dr. Volcker' - the dreaded enemy of inflation - reappear. In our April Letter, we warned that money had not been growing for three months... and that it had so far gone unnoticed... in our August, 1987 Letter we really took the lid off the story and told you that we thought it was too early to worry... but it was not at all too early to grow alert to the possibility of a sudden, mild, surprise mini-recession... or at least a period of flat, zero growth in the GNP...

"We drew a line across the point M1 hit on New Year's Day, 1987. After that, it dipped and rose again, reaching $758 billion on two occasions in April and May... WALL STREET HAS STILL *REFUSED TO FACE THE FACT* THAT MONEY HAS BEEN FLAT FOR SEVEN MONTHS AND SHRINKING FOR THREE!! It is a fact that after money growth slows for six months, a recession usually appears. And we are no longer talking about the relatively mild medicine of slowing down the growth of money. We are long past that. When bonds fell and gold rose on the basis of inflationary expectations, *Volcker and the Fed took the much tougher measure of actually REDUCING the money supply.* If they continued to do so, there would be less money circulating at year-end than was the case in the spring. Yet prices are clearly up... mostly because people expected them to go up and businessmen obliged. When you get into that kind of situation (and America did get into a remarkably similar bind in late 1981) *it is just like the old game of musical chairs.* You remember, everyone walks around the chairs

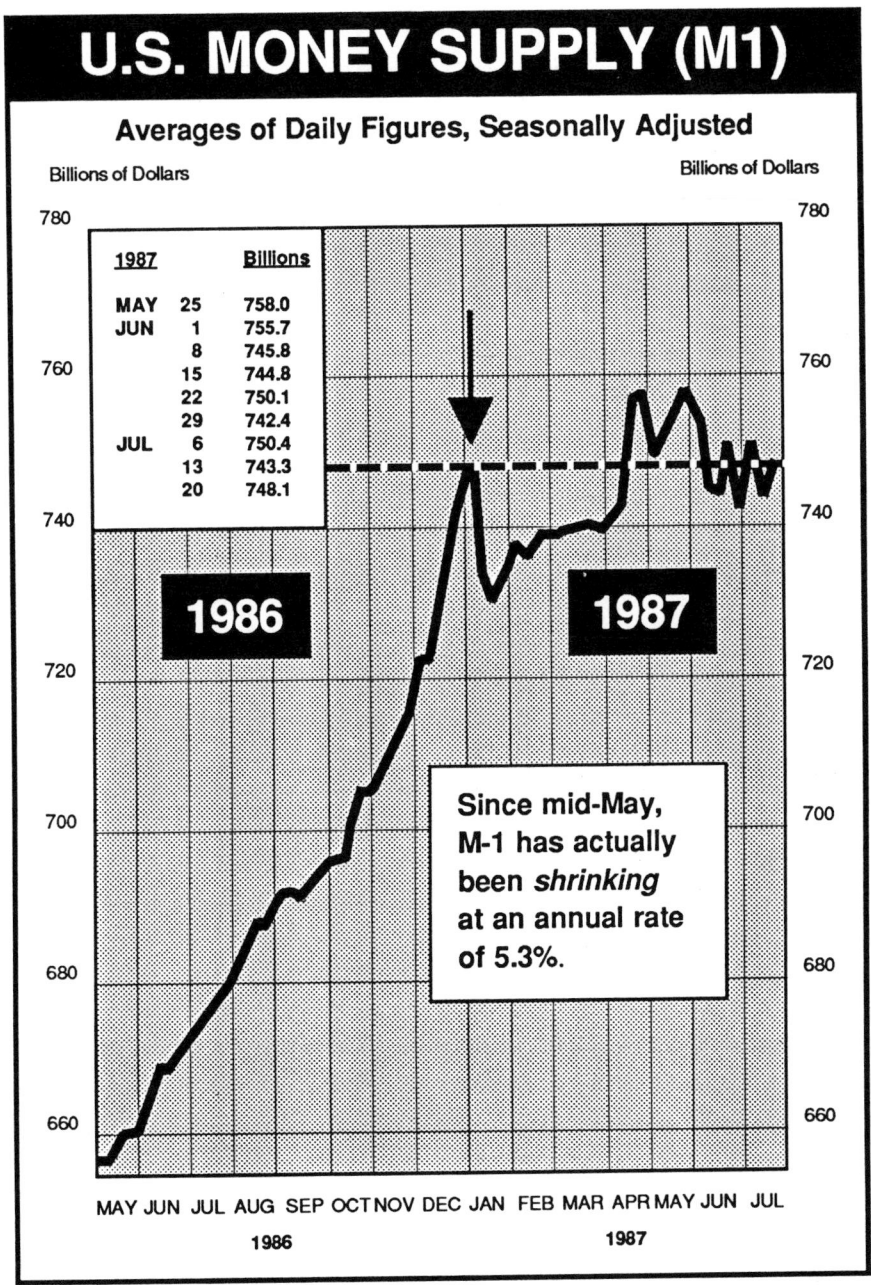

U.S. MONEY SUPPLY (M1)

Averages of Daily Figures, Seasonally Adjusted

Billions of Dollars

1987		Billions
MAY	25	758.0
JUN	1	755.7
	8	745.8
	15	744.8
	22	750.1
	29	742.4
JUL	6	750.4
	13	743.3
	20	748.1

1986

1987

Since mid-May, M-1 has actually been *shrinking* at an annual rate of 5.3%.

MAY JUN JUL AUG SEP OCT NOV DEC JAN FEB MAR APR MAY JUN JUL

1986   1987

as the music plays. When the music stops, one person is left standing and is 'out.' One chair is taken away... the music starts... and everyone begins to walk around the chairs. It is the game Volcker has been playing since 1979. He left the Fed with the music still playing. But he took one of the chairs away with him!

"Folks at the White House seriously believe that Alan Greenspan will now bring in new chairs to make sure there is a seat for everyone and anyone. They do not know their man. Alan Greenspan is going to surprise just about everyone on Wall Street and in Washington. We predict that when the music stops and the speculators on inflation and the debtors discover how tough and *mean* Greenspan is, *they are going to cry and moan and say they wish they had Paul Volcker back.* The two Chairmen are different. We warned readers eight years ago that Volcker was like a chunk of granite in the middle of the road in the New Hampshire mountains. We compared inflation to a speeding car rounding the curve. *ALAN GREENSPAN IS THE STATE TROOPER!"* (End quote from my Letter mailed mid-August, 1987.)

When the market fell some 1,000 points between late-August and October 19th, Washington and Wall Street grew frightened. Ironically, I began to breathe easier. It is not that I am a contrarian. It is just that I knew why (and so did you, if you read my Letters) the Fed had forced the situation.

When Greenspan and the Fed pumped reserves into U.S. banks while officials counted noses to see who would survive and who would be shut down, I did not join the chorus of those who predicted inflation. And sure enough, the Fed drained all of those reserves out of the banking system. America ended 1987 with M1 standing at almost precisely the same total on December 31st as it had back on January 1st. I had not seen that phenominon since Eisenhower's years in the 1950's. Frankly, I found it bullish. Ike forced three recessions in his eight years. He and Congress balanced the Federal budget often. He kept interest rates low. Inflation averaged 1% a year. Investment in plants and equipment was high. Corporate profits averaged 15% of sales, compared to 5% of sales in recent years. The Dow Jones average tripled during his two terms. Skeptics said it was over in 1959. They predicted a crash just like that of 1929. (They had said the same thing in 1949, too. They predict it for every year ending in nine.) No crash came. John F. Kennedy was elected. He continued Ike's policies. America was afraid of his economics at first. They did not realize he was "his father's son." His speeches were liberal. His policies were conservative. He resisted communism abroad and pushed for factory modernization at home (introducing a 10% investment tax credit). The Dow fell sharply in 1962... and as a result everyone thought a recession was coming. But none came. In fact, his policies stimulated a strong industrial growth Boom with low interest rates. No one seems to remember those facts today. Because it is all happening again... and people say it is an impossible combination. People do say that... but Alan Greenspan and the Fed Board do not say that. And I think they are important people.

Greenspan and the Fed are now determined to shove the U.S. economy right back onto and along the path it followed in 1953 to '63... high investment in modern plants, high profits, low inflation and low interest rates. Do not "bet against" the Fed on this one. No one who bets against them will win!

I warned readers when Volcker recommended Greenspan as his successor (and the President went along with the choice), that Alan would want the *same* things Volcker wanted. I had already said in these Letters that *Volcker had evolved* into a strong believer in the possibility of growth without inflation. Greenspan believes in it too. I said in August, 1987 that: "There are powerful cross-currents battling each other... consumer borrowing and spending are weak... maybe already trending down in real terms. But industrial activity is getting stronger. *And we think industry will surprise everyone with its vigor in the next eight years!"* (End quote.) And sure enough, numbers began to pour out... showing consumer spending down and business investment in capital equipment going up. We have a generation of analysts today who do not remember the Ike-JFK Boom years... so they cannot quite figure out what is going on. They keep waiting for capital investment to collapse... even stop altogether. Poor, poor souls. Years from now, in 1995, they will look back on the 1988 to '95 period as one of the greatest industrial modernization Booms in the history of America. They will look around them and see super-efficient factories in all corners of the United States... they will see an America running a substantial trade balance. And they will wonder how they missed the early days of the Boom. By then it will be old hat... and they will be able to look back at the history that to us, today, is still the unseen future. It will be all so very clear to them by then. They will curse themselves for having believed scare stories crafted by opportunists catering to the frightened mass mind of early 1988. But you will not be cursing yourself by then. You will be counting your new wealth... the personal and business gains piled up in 1988, 1989, 1990, 1991, 1992, 1993, 1994 and 1995!

But I have to warn you: The greatest danger to you and your money in these next seven years may come in the *next several months*. If you prudently guard against speculation, you should avoid downside risks that threaten precious *capital accumulations*. But others will try to tempt you into such speculation. I EXPECT THE USUAL SCREAMS, SHOUTS AND CHEERS. THEY WILL ASSUME THAT GREENSPAN IS SELLING OUT TO THE WHITE HOUSE. THEY WILL START CRANKING OUT LETTERS ABOUT *INFLATION*. YOU MAY EVEN HEAR THE OLD TALES ABOUT GERMANY AFTER WORLD WAR I AGAIN. (OR MAYBE THEY WILL TALK ABOUT MARXIST NICARAGUA, WHERE THE GOVERNMENT CAN

NOT AFFORD NEW PAPER TO PRINT ANY MORE MONEY... SO THEY ARE RUBBER-STAMPING HUGE NEW DENOMINATIONS ON OLD SMALL BILLS AND RECIRCULATING THEM.) PLEASE COVER YOUR EARS AND BLOCK YOUR EYES TO ANY SUCH MESSAGES. Just tell yourself the truth. Shout it loud enough to drown out any wild scare messages directed at you. And the truth is that the Fed is still engaged in balancing the growth of money, offsetting money growth in 1986. Volcker used to do it too. He did it deliberately, to get a rise out of politicians, bankers, etc. He would force them to demand that he stop the rapid growth and "obey" their wishes. He alternated *short* bursts of rapid growth with *long* stretches of very slow growth. When all was said and done, *it broke the back of inflation that was reaching 20%* (annual rate) in a month shortly after he took office in 1979. (You may, if you go way back with me, remember how clearly that incident revealed a *weakness* I have. In late 1976, with inflation running at 2%, I looked at the way money was being created to pay for a big new tax-cut caused Federal deficit. I said it would cause 20% inflation. And I thought that rate would be reached within two years, maximum. It did cause 20% inflation, annual rate. But the process took more than three years. You have to watch out for me in that regard. Things look too clear to me, so I believe coming events are closer in time than they turn out to be. Oftentimes, just before something I have forecast actually explodes "out of the blue, without warning" - according to the media - I start to get letters from faithful readers asking if maybe this time I may possibly be wrong. So keep that in mind. But remember I have been on target as to direction of events and final result!)

For example, in November 1987 I said: "MONEY IS NOT A SIMPLE SUBJECT. IT IS COMPLEX. IF YOU ARE GOING TO UNDERSTAND MONEY, YOU MUST BE PATIENT AND MASTER THESE COMPLEXITIES. *THERE IS NO SHORT CUT.* And we refuse to say something silly like: 'Trust us. We understand. We will do your thinking for you!" No way. Even if you would allow that (and we do not believe you would allow it!), we just cannot operate that way. *It is a matter of deep pride to us that letters from our readers reveal a depth of understanding about money so great that we know we are dealing with equals... and even superiors!*

"There are three things you must know about money. One is that the *turning points in money supply are almost always your best indicator of a coming turn in the economy.* The C.P.I. (Consumer Price Index) will often turn down after money growth does. *Then turn up after money does.* And GNP (real growth, adjusted for inflation) often turns up or down *three to six months after money does.*

"The second thing you must know is that *before a TURN in money growth can have a major influence on the economy it must go on long enough and be large enough to significantly alter the balance between money and GNP.* That is trickier than it sounds on the surface. Too many people fail to appreciate the subtle nature of money! They see money growing fast and immediately they start to see visions of double-digit inflation. Maybe so and maybe not. It depends! We are not hedging or fudging. We are telling the truth. To begin with, *you have to put money growth in a long-term context. The reason flat growth in money during the first ten months of 1987 did not send the economy into and immediate tailspin is that money had grown so fast during the last half of 1986. That was a favorite trick of Paul Volcker:* Go like a son-of-a-gun and get everyone all worried about inflation. Then slam on the brakes so that the economy hits the windshield!

"Our view, as you know, is that Paul Volcker had a plan in mind on New Year's Day. He knew that by 1988 the politicians would fight him tooth and nail (if he were still at the Fed) on the subject of money growth. So he decided to get the job done *a year early. He pulled the pin on a financial hand-grenade on January first.* Then he started counting... ONE... TWO... THREE... FOUR... FIVE... SIX... SEVEN... EIGHT! Long enough, he decided, for him to stick around. So he let it be known that he would only stay if the President begged him to stay. This President was not going to do that. *So Volcker left. And he took his secret with him. (Although you knew, if you were with us in late-spring or summer or early-autumn.)*

THE FINANCIAL GRENADE KEPT 'TICKING'... NINE... THEN TEN! IN OCTOBER IT BLEW UP IN WALL STREET'S FACE. MOST PEOPLE NEVER EVEN KNEW WHAT HIT THEM. WE SAW ARTICLES RIGHT THROUGH 'BLACK MONDAY' OF SELF-STYLED 'EXPERTS' ON WALL STREET SAYING THAT THEY HAD NO IDEA WHY THINGS HAD GONE UP IN SMOKE... BUT THEY WERE SURE IT WASN'T MONEY CAUSING IT BECAUSE THEY KNEW THE FED WOULD NOT BE SO CRAZY AS TO TIGHTEN MONEY WITH AN ELECTION YEAR COMING UP SO SOON.

"Now, of course, the same people who did not see money get tight are worried sick that money will now be tightened to "save the dollar," causing a Great Depression. Goodness gracious! Where do these folks get such ideas? Depression? The United States is about to enter its greatest Super-Boom of this century. *Nothing like it has been seen since 1894... the end of the last great Super-Boom!* This new Super-Boom, which we see running on until the mid-1990's (perhaps with a correction / recession or two along the way) *will feature the two elements that really caused the Super-Boom of the late 1800's: Low interest rates plus low-inflation. Both have to go together to make a Super-Boom happen! And they will now both come at the same time - surprising America and the world.* We are positive that Volcker knows what is coming... After he finished his Harvard graduate studies, he went on for Doctorate work at the

London School of Economics. (That is were John F. Kennedy, also a "Harvard man," took his graduate studies in economics. His father, U.S. Ambassador to England Joseph P. Kennedy Sr., was determined that JFK gain *a solid understanding of how and why England had prospered during the long era of Queen Victoria.* When JFK was in the White House, America got a taste of this formula - low interest rates and low-inflation. He began *a genuine capital investment Boom.* His untimely death changed everything around, and America went into an unsustainable high interest rate, high-inflation Boom. NOW WE ARE GOING BACK TO THE GENUINE ARTICLE." (End quote, November 1987.)

The secret of my success, in that regard, is that I listen closely to what the Federal Reserve Governors say about their own long-term goals. MONEY CONTROLS EVENTS IN AMERICA. AND THE FED *IS* MONEY!

I found one public statement by a Fed Governor extremely revealing. *I take it very seriously. You should too.* These were remarks before the National Investor Relations Institute by Governor Edward W. Kelley, Jr., last November 9th. *(Remember that was only three weeks after the October 19th experience.)* Mr. Kelley said: "Our business and financial communities have a strong orientation towards *short-term profits, whereas I believe we need to be much more oriented toward long-term profitability.*

"We have just been through a major shock to our system. That gives us an opportunity to reassess ourselves and reorient, if necessary... Over the past several years, there has been a great deal of concern that the United States was losing its competitive edge and was on the way to being a second class economic power. We all saw scare headlines in the media about how the West is at last coming to the end of its vibrant era and is losing its will to keep pushing ahead. These claims were greatly overstated... Industrial production is up strongly and the area of greatest concern, our export volume, has been growing at a real rate of 16 to 18% a year... This holds great promise for the future. BUT WE MUST NOW REORIENT OUR THINKING TO THE LONG-TERM. We need to redefine success as generating consistent, dependable, sustainable, long-term profitability... We have a 'Catch 22' here. In an attempt to maximize profits right now, we severely jeopardize our ability to maximize profitability over the long run... Over the long haul... cost-cutting is a forever job... This basic presents an opportunity to cut corners and thereby raise current profits for a while...

"THIS IS PARTICULARLY TRUE IN THE AREA OF INTERNATIONAL TRADE... An underlying reason for this situation is that so many *American companies are short-term oriented* whereas our foreign competitors take a long-term view. The United States is a huge and dynamic market and other countries know this. In order to get into this market, they have been willing to pay a very large current cost of admission. They sent people to study us, they tried products out on us, and many of those products were expensive failures for a while. But they stayed with it, and they learned, and they got those products right. Furthermore, they priced them very aggressively and went for market share as opposed to those short-term profits. Now that they have that market share, I might add, they are not going to give it up very easily. All this was very costly to them in the short-term but it has begun to pay off in the long-term.

"With the important exception of a handful of major international companies, our business community has *not* done that. We can and must do the same thing and our opportunity is vast. As a nation, *we are not nearly aggressive enough as exporters*. We export 5.5% of our GNP. West Germany, on the other hand, exports 25.8%, the United Kingdom 19.8% and Japan 9.7%. There are huge market opportunities out there for us, just as there have been for our trading partners. In the industrialized countries we had a $91.6 billion adverse balance of trade in 1986. *We can cut deeply into this.* In the emerging industrial countries there are big markets that are starting to open up. And as time goes along, the Third World (at varying rates of speed) surely will also open up. *We need to get ahead of this by getting into those markets now.* I am satisfied that the United States can and will become a fearsome worldwide competitor. We have the managerial talent and *the entrepreneurial drive that is required to be successful.* What we need to do is be willing to accept the up-front expense that it takes to get a long-term pay off.

"SO HERE IS THE CHALLENGE: Nothing less than to change financial-America and business-America's mind-set. Change it away from a fixation on short-term profits toward long-term profitability. I would submit that right now is a perfect time to do this. In the aftermath of the recent financial shock you can just feel America start to rethink itself. Where are we? What are our strengths? What are our weaknesses? What can we do well? Where do we want to go and how do we want to get there?... The general investing public has been fed a steady diet for a long time of 'right now, this quarter, next quarter.' It has been an exciting and easy concept to digest, but it is not adequate.

"THE LONG-TERM MAY BE A LITTLE LESS GLAMOROUS BUT IT HAS TO BE SEEN FOR WHAT IT IS - WHERE THE FUTURE LIES... There is a story here for the value investor, for the growth investor, and even for the contrarian. The only group I do not believe will be interested are the professional short-term traders and the market timers - but I don't think we need to worry too much about them." (End quote from Federal Reserve Board Governor Edward W. Kelley Jr.) I urge you to study these remarks carefully. They clearly sum up the mind-set of the Fed today. Anyone who expects this Board to fool around with M1 and M2 just to help promote a short-term election-year surge in the economy, do not know their men very well. (One person on the

board would love to do so. But she only has one vote and her calls for easy money have opened up a gap between her and her fellow Governors.) This Board was aware that Chairman Volcker was pinching money growth. All the members realized that Chairman Greenspan continued this brutal anti-inflationary policy. They knew America would pay a short-term price... but it is a price they are willing to pay in order to get America onto a track of strong growth, low inflation and low interest rates. They know full well that when the marketplace understands and accepts how serious and determined they are, inflation fears will melt away... and interest rates will tumble naturally. *This is the way Volcker got rates down in 1982, 1983, 1984, 1985 and 1986.* The Fed gave up trying to manipulate interest rates artificially in 1979... just as I had predicted almost a month before Volcker made the big switch in policy. Yet, even today, it seems that almost everyone still waits in vain for the Fed to attempt to manipulate interest rates. It cannot be done now. The market is too sophisticated. If the Fed tried to force down rates by printing a lot of money, the market would raise its inflation premium and rates would go up! We saw that happen in 1987. So the only way to get rates a lot lower is to reduce inflation expectations. THERE ARE TWO WAYS TO CURB FEARS OF INFLATION. One is the West German way... slow the growth of the economy way down, close to zero. The other is the Japanese way... invest in cost-efficient new plants and equipment, increasing output and force down prices. The Federal Reserve Board is now committed to forcing

America onto the Japanese type of economy... with strong growth in productivity, low interest rates and low inflation!

Governor Kelley is not the only Fed member who tips his hand in public remarks. Chairman Greenspan does so himself. *I notice he has adopted the old Volcker habit, of making his most important policy remarks at out of the way events... where the financial media is rarely present to cover him.* I used to get my best insights into Volcker by carefully studying his speeches at places that did not even get reported in the newspapers. He loved to do that. It was part of the man's make-up... sort of his private joke. He always insisted that he had revealed in advance and in public everything he planned to do... but almost no one could ever remember him making any such remarks. It looks to me as if Greenspan has the same wonderful dry wit. I keep tabs on his public remarks. And I can now say I have nailed him... nailed him good!

On January 15, 1988, Chairman Greenspan spoke at the Martin Luther King Jr. Social Seminar in Atlanta, Georgia. After opening by saying that he had never met Dr. King and had disagreed with him considerably on many aspects of economic policy - *a sure tip-off that this was to be a major statement of Fed intentions and not merely a polite speech* - the Fed Chairman went on to say:

"THE ISSUE OF INTERNATIONAL COMPETITIVE-NESS DID NOT ARISE IN A VACUUM... Our evolution from an agrarian nation at the turn of the century to a first-rate industrial power was greatly facilitated by the adoption of *labor-saving technology...* Our competitiveness in world markets - as well as prospects for economic growth in general - *will depend upon our ability to develop and apply technology...* We have been slow to convert many of our scientific and technological breakthroughs into commerically-viable products. Notable examples include the transistor radio, the color television and most recently the VCR. The initial development work on all of those products was performed here. But it was the Japanese who made the necessary improvements and adaptations to introduce them on the mass market... Many foreign firms have established extensive distribution and service networks here, and American consumers have developed loyalties to foreign brands... Protectionist measures would merely raise prices to American consumers and lead to an atrophy of American competitiveness... Prospects for improved economic performance hinge on our ability to overcome our problems with productivity and with quality... We must maintain a high level of business investment, in order to equip our factories with the most up-to-date technology and machinery... Meaningful cuts in the Federal budget deficit will raise the amount of saving available for capital formation... *We can modernize service businesses as well as manufacturing.* New data processing and communications systems have revolutionized the control of inventories and reorganized the flow of work... THE POTENTIAL FOR FURTHER

GAINS IN EFFICIENCY IS IMMENSE... SUBSTAN-CIAL BENEFITS WILL FLOW." (End quote, Alan Greenspan.)

And there you have the Fed's own blueprint for the U.S. economy over the next three years (the balance of Greenspan's term). It is exciting... even exhilarating, don't you agree?

CHAPTER TWO

Van Eck's Record (How We Got Here)

MONEY makes the world go 'round. Or at least that part of the world including Western Europe, the Americas, Japan, South Korea and Taiwan. *PEOPLE control MONEY.* Thus it is my belief that if you keep pretty good tabs on MONEY and PEOPLE you will have a good grasp of where the economy is and where it is headed. For the past dozen years, I have made that belief the *basis* of my Letter. So far it has not let me down. Nor has it disappointed my subscribers.

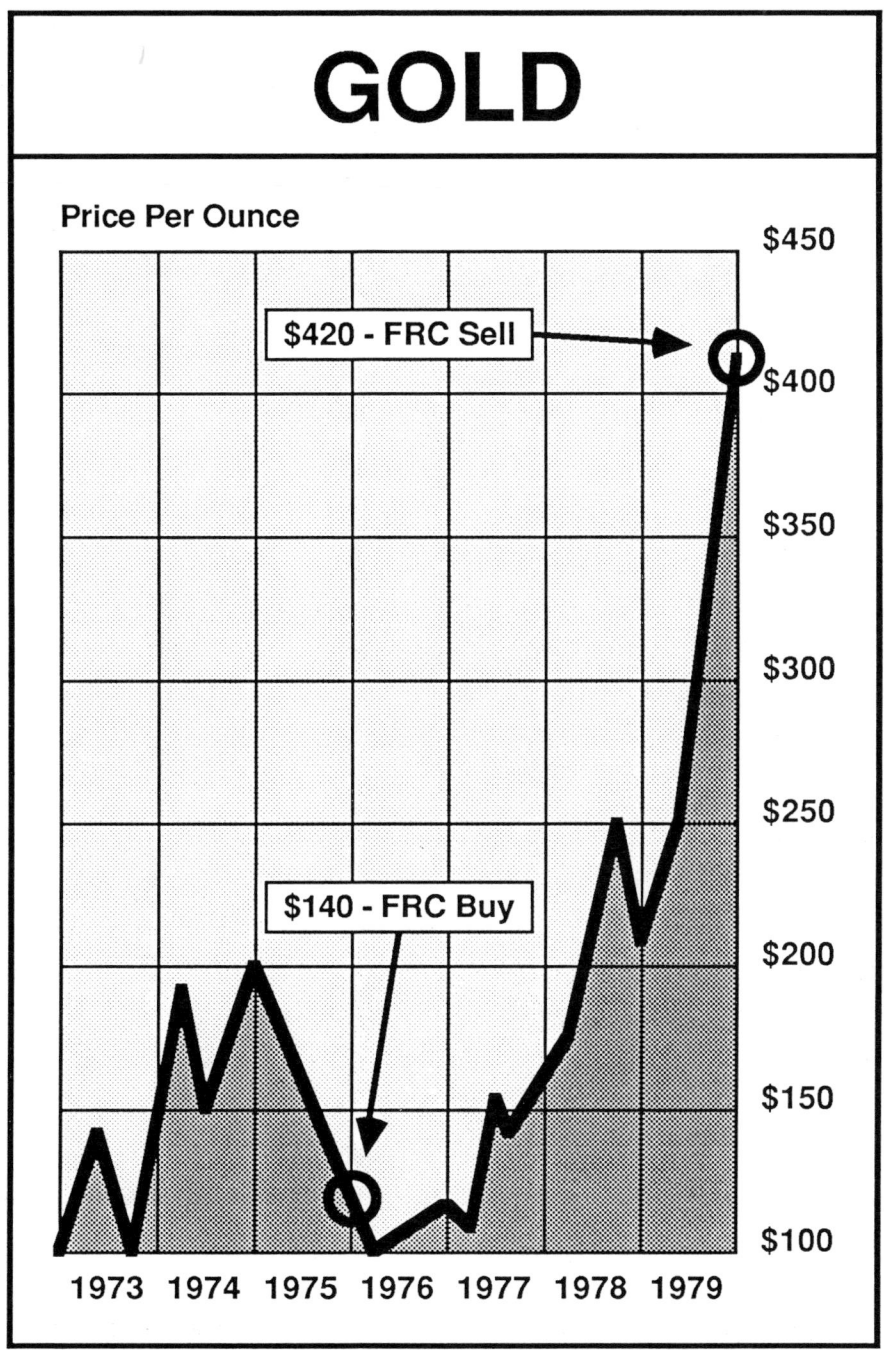

Not so long ago, for example, I received a note from a subscriber who happened to be a stock broker in New York State. In it he wrote: "I've been amazed over your ability to foresee trends developing a good bit in advance of the actual event. Your advice has helped me steer many of my clients to the right course in the past three years." *(Note: I am intensely proud of the number of financial professionals who read my Letter today.)*

The only problem that has turned up so far in using my PEOPLE PLUS MONEY Forecast Formula is that it tends to get me out ahead of events just a little bit. I am constantly responding to events that have so far happened only in my own mind *(where I see them so clearly, I sometimes convince myself they will immediately take place)*. In the beginning, as a result, my forecasts were met with disbelief.

For example, when I issued a "BUY GOLD NOW" message early in 1976, it seemed to many of my readers (who numbered only in the hundreds at the time) as if I had lost my mind. (And some of them wrote to tell me so.) After all, inflation was down around 2% a year and seemingly headed down. But I told our readers that new developments in MONEY behind the scenes, developments involving powerful PEOPLE in Government and finance, made it likely that inflation would soar to 20% a year in just a few years.

GOLD WAS $140 AN OUNCE WHEN I SAID BUY. It

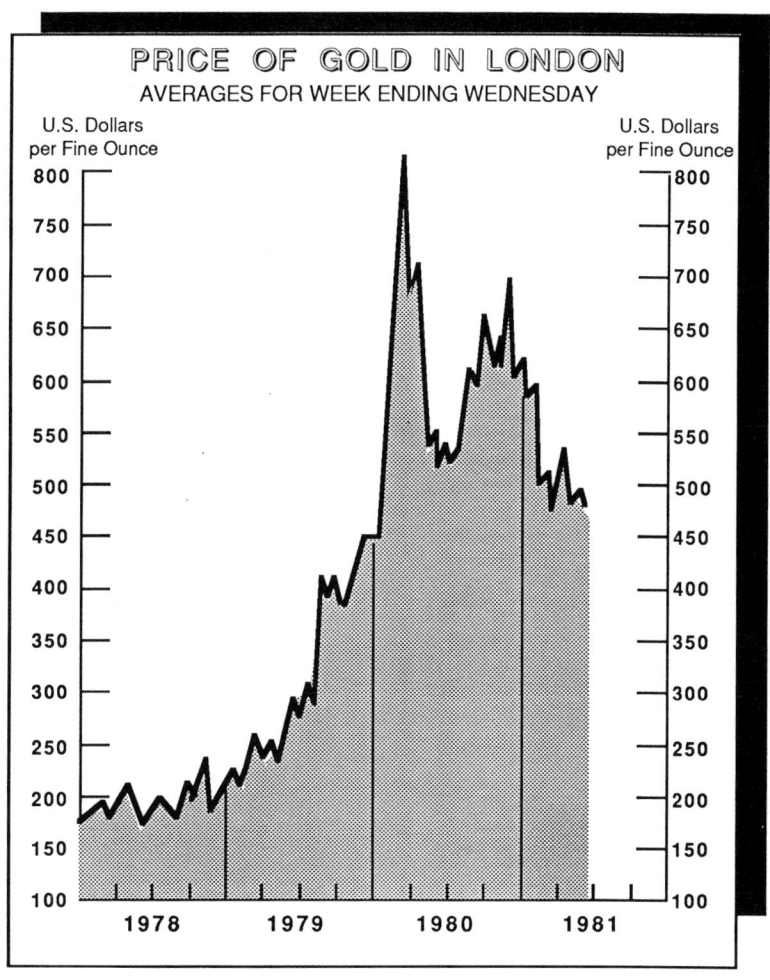

slipped and slid to $100 over the next several months, while I kept repeating my new inflation warning. Then, late in 1976, just about on Election Day, the tide began to *turn* for GOLD and inflation. Over the next three years, prices rose at an ever-faster rate in America... as the very forces I had warned about in January, 1976, simply exploded across the landscape. GOLD rose too... back up to my $140 buy point... then on up to $200... $250... $300... $350... $400 an ounce. Inflation hit double digits... 15%... shot up for a single month to the exact 20% annual rate I had seen so clearly and had predicted more than three years earlier. *But by that time I was seeing a brand new picture in my mind's eye... a scene of falling prices and panic selling in GOLD.* Paul Volcker had been named Chairman of the Federal Reserve Board. I had followed his career and knew his mind well. I warned my readers that he was now likely to shift from controlling interest rates to restricting the runaway growth of the MONEY supply. Three weeks after I predicted Volcker would do this, he and the Fed voted for this shift. In fact, to do so Volcker called the first emergency Saturday morning meeting since the Great Depression of the 1930's - that is how urgent he considered the problem! Wall Street was *stunned!* My readers were ready!

I had advised subscribers to cash their gains in GOLD. (It had tripled from $140 to $420 since I had said BUY GOLD.) Some readers did as I urged. Others ignored Volcker and the Fed and bought more GOLD. As usually happens, most PEOPLE respond to recent events... rather than to coming events! They came *late* to the market. Their buying pushed GOLD up to a new all-time high. Over $800 an ounce. One night I watched national television news and saw a long line of PEOPLE snaking outside the office door of a Chicago GOLD dealer. So many PEOPLE were waiting in line to buy that the dealer could not close at 5 p.m. It had to stay open and take the PEOPLE'S MONEY. The television news reporter interviewed one Chicago nurse who had just cleaned out her savings account - $8,000 - and had bought ten GOLD coins with the MONEY. *She was ecstatic.* The television reporter then asked the manager if he was buying GOLD for himself. "No," he said. "I'm so busy taking care of these folks that I have no time to buy GOLD for my own account." I shook my head. *I knew this had to be the peak of madness. It would be all over within hours I felt. And of course it was!* GOLD stalled out just a few days later and began a steep panic decline, just as I had foreseen late in 1979.

Some PEOPLE bought more GOLD as prices fell, thinking it to be just another correction. I knew better and *said so!* I WARNED THAT WALL STREET HAD MISREAD A STATEMENT BY FED CHAIRMAN VOLCKER, IN WHICH HE SAID THAT HE WOULD NOT IMPOSE *GENERAL* CREDIT CONTROLS. He used his words with the precision of a surgeon, I told readers. If he meant to say NO controls at all, he would not have added the word "general." It could only mean one thing, I said: *SPECIFIC CREDIT CONTROLS*, just like those imposed by IKE in the early 1950's. The back of inflation would be busted, I warned. Both GOLD and STOCKS were sure to *collapse*. But when Wall Street discovered how bullish the end of inflation could be, stocks would come back sharply. *Within a month, Volcker imposed specific credit controls. Everything I had foreseen and warned about came to pass.* (It seemed fewer PEOPLE criticized my MONEY PLUS PEOPLE Forecasting Formula after that. In fact, more readers joined my Letter on the advice of their friends.) And thus began the 1980's.

I correctly predicted that Reagan's historic Tax Reduction Program would pass - and that it would *not be inflationary*, as so many others believed! The reason it would not be inflationary, I said, was that Fed Chairman Volcker would restrict the growth of MONEY. He would refuse to buy much in the way of Government bonds, thus forcing private savers to fund the debt. MONEY would grow tight. The result? I said it would be a virtual *end* to huge annual raises at unionized big business manufacturing plants. Workers were signing three-year contracts with 1% a year raises plus cost of living increases. They were expecting paychecks to grow by 15% a year or more. I said they would be lucky to see 5%. *When the nation's air traffic controllers struck, I told readers President Reagan would fire them all and never rehire them.* (I will tell you how I knew that later on.) And I said that plus Volcker's tight MONEY would end the rash of strikes that pushed inflation up. *Everything happened exactly as I had foreseen. (And again more of my subscribers became believers in my MONEY PLUS PEOPLE Forecasting Formula!)*

There were, of course, opposing Forecasts. Indeed I found myself a lone voice here in the New England wilderness most of the time. In 1980 for example I was all alone in America, or the rest of the world for that matter, in predicting that a soaring U.S. dollar would be the number one story of 1981. I even named a target value - three marks per dollar. At the time of my forecast, the dollar was trading at just under two marks and the idea of a three-mark dollar was seen by Wall Street analysts as quite unlikely. As so often happens, *I was right-on with my forecast* but a little premature. (I constantly warn subscribers of this habit I have of seeing coming events so clearly that I think they are closer in time than they eventually prove to be!)

In 1981, Wall Street's favorite guru, Henry Kaufman, dazzled and delighted the media and the very rich customers at a series of breakfast press briefings. I disagreed with him every time! Inflation would head upward, he said. *(I said it would trend down.)* He predicted a 25% prime by the end of 1981. *(I said rates would be down by half in four years.)* I warned that *deflation* might result from overkill by the Fed. And I said that the long *Housing Price Boom* of the 1970's would be curbed. I even gave the month it would end:

August, 1981. I hit the end of the Housing Boom on the nose. It ended just before Labor Day, 1981. (And in places like Houston, Texas, the crash brought down some big banks.) But I was a little early with my overall deflation warning. America was ninety days into 1982 before the first month of *declining prices* shocked Wall Street right out of its shoes.

The 1982 recession and bear market brought the first of many claims that "Another 1929" was close at hand. *I said otherwise.* In the spring of 1982, I spoke of a recovery soon that would turn into a Boom quickly. I said interest rates were being held up by mirrors and hot air... and told my readers *rates would collapse by autumn.* I also pointed out that bull markets had often begun in the middle of the second year of a new Presidency... and noted mid-1982 was such a time!

THE KIPLINGER LETTER, a famous Washington-based Letter, seemed to speak for just about everyone in July of 1982 when they said that interest rates had gone about as low as they were going to go and the stock market had gone about as high as it was going to go for some time. In fact, Kiplinger suggested that stocks were about to go down in anticipation of *rising interest rates.* I have got to admit: I felt very lonely right at the moment. I had read Kiplinger myself for a lot of years... since the mid-1950's. No one had more respect for Kiplinger than I did. But then, *my own studies and my own instincts said that this one time they were dead wrong. So I had to call*

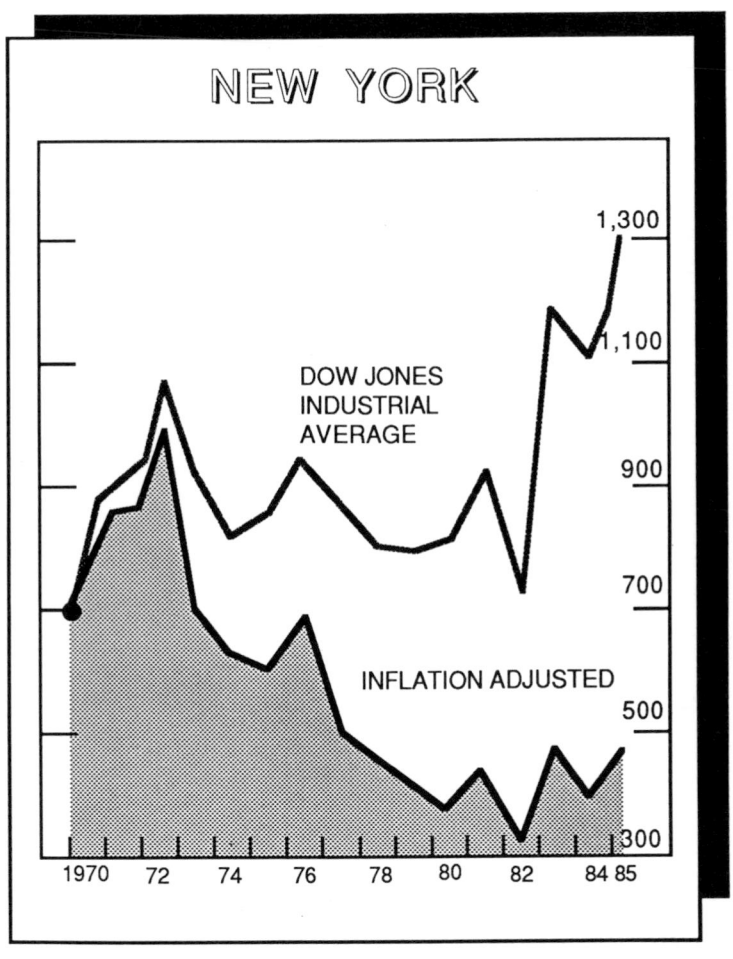

it as I saw it. I told my subscribers that I stood by my belief that America was then repeating the inflation-smashing recession of the early 1920's and that a major decline in interest rates was close at hand. (I did not realize it then, but the decline in interest rates I was predicting had already barely begun a few days earlier.)

As I had said with such confidence would happen, interest rates *collapsed* before the election. In four months, they fell four points. NOT RECOGNIZING THE PARALLEL TO THE EARLY 1920'S, *WALL STREET HIT THE PANIC BUTTON.* THEY THOUGHT RATES WERE FALLING BECAUSE WE HAD BEGUN A NEW 1929 - A NEW DEPRESSION. (IT WAS TO BECOME A FAMILIAR THEME ON WALL STREET, BEING REPEATED MANY TIMES DURING THE YEARS TO COME.) In November, 1982, I said: "The stock market has just completed its worst day since the terrible collapse in October, 1929... Let us examine the very important difference between now and 1929. *We are now almost seventeen years past the time (February 1966) when the Dow first reached 1,000. Seventeen years! In those seventeen years, the cost of living has just about tripled in America.*

"So, adjusted for inflation, you could say that 1,000 on the Dow today equals a 1966 level equal to 333. That is a 67% decline. What is more, the stock market has made a run at the 1,000 level several times since 1966. One more fact: In 1929, the Dow had been roaring up for years...

Like Chicken Little, some people worry a lot that "The Sky Is Falling!" They are missing a chance to get rich!

during this bull market (of the 1920's), the Dow rose 300%... the U.S. was mad with enthusiasm in 1929. By way of contrast, *America today is wallowing in self-doubt and fear such as been seen only on a very few occasions...* such as the winter when George Washington and his troops were freezing at Valley Forge. PEOPLE seem to crave awful predictions... eat them up... thrive on them! *It seems as if the worse the prediction, the more folks agree with it.* Subscribers send us a lot of this stuff. We read it, smile and file it away."

Of course, it was not just lower interest rates and a review of the Boom of the 1920's that dominated my predictions in that crucial year of 1982. I also told subscribers (back in March of 1982) that: "THE RECOVERY, WHEN IT COMES, WILL *NOT* BRING A RESUMPTION OF DOUBLE-DIGIT INFLATION - AS SO MANY INVESTORS AND BUSINESSMEN NOW FEAR! *SO FAR, THE ECONOMY HAS BEEN FOLLOWING A COURSE REMARKABLY SIMILAR TO THE EARLY 1920'S...*

"Somehow all of this history has been forgotten. That is probably why so many PEOPLE do not now understand or believe that the current economic conditions have traditionally been the PRELUDE to a real Boom... not a phony Boom where unit sales stay even while dollar sales go up... but just the opposite - *a Boom where dollar sales stay even but unit sales go up each year.*" (End quote.) Of course, *this was not my first bullish prediction of 1982.*

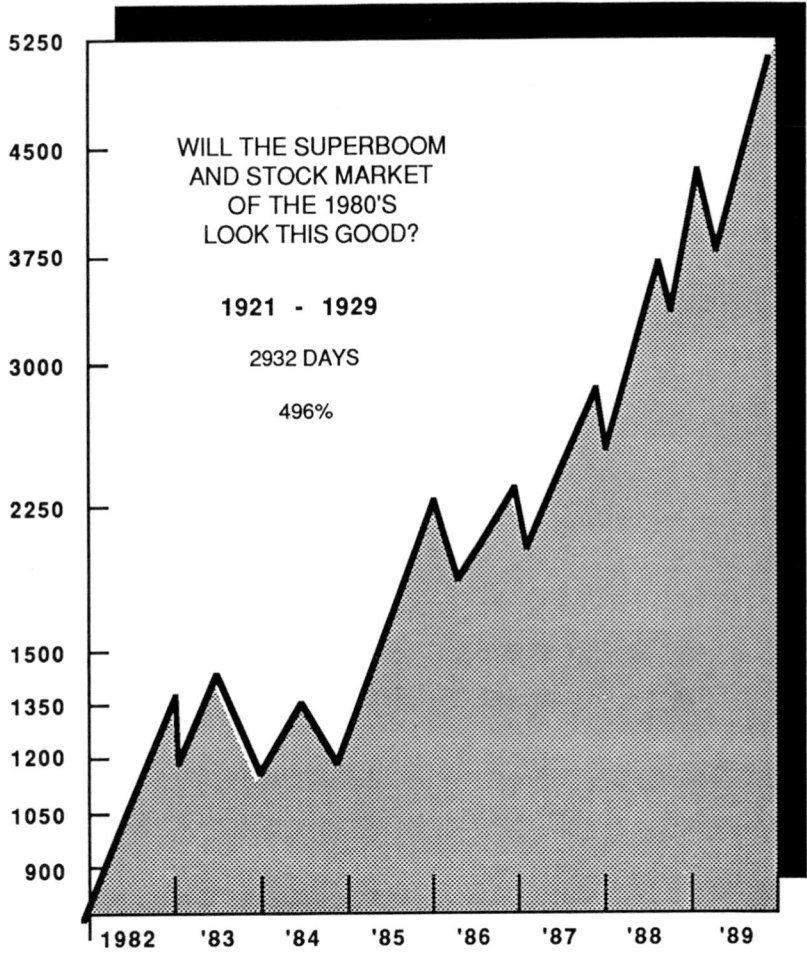

This chart shows the bull market of the 1920's recast in 1980's terms. We ran it in our Letter several times starting in 1982. Isn't it fascinating?

Two months earlier I said: "WE PROMISED YOU A COUPLE OF BLOCKBUSTER PREDICTIONS. HERE THEY ARE: FIRST - *this recession is not going to last much longer... The timing of the turn is not so important as the angle of the upturn. The angle will be very steep. The recovery, led by explosive growth in defense spending, will be breath-taking in its power and momentum.* SECOND: Do not waste your time worrying about the new business upturn bringing a confrontation in the MONEY markets... *Lower inflation* will allow a Boom with moderate M1 growth. Interest rates will continue to decline for months to come. *Wall Street will BOOM despite itself."* (End quote.)

IT ALL DID HAPPEN PRECISELY AS I PREDICTED IT FOR MY SUBSCRIBERS (WHOSE NUMBERS KEPT GROWING AS BROKERS, BANKERS, BUSINESSMEN AND INVESTORS TOLD THEIR FRIENDS ABOUT MY RECORD). Later on, advisors would come out of the woodwork and claim that their writings, *properly interpreted*, had seen the upturn coming. You did not have to interpret *my* work. I made my forecasts so clear that no one needed any special training in finance to follow them! *You saw how right my predictions were!*

Late in 1983, the business media was packed with predictions that the Fed would loosen MONEY for the election year, forcing interest rates down in the first half of the year. But almost everyone said that inflation would erupt again in mid-1984, forcing interest rates back up during the second half! *ONCE AGAIN I WAS A LONE VOICE IN THE WILDERNESS. I SAID LATE IN 1983 THAT VOLCKER WOULD GO AGAINST THE CONSENSUS VIEW - TIGHTENING MONEY IN THE FIRST HALF OF ELECTION YEAR 1984. "THE FINAL TWIST OF THE SCREW TO KILL INFLATION," I SAID.* THEN IN MY JUNE, 1984, LETTER, I PREDICTED THAT VOLCKER WOULD EASE UP FAST, HAVING DONE IN INFLATION. *INTEREST RATES, I SAID, WOULD FALL IN THE SECOND HALF OF 1984.* (A TIME WHEN JUST ABOUT EVERY OTHER FORECASTER HAD SAID THEY WOULD GO UP.) *Once again I was right both times - and almost 100% of the other economic forecasters were wrong!*

BUT ALL OF THESE CORRECT PREDICTIONS MAY HAVE BEEN ONLY A WARM-UP FOR A SERIES OF *STOCK MARKET FORECASTS IN 1985* THAT WERE, SO FAR AS I KNOW, *UNMATCHED IN ACCURACY* FOR TIMING, DIRECTION AND THRUST. 1985, AS YOU KNOW, WAS A YEAR WHEN TALK OF "IS THIS ANOTHER 1929?" NOT ONLY FILLED THE BUSINESS MEDIA... IT EVEN SPILLED ONTO TELEVISION NEWS SHOWS. *BY LABOR DAY, INVESTORS WERE FRIGHTENED! BUT MY READERS WERE READY FOR A FAST MOVE UPWARD!* AND IT CAME, AS I PROMISED. HERE IS WHAT I TOLD THEM - *IN ADVANCE* OF

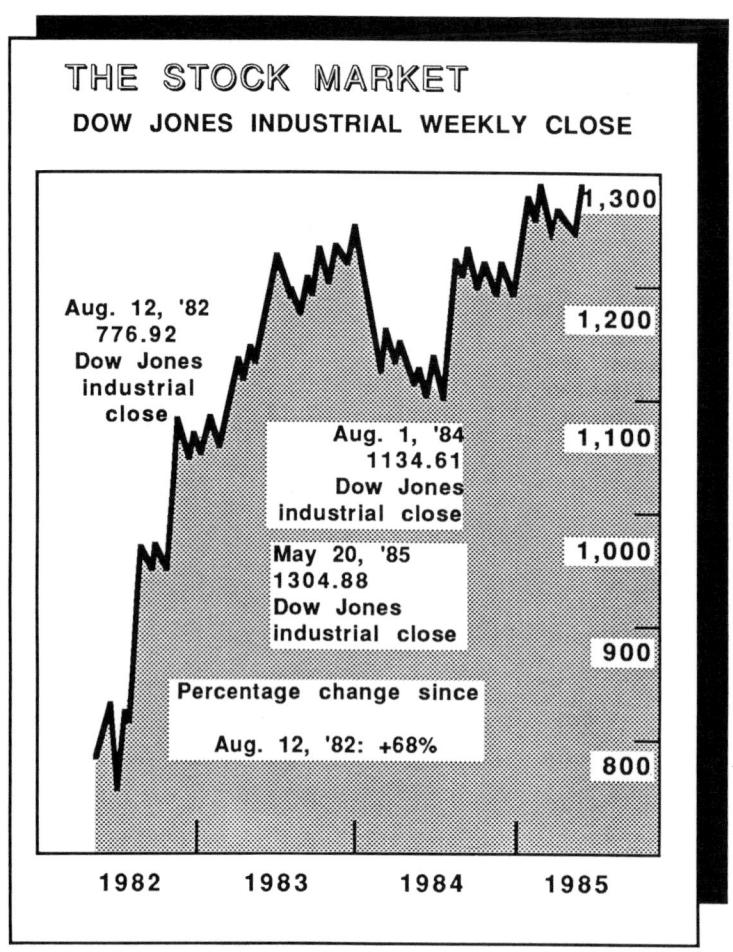

People forget now, but in September, 1985, as the market was about to explode, a crowd of self-styled forecasters were talking of "another 1929" at hand. Not us. We predicted a 2000 Dow by the end of 1986. It turned out we missed it by *one week!*

THE MARKET EXPLOSION. (IT WAS TO ADD $400 BILLION TO THE VALUE OF U.S. STOCKS IN UNDER FIVE MONTHS, SHOCKING WALL STREET.)

In my January, 1985 Letter (after a market dip had taken stocks as low as 1134 on the Dow): "It is probably impossible for a major bull market to get underway and stay in force while bond rates are high... (but) we very definitely are looking for lower bond yields over the second half of this decade. *Much lower bond yields!* We are talking here about a LONG-TERM MOVE, and this by no means rules out shorter-term bear markets along the way. It is just that you will not have to worry so much about bear markets when you have a pretty clear idea that they represent merely a temporary pause on the long upward slope." (End quote.) By August, 1985, the market was up 150 points and talk of "Another 1929" was dominating Wall Street chatter. *I disagreed strongly.* And I said: "RIGHT NOW THE DOW HAS JUST BROKEN INTO NEW HIGH GROUND NOT THAT FAR FROM 1,350..." (End quote.) *I suggested the Dow could take off from this point and blast into orbit by 1986!*

I concluded (again August, 1985): *"All of our comments have been based on... the 'itch' PEOPLE have to find ways to make profits..."* (End quote.) SO CONVINCED WAS I THAT IT WAS A TIME TO *BUY AND NOT TO SELL* THAT IN MID-SEPTEMBER, 1985, I

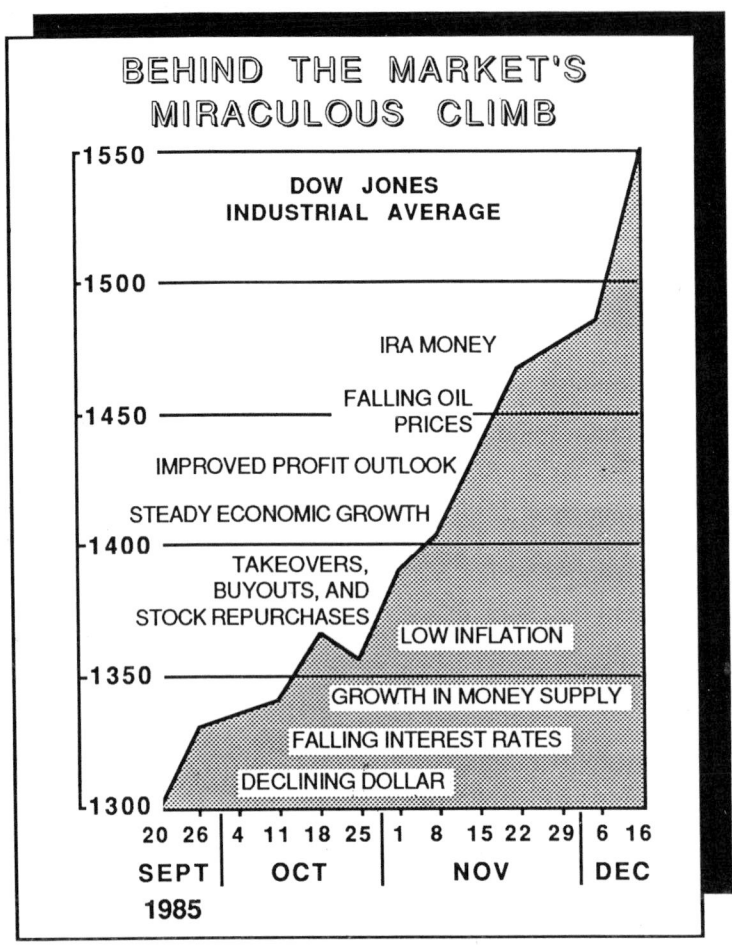

The bull market move I saw coming in mid-1982 took the Dow up 500 points by mid-1985. Most investors missed it... then refused to believe it was for real and could "stay so high."

LAUNCHED A BRAND NEW SUPPLEMENTARY MINI-LETTER ON INVESTMENT-PLANNING. The Dow was still around 1300 then. Within days it was roaring upward. By mid-December, 1985 - during a period that other forecasters said would mark a repeat of the late-1929 stock market crash - the Dow moved up a then incredible 250 points to 1,550!

In October, 1985, when the Dow had achieved only fifty of the 250 points it was to climb before year-end, *I told readers to ignore the Doom and Gloom warnings.* I said: "Unless someone changes what they are doing now - and does so fairly soon - we are in for one heck of a Boom and bull market... *The fun period for stocks has yet to begin. Adjusted for inflation the Dow stands at only half its 1966 level...* STOCKS COME ALIVE DURING TIMES OF STABLE PRICES OR MILD DEFLATION! THE TWO GREATEST BULL MARKET SURGES IN THIS CENTURY CAME DURING SUCH PERIODS... the 1920's and the 1950's... Let the Boom begin!" (End quote.)

That is what I was saying as the stock rise got under way. Two years later, stocks had doubled. My message had changed. It is still very timely, and I urge you to read it now.

Quoted from the October 15, 1987, FRC Investment-Planning Letter: "LOOK ON THE BRIGHT SIDE! THE SLIDE IN THE STOCK MARKET AND THE RISE IN

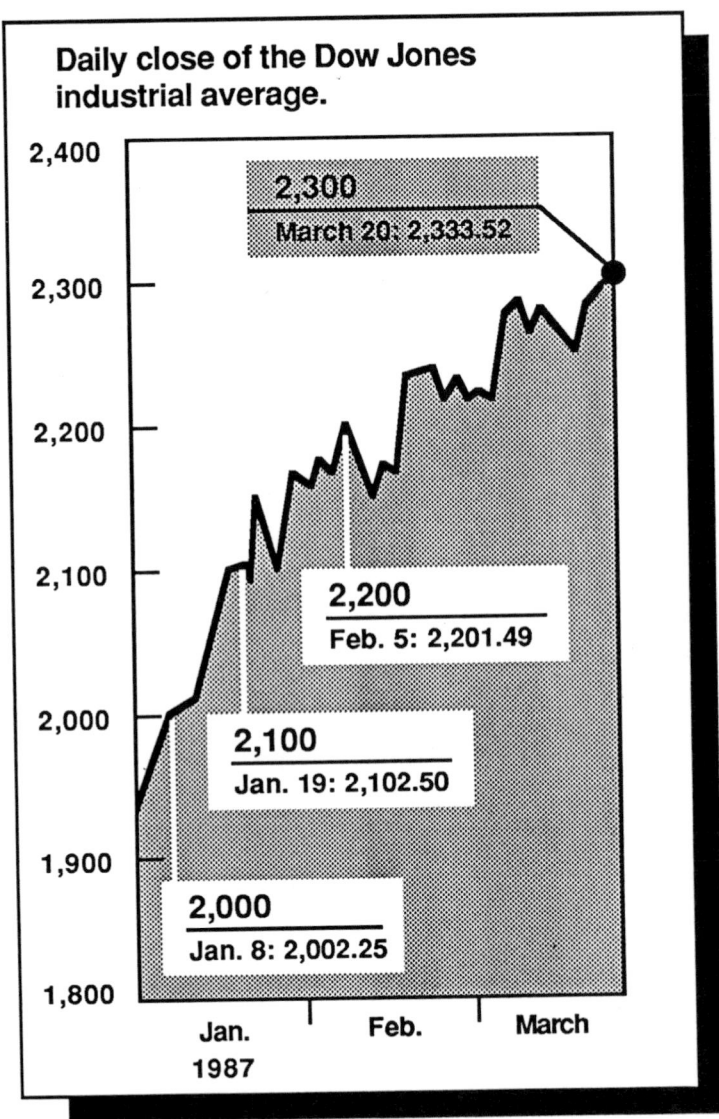

Daily close of the Dow Jones industrial average.

2,300
March 20: 2,333.52

2,200
Feb. 5: 2,201.49

2,100
Jan. 19: 2,102.50

2,000
Jan. 8: 2,002.25

Jan.
1987   Feb.   March

As 1987 began, I said the market rise was far from over. Sure enough, the Dow shot up again... climbing higher and higher. By then, most people had finally started to "believe."

INTEREST RATES MEANS THAT TALK OF A MAJOR CRASH IN STOCKS AND BONDS IN 1989 - AND A DEPRESSION BY 1990 - CAN NOW BE SAFELY STUCK AWAY IN THE DUST-BIN OF HISTORY, ALONG WITH ALL THE OTHER POPULAR DELUSIONS AND MADNESSES OF THE CROWDS. *TALK OF A CLIMACTIC BLOW-OFF TOP IN STOCKS, FOLLOWED BY A DEPRESSION CAN NOW BE FILED AWAY UNDER THE CATEGORY OF 'NEXT JOKE, PLEASE!'*

"WHAT WE ARE SAYING IS THAT THE SLOGAN OF THE FITNESS FOLKS IS NOW BEING APPLIED TO THE ECONOMY: *"NO PAIN, NO GAIN!"* TREASURY SECRETARY JAMES BAKER III SAID AS MUCH ON OCTOBER 9 (THE DAY THE STOCK MARKET WAS ENDING A RECORD SETTING ONE-WEEK DECLINE OF 158.78 POINTS). DEFENDING THE DECISION BY THE FED TO PUSH UP INTEREST RATES TEMPORARILY, BAKER SAID: *'A LITTLE BIT OF (INTEREST RATE) MOVEMENT EARLY CAN SAVE A LOT MORE LATER ON.'* HERE YOU HAVE IT - THE OLD SAW THAT A STITCH IN TIME SAVES NINE! *PREVENTATIVE MEDICINE.* AS WE SEE IT, THE FED IS NOW DOING WHAT PROFESSIONAL FIRE-FIGHTERS ROUTINELY DO IN BLOCKING OFF A FOREST FIRE, TO KEEP IT FROM GROWING AND CREATING A BIGGER DISASTER. THEY START A NEW, SMALL, CONTROLLED FIRE AHEAD OF THE BIG BLAZE.

BLUE CHIP STOCKS MAY TEST DOW 2000 BEFORE STARTING UP AGAIN TOWARDS 4000!

DOW JONES 1987

Just before the 1987 peak, I warned of a "time-out" ahead in stocks. Even as the Dow tipped over, few outside my subscribers believed me. I repeated my warning on September 17, 1987 - running this chart. Events a month later proved how correct I was. I urge you now to pay attention to our new forecasts!

THEY BURN OUT THE AREA IN FRONT OF THE DANGEROUS CONFLAGRATION. WHEN THE FIRE REACHES THE "BURN OUT," IT IS STOPPED AND IT SOON DIES OUT. *THE FED IS DOING THAT TO THE SIGNS OF EMOTIONAL, PSYCHOLOGICAL FIRE THAT THREATEN TO REKINDLE INFLA-TION. ONCE THE FED HAS FINISHED ITS JOB, STOCKS WILL - AS WE SEE IT - WANDER AROUND IN A TRADING RANGE FOR A PERIOD OF MONTHS AS THE BASE IS BEING BUILT UP FOR THE COMING SUPER-BOOM AND SUPER BULL MARKET...*

"In July of this year we warned that *"A TIME OUT"* was coming in the roaring stock market. *Again we were right!* WE SAID THAT OTC SPECIAL SITUATIONS WILL NOW HAVE THEIR DAY. AND SURE ENOUGH, YOU HAVE EVEN SEEN OTC STOCKS GOING UP ON SOME OF THE MARKET'S WORSE DAYS. *We see what is coming! And when you listen to us, you know what to expect. It is our belief that knowing what is coming is just as important as knowing in advance what to buy.* We apply the MONEY-FORECAST LETTER'S insights into Federal Reserve intentions to specific market forecasts. The hard fact is that all of the theories and beliefs and myths and fears on Wall Street - and all of the formulas for market-timing of selected forecasters - must all by necessity *bend before the all-powerful will of the Federal Reserve Board.* Some of our readers do not like that. To be honest, we are not sure (at

Soon after we ran this chart in our October 15, 1987 Investment-Planning Letter, bonds did indeed shoot up like an arrow shot from a bow. When you understand the BIG PICTURE, you won't be surprised by sudden changes!

least on some days) that we like such an inroad by the Federal Government into the art or science of managing the economy. But like it or not, it is a fact today. If you value the money you work so hard to earn and save, *you will by gosh pay attention when we tell you what the Fed is doing and what this means to your investments. For if you do not, you will join the pack... the mob... the uninformed, emotional rabble on Wall Street who sweep back and forth almost hour by hour... befuddled... foolish... frenzied!*

"THE CURRENT MOVE TO HIGHER INTEREST RATES IS *NOT* A SIGN OF AN ECONOMY OUT OF CONTROL, AS SO MANY WOULD HAVE YOU BELIEVE. IT IS, AS TREASURY SECRETARY BAKER HIMSELF OBSERVES, A CLEAR PROOF THAT *THE FED IS IN CHARGE.* THERE WILL BE A DELAY... A TIME OUT. EXCESSES WILL BE WRUNG OUT OF THE MARKET AND THE ECONOMY. *BUT THAT IS HEALTHY AND IT IS GOOD.* ONCE THE JOB IS DONE, THE YIELD ON THIRTY-YEAR T-BONDS WILL *PLUNGE ALL THE WAY TO 6%.* Because we know all of this so clearly, we do not worry about a stock market crash. *(Even though we stand by our warning that the 'correction' or bear market may reach 25% before turning up! That will not be the end of the world. So do not let anyone panic you as it unfolds.)* We are impressed ourself with the calm and cool patience of our own personal 'guru' on the FRC staff. We have told you about him before. His name is

Adrian Van Eck

Miller Laufman - class of *1929*, Harvard Business School and former chief trader with the gigantic *Fidelity* Mutual Fund organization here in Boston.

"Miller has seen it all on Wall Street, often from a seat of power. (He had banks of direct phone lines running to every major brokerage firm.) Miller watches our numbers on money and the economy. *He holds a personal portfolio that gives his opinions weight in these offices...*

"Always keep firmly in mind the story of Bernard Baruch, advisor to several Presidents. He missed one of the worst one-day panics in American financial history early in this century. It came on a Saturday - back when the market was open on Saturdays. He had spent the day at his Temple, keeping a promise to his mother. He came out to learn of *a crash... followed by a huge recovery.* He said that had he not kept his promise to his mother, he probably would have sold at the *emotional lows.* His mother saved him a fortune in losses, he told U.S. Presidents. His message was clear: *When you keep your head while others around you lose theirs, you can come out far ahead of them in the long run!"* (End quote, October 15, 1987.)

I urged subscribers to my Letter - and I now urge you: KEEP THIS UNBELIEVABLY BULLISH PICTURE OF 1989 TO '95 FIRMLY IN MIND... EVEN IF, AS I EXPECT, THE STOCK MARKET SUFFERS PERIODIC QUICK, NASTY CORRECTIONS THAT

GET THE DOOM AND GLOOM FOLKS WHOOPING IT UP AND HOLLERING THAT, AT LAST, 1929 IS HERE AGAIN. This was my advice *before* October 19, 1987. It is still my advice today... more timely than when I first gave it.

Adrian Van Eck

CHAPTER THREE

Why A Boom Every Thirty Years?

I am not an economic technician. I do not have any rigid framework that I use to make financial forecasts. Rather, I look to such factors as emotional momentum. WHAT PEOPLE DO WITH THEIR MONEY! That is what interests me. But you cannot look objectively at the economic history of the United States of America without seeing *a major pattern repeating itself.*

America had uncommon economic Booms in the 1860's, the 1890's, the 1920's and the 1950's. In each case, many new fortunes were made.

Why every thirty years? Common sense seems to lead me

After each thirty-year period, the previous boom seems like anchient history. Then it happens all over again!

towards a simple generational theory. Some young men and women marry before they are twenty and start their families. Others marry during their twenties... and begin families. By the age of thirty, and this can be proven quickly by a glance at the available statistics, the majority of young men and women who plan to get married and start a family have done so.

What this means, quite simply, is that after thirty years have gone by *we have in place a whole new generation of hopeful, optimistic young men and women who do not have personal memories of losing money in an economic Boom.* Thus conditions are ripe for a new Boom to come along. It can be fed by the expectations of this new generation.

Remember not so long ago when the rallying cry of America's young was: "Don't Trust Anyone Over Thirty!" Here again you have a fairly concrete example of how the period *THIRTY YEARS LONG* is instinctively seen as a generational dividing line in America.

What this means is that by the time the "Roaring Twenties" rolled around, America was being pushed and driven by a generation that either had no real memories of "The Gay Nineties" or had decided that long-ago decade had no message at all for the 1920's.

Of course, events proved them wrong. *The Boom of the*

1920's did indeed have something in common with that of the 1890's. And that element was its swift, unpleasant ending!

After the 1920's hit a peak (1929), the bad times that followed were so unpleasant and lasted so long (really until World War II stimulated the economy again in the early 1940's) that *the new generation taking power in the 1950's still had vivid personal memories of the "Morning After" years.* And so it happened that when a Boom got underway pretty much on schedule during the 1950's, a rather surprising and unusual response developed. Presidents Harry S. Truman and Dwight D. Eisenhower sternly resisted letting this Boom get out of hand.

The public supported Government moves to tamp down speculation. Just as in the 1920's, common stocks quadrupled in value. And a lot of people worried that this meant another "Morning After" was at hand. But as events turned out, the stern measures adopted by Presidents Truman and Eisenhower (with the cooperation of equally prudent Congressional leaders, bankers, brokers and business executives), left America in such solid financial shape by the end of the 1950's that *still another decade of Boom was piled on top of the 1950's,* with stocks not peaking until 1966 and late-1968!

The very fact that the economy and stocks set new highs in the 1960's has thrown off America's sense of history when it comes to finance. Very few people actually know or sense the *true underlying thirty-year tide* that seems to carry America's economy forward... either rising or falling. There is, in fact, a great deal of confusion today as to just where we stand in the larger picture... *the long view.*

Probably it is this lost sense of history that accounts for so much of the just plain wrong predictions that have bombarded your ears since the 1980's began. Year after year, *the same voices cry out* to warn you and everyone else that "1929 is here again!" Of course, as you know, events have proven them wrong each year. They are at it again *this* year. They will be shouting louder than ever *next* year. And they will be wrong again. But do not get the idea that I am amused by these false prophets. Quite the contrary. I suspect they are doing an enormous amount of damage *in a cumulative manner*. Permit me to explain what I mean.

By the time America moved into the 1980's, it had been not one but two thirty-year generations since the last big Boom-And-Bust Cycle. *Many* people remember 1929 personally in this day of extended health and long lives. That is normally a very good thing. Such bright-eyed and bushy-tailed senior citizens form a reservoir of experience and wisdom that makes them one of this country's most valuable assets!

But here we have a senior generation plus a still-young middle generation... both of whom remember the last

Boom, thirty years ago. And what do they remember? A very important fact: If America has the political and economic will, it can avoid the bad after-effect of a Boom just by not permitting speculative excesses to develop during the Boom itself! Okay. That is good to remember... so long as they remember the *whole* message. If, as can happen, all they choose to recall is that the last Boom did *not* end with bad times, they can delude themselves into thinking there is no risk at all involved with a Boom.

I can think of nothing quite so likely to make people *lose their fear* of a Boom as will these constantly repeated false warnings of "Another 1929." Each time such a warning message is carried in the newspapers and on television news programs - and the most recent time was October 19, 1987 - *it grows less and less likely that people will respond correctly to a real time of danger, should one materialize by 1995 to '99.* (It is simply the oft-told tale of "The Boy Who Cried Wolf Too Often.")

And so I urge you: Burn the correct historical view of America into your memory. Remember that in the 1920's America had a roaring Boom followed by a most-unpleasant "Morning After." But the Boom of the 1950's was followed by *an even bigger Boom!* Much of the reason for the success of the 1950's and 1960's in *avoiding* the kinds of speculative excesses that lead to later troubles stems from the active fears of that time... fears about 1929! Should the false prophets, with their repeated warnings about 1929, cause us to lose our fear of "Another 1929", *we might stop* preventing speculative excesses from getting out of hand. Should that occur, we could someday be in danger of a serious "Morning After." Later on, in another chapter, I will explore the odds on a Happy Ending vs. a Sad Ending. But for now, let me concentrate not on the ending, but on *the coming HEART of this new Boom!*

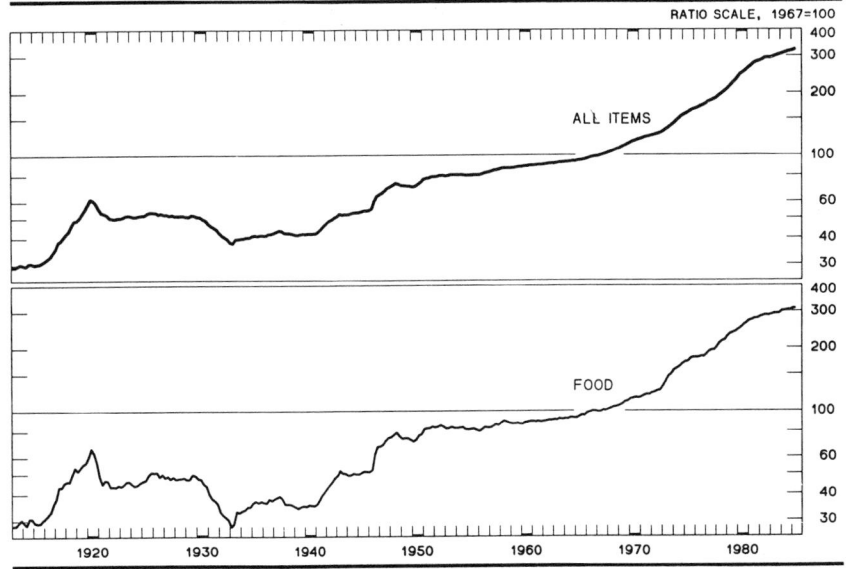

CONSUMER PRICES
ALL ITEMS AND FOOD
QUARTERLY AVERAGES

It comes as a shock to many investors when they learn that inflation has not been the norm for America since the Civil War. In the late-1800's, gentle deflation actually forced companies to invest in labor-saving machines in order to cut costs and survive. You can see that prices were mostly flat in the 1920's and from 1950 to '63, as Truman, Ike and JFK sought and got growth without inflation. *The 1970's were a fluke. People who are now waiting for them to come back will get hurt badly!!*

- 127 -

Adrian Van Eck

CHAPTER FOUR

Back To The Normalcy Of Very Low Inflation!

During the 1970's, inflation exploded across most of the Western World. In the United States in particular, this inflation was caused by spending on the war in Vietnam. Presidents Lyndon Johnson and Richard Nixon both realized that the war was not popular. So, they did not levy taxes to pay for the war. *Instead they simply printed money to pay the troops and buy the war materials.* (Actually, they used a complicated and sophisticated financing technique that involved the Federal Reserve Board buying new Federal Government bonds with money created out of thin air by the Fed. *But the end result was just the same* as if the Government had simply printed lots of new money.) President Nixon tried to stop the inflation that came as a result of his "funny money" creation by slapping on price and wage controls. He found out - as others have before him - that such controls are just as effective as a king standing on a beach during a time of incoming tide and *shouting at the ocean water to "STOP RISING!"*

After a while the price controls stopped working altogether. They grew uncomfortably tight and many people complained about the way the Government was making life difficult. *So the politicians took off the controls. And of course, prices shot up fast to make up for the time controls had been on.* It did not take long for people in foreign countries to complain that everything they bought from the United States had suddenly become very expensive. In the Middle East, for example, the nations which had a lot of oil under the big deserts complained loudly that *the food they were buying from Americans now cost so much* that their children were forced to go to bed hungry. One day, when the people with oil got angry enough, they all sent leaders to a meeting. And these leaders decided to *get even* with us for our high prices. They did so by raising the price of the oil they sold to us. And when they found out they could get away with raising the price of oil once, they did it a second time. And then a third time. *And soon the price of everything that was made from oil or used oil*

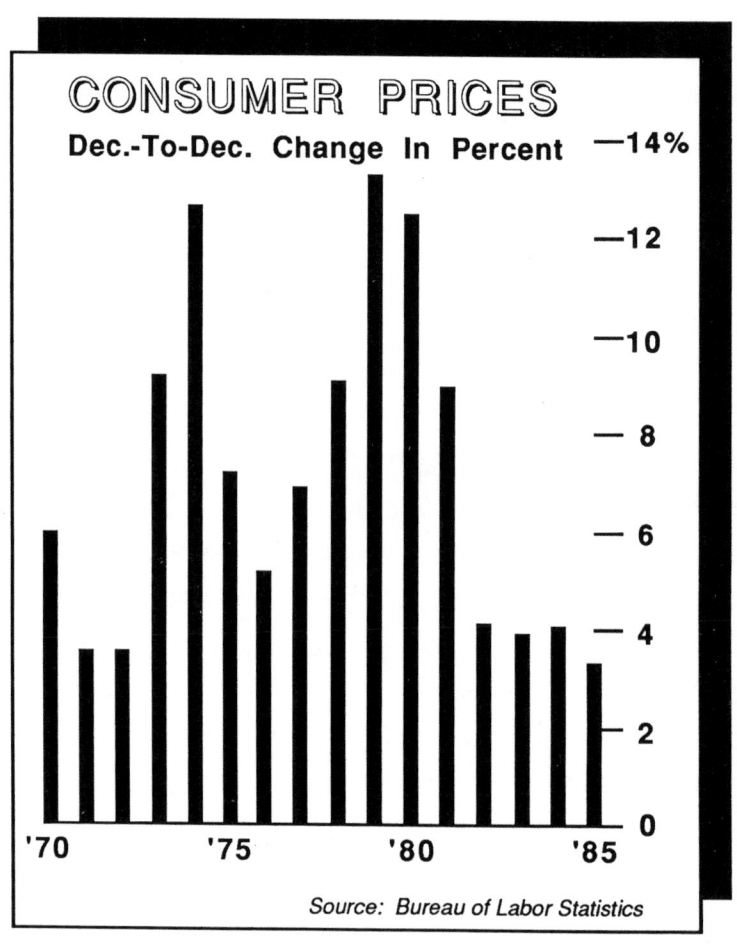

CONSUMER PRICES
Dec.-To-Dec. Change In Percent

Source: Bureau of Labor Statistics

began to go up fast in the United States and Europe. As we were to discover the hard way, that included just about everything!

When America's prices began to go up faster, people complained. And when people complain in a democracy the politicians listen. What they heard made them unhappy. They heard grumbling noises that made them fear for their own jobs. *And you know what politicians do when they fear for their own jobs: They give money away to the people. Lots of money. FREE MONEY!*

Pretty soon the Government was paying for things the people had earlier paid for themselves. Naturally the politicians did not want to tax the people to pay for all this spending. So they printed some more money. They printed so much money so fast that pretty soon the country was simply awash in new dollars. There were so many dollars around that no one wanted to hold onto them anymore. Dollars got to be like leaves falling from the trees in the autumn. Almost a nuisance. So people started to *swap their dollars for other things. First it was houses.* There were only so many houses standing around. And an awful lot of people were trying to swap dollars for them. You know what happens when a lot of people are *competing* to swap their dollars for houses or anything else. They bid against each other. They keep offering to pay more and more money for each house. *That makes the price of a house go up.* And when people hear about the price of houses going up, two things happen pretty

During inflation surges, people squirrel away money in gold, silver, diamonds and rare paintings. This can be costly later when inflation ends.

quickly: First, the people who have houses to sell start to demand *more dollars* for their houses. Secondly, the people who want to buy houses begin *agreeing* to pay more money for the houses. This turns into a game. And so long as the Government is willing to print more and more money to play the game - sort of like happens in a Monopoly game when the players borrow more and more money - *the prices keep going up and up!*

After a while, people look around for other things to *swap* their dollars for. They do so because the word is getting around that with more and more dollars being created, *the value of each dollar is going down very fast.* People are afraid that some day their dollars will not be worth anything at all. And they hope that the things they buy - whatever they are - may *go up* to protect them against this event. So they buy gold, because they have been told that will help protect them against this inflation. And they buy silver. And diamonds. And rare paintings. And they buy farm land. *Lots and lots of farm land.* (Sellers tell potential buyers: "They're not making any more land. Better get some while you can!") And the more they buy, the faster prices go up. People soon forget that this is not the way it used to be. They get so used to inflation they begin to think that this must be the way it always was. And even if they do not believe that, *they began to think this is the way it always will be from now on. For ever and ever!*

It is a shame when people start to think like that. They do

strange things. *They borrow a lot of money, thinking it will be easy to pay it back later when inflation has pushed their income up so high that it will be very easy for them to take care of the loan.* And they pay more for things - like houses - than they really think they ought to pay, just because they are so sure that some day, later on, they will find someone to buy it from them at an even more ridiculous price. The saddest part of all this is that most people really believe this is something *NEW* - something that has never happened before to anyone else. But, of course, that is not true. Not at all. America has seen INFLATION many times, in many places. Each time that it happened, the people then and there were sure inflation would never end. *But each time, end it DID!*

That is the way it was *after* the American War of Independence (1775 to 1781). That is the way it was *after* America's Civil War (1861 to 1865). That is the way it was *after* World Wars I and II. And that is the way it has been *since* 1980! *INFLATION, IT TURNS OUT, IS ABNORMAL AND TEMPORARY.* BUT THE LACK OF INFLATION - EVEN ACTUAL DEFLATION - HAS REALLY BEEN NORMAL AND ALMOST PERMANENT DURING THE LAST 200 YEARS. WE ARE NOW BACK IN NORMAL TIMES. MOST PEOPLE DO NOT YET REALIZE THAT. THEY HAVE NOT YET ADJUSTED. THEY KEEP WAITING FOR INFLATION TO COME BACK. WAITING... AND WAITING... AND WAITING. THEY MAY HAVE A LONG WAIT!

Perhaps the biggest problem with inflation is that it encourages people to borrow money. When deflation hits, they can't pay back their loans... and creditors take away everything they own. It is a lesson learned many times in American history. It may be learned again!

Adrian Van Eck

CHAPTER FIVE

The Innocent Suffer Most!

Farming has long been an important part of what we call The American Way of Life. Thomas Jefferson - author of The Declaration of Independence and third President of the United States - believed deeply that farmers and small farm towns were *vital* to America.

Farmers have maintained the traditional work ethic in a time of growing welfare support in our larger cities. Farm towns still have a friendly neighborliness that defies description. You have to actually *live* in a farm community to know first hand just how special these towns can be. No matter how large our cities become, no matter how rich and sophisticated some people become, *it is still the farmer that is seen as the strength and backbone of our nation.*

Life on the farm has never been easy. Farmers are born knowing that fact. They accept it. Many farmers go beyond accepting that fact. They take great pride in the hardships of farm living. Or, more to the point, they take *uncommon pride in their ability to live with and overcome the natural hardships of farm living.* Drought... insects... even floods. All these and more have done their best to defeat farmers and have failed. But, alas, man-made inflation, debt and deflation are succeeding where natural hardships and even disasters have not... in hurting farmers so badly that many of them are *now being forced to give up the life they hold dear!*

You have seen on the news how farm auctions have ripped land away from farm families... land that in some cases has been in the same family for 120 years or more. (Many of America's family farms date back to the Great Migration West that was *unleashed after the Civil War.)* This is land and these are families that survived even the Great Depression of the 1930's. That is how terrible today's DEFLATION is on the farming heartland of America!

A measure of just how cruel deflation has been to farmers comes in the fact that here and there *farmers have resorted to suicide to try and save the land for their wives and children.* City folks cannot understand how land can mean that much to a farmer. But anyone born and raised on a farm instinctively understands what drove these desperate men to make the ultimate sacrifice - their own lives - in the hope and belief that money from their insurance policies (where the law allows it) might pay off or at least reduce the debt on their farms by enough so that the bankers or Federal Government would *leave their families alone.* TRAGIC!

And the worst part of it is that just about everyone - farmers, bankers, politicians - *underestimates* just how serious the long term problem really is. Most people involved in the farm deflation situation are under the *false belief* that this situation is probably temporary... or that it can be changed by some simple political act. The most popular idea is that a strong U.S. dollar is the *only* villain. *If only the dollar can be pushed still lower, goes this emotional belief, then foreign nations will once again line up America's export docks and good times will return to farming communities.* Oh, if only it were that easy! Then America would cure this evil situation. For who among us can stand to see the sight of grown men weeping at farm auctions... or even worse - to see widows and orphans weeping on television news as a farmer who committed suicide to save his land is laid to rest *before his time!*

Unfortunately, a cheaper dollar cannot by itself save American farm export markets. *(Although it can and is reducing the suffering a bit!)* But in country after country, around the world, local farmers have learned how to *increase* their production of food. In some cases it is the development of irrigation systems. In other cases it is the use of the new "miracle seeds" that offer greatly increased yields. But by far the greatest change has been the new awareness by Governments, *even socialist and communist Governments,* that farmers must be allowed to profit directly from their own hard work on the land. Communist China, for example, has *busted up its communes* and, in effect, gone back to a system that permits private family farms. The Red Regime now requires only a modest quota of produce to be turned over to the state as a form of rent *(really a tax)* for the land. The rest of the produce is left in the hands of THE FARMERS. What is more, the Chinese farmers no longer have to sell their produce to the state at a low, fixed price. They are allowed to sell it directly to the public at private, open-air farm markets in the towns and cities. *A hustling and bustling commerce has sprung up.* Farmers who adopt improved techniques are fast developing into a prosperous new middle class. The total result? Farm output has doubled in Red China in just five years, under this new system. Here is a nation of one billion people that - in the darkest days of communist rule - was faced with chronic starvation on a mass scale. Today it grows most of the food it needs, effectively *snuffing out much of a potentially huge export market for American farm products.* Good news for China. Bad news for U.S. farm towns!

And so it is that the misery of American farmers has spread from their land to the shops and stores... the farm equipment, automobile and truck dealers... to local schools and Government... and most urgently of all to the local banks in farm towns. Since the larger cities of farm states depend too on whether or not the farmers prosper, we have a situation that has spread and grown like a cancer. *And like a cancer it can result in death... not just to a farmer or a farm but also to farm towns and farm states...* even to a whole way of life that stands at the very CENTER of what has from the beginning been called American! Fortunately, we see forces at work that can and we think *will rescue* the farm states.

Adrian Van Eck

CHAPTER SIX

American Business Managers Hit Back!

When President Ronald Wilson Reagan *fired* thousands of illegally striking air traffic controllers early in his Administration - an action I foresaw in my Letter - *he did more than regain control of the towers at America's airports. He sent a signal to private business owners and managers all over America.* He told them, in effect, that it was okay to seize back from unions the right and the ability to manage their own operations effectively. As strange as it may seem even today, that right to manage had been all but given up during the inflationary 1970's.

Unions had struck again and again to demand raises that could *not* be justified on the basis of either worker need or worker production. It had come down to sheer union muscle. And sometimes it was just exactly that... the *physical intimidation* of managers by brutal union "goons" imported from out of state just for the duration of a strike. The problem had become most acute in those industries that were regulated. The Federal Government stepped in on behalf of union workers whenever management seemed to be on the verge of winning a strike. (That happened in the mid-1970's, when the tire companies were about to *defeat* the Rubber Workers' Union in a long and bitter strike. The White House suddenly intervened and threatened to break Government contracts for tires (a clearly illegal threat) with any company that refused to grant the Union's demands. *Faced with the loss of business from the Armed Forces and the Post Office - huge and essential contracts - the companies gave up and gave in!)* THE SHARPLY HIGHER WAGE COSTS AND SCANDALOUSLY POOR WORK OUTPUT PER HOUR RAISED THE COST OF TIRES FOR EVERYONE. AND SO IT WENT IN STEEL AND OIL, TRUCKING AND AIRLINES, COAL AND ALUMINIUM! It all came to a head when the air traffic controllers *defied the law* and moved to close down U.S. airports!

This kind of union arrogance had shown up before in U.S. history. Right after World War I for example, the Boston police went out on strike in defiance of a Massachusetts law forbidding strikes by public employees. The mayor of Boston was so afraid of PRO-UNION SENTIMENT amongst Boston voters that *he did absolutely nothing about the situation, even when looters and rapists started to turn Boston into a criminal's paradise and a citizen's Hell on Earth.* But Governor Calvin Coolidge hesitated not one single minute. Declaring that public employees did not have the right to strike against the public at any time, under law, this *tough-minded former Vermont farmer* turned Massachusetts politician fired all of the striking Boston policemen. He called up the state militia to keep order... then hired all new police officers. He vowed that not one of the striking Boston cops would ever wear the blue uniform of an officer of the law again. And *he stunned the union* by making good on that pledge. America knew a real leader when it saw one. Three years later he was in the Oval Office of the White House - President of the United States! It was a time much like the 1980's were later to be - a time of deflation. As in the 1980's, companies asked unions to take pay cuts so they could survive. As in the 1980's, the unions responded by going on strike! Coolidge announced that when the workers got hungry enough *they should go back to work* at the wages their companies could afford to pay. As time passed, that is just what they did. Plants reopened with lower wages and lower prices. They were able to profit and grow. Ronald Reagan was a youngster in a town in Illinois as all of this unfolded. *He found a personal hero in Calvin Coolidge.* That was to be important to America sixty years later. And it may now be the economic

Following World War II, President Harry S. Truman used the army to crush a railroad strike and break inflation in America.

salvation of farm towns.

It is no accident that *the last tremendous social migration in America - the rush to the suburbs - also came at a time of declining inflation and bitter union resistance to management's requests for reforms.* That was in the 1940's, when Harry S. Truman was in the White House. Unions had been given enormous power by the Federal Government during Franklin Roosevelt's thirteen years in the White House. So *arrogant* had unions become that John L. Lewis' COAL MINERS UNION actually dared strike and shut down the mines during World War II, at a time when American industry ran entirely on *coal power* and needed this energy to produce goods for eleven million men and women fighting overseas!

Truman, upon finding himself President, dropped the first two A-Bombs to end the war. When Russia sent tanks racing into Iran to grab its oil fields, Truman gave the Soviets forty-eight hours to reverse engines and get out of that nation. Russia backed down and pulled out of Iran, *biding its time to wait for another opportunity* to go for the oil. Then Truman turned to his number one domestic problem: *Postwar strikes by labor unions mad with their own power.*

In those days before the interstate highways were built, railroads were the only means of moving goods and people. The Rail Union struck, shutting down the U.S. The feisty Truman used the army to break the strike.

When he did so, he broke the back of inflation in America. An exciting new age of growth and expansion began. Millions of Americans, many of them young veterans just getting married and starting families, rushed out of the cities of America and *bought small homes springing up on what had been farm land.* The suburbs were born! A whole new way of living emerged in America.

Now, four decades later, America is on the verge of another important change. Unions that were forced to accept pay cuts and work rule changes a few years ago have elected militant new leaders. These leaders are demanding restored pay levels and a return to *wasteful* work rules.

Some companies have responded by shutting down American manufacturing plants entirely - moving them to Mexico or Taiwan. *But others are moving operations out into farm towns and farm states.* They are hiring farmers and the sons and daughters of farmers to work in modern new plants. They are looking for and finding workers who give a day's work for a day's pay. And in doing so they offer a new hope to *save the farm towns.* The success of these farm town plants - including huge auto assembly plants built by Japanese manufacturers - has attracted attention and interest from America's surging *service industries.*

Already one giant New York bank has moved its national

Adrian Van Eck

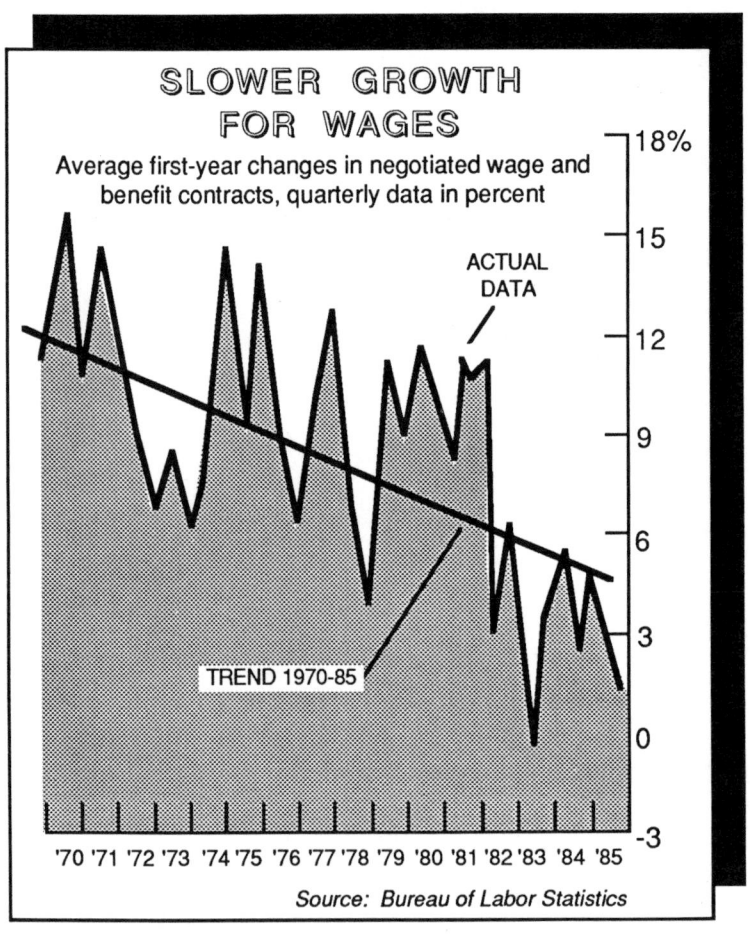

SLOWER GROWTH
FOR WAGES

Average first-year changes in negotiated wage and
benefit contracts, quarterly data in percent

ACTUAL
DATA

TREND 1970-85

'70 '71 '72 '73 '74 '75 '76 '77 '78 '79 '80 '81 '82 '83 '84 '85

Source: Bureau of Labor Statistics

credit card operations to the Dakotas, where telephone lines and computers link the workers to the whole nation... even the whole world! Others are following... insurance and leasing companies, publishers, high-technology firms. In the months to come, a new BOOM may well emerge in farm states, *allowing farm families to keep their farm roots*... even farm part-time if they would like. The money flowing in to the farm towns may revive their economies. So too will the business created by migrants from cities and suburbs... looking for the good old-fashioned way of life! This may prove to be the biggest development of the early 1990's!

Adrian Van Eck

CHAPTER SEVEN

Here Come Lower Interest Rates!

There is a surprising bias in many forecasts these days. *They assume higher interest rates for America in the future.* Some think the higher rates will come in a few months. Some think they will arrive in a year. But almost all agree higher rates are inevitable. *They are all wrong!* I believe, and I have been telling my subscribers this for some time now, that the Fed has stopped new inflation fears, interest rates will again fall until they get back to the levels of the early 1970's (before inflation really began to heat up). That would mean a thirty-year treasury rate of around 5.5%. And it would mean an *FHA guaranteed 30-year fixed mortgage rate of perhaps 6.5%.*

Even this, in my opinion, could possibly prove to be just a temporary way station en route to even lower T-Bond and FHA mortgage rates. We may see them falling back again to the *5% to 5.5% level* under certain circumstances!

Such declines in interest rates would create a bull market in bonds. (I told my readers to lock in long-term yields of *14% on thirty-year bonds* at a time when almost everyone else thought I was crazy. I warned subscribers that expectations of still higher rates were doomed to disappointment. *I was proven correct by events.)*

The only reason borrowers could justify paying sky-high rates in 1981 (a time when corporate debtors rated Baa by Moody's were paying 17% interest on their long-term bonds) was that they seriously believed *inflation was scheduled to cross right through the 25% a year mark and keep right on going up for years to come... to 30%... and even higher. I said at the time such fears were nonsense. Yet even today I hear the same fears expressed. It is still nonsense!* THE FACTORS THAT CAUSED INFLATION IN THE 1970'S ARE DEAD. Deflation is now and is likely to continue as the number one threat to the world economy. The debt outstanding everywhere is *deflationary* all by itself. I cannot understand why it is so hard for Wall Street to understand this simple fact. But in due course, *facts will win out over myths* and false expectations!

It is part and parcel of the myth of coming higher interest

rates to believe that the level of interest rates depends on *how much money* the Federal Reserve System chooses to "print" and pour into the nation's banks. If the link was as close as some would have you believe, then every move up and down in interest rates in the past decade would have been accurately predicted by economists. *The truth is their predictions, for the most part, have been far off the mark.* In fact, I will go so far as to say that YOU COULD HAVE DONE A BETTER JOB PREDICTING INTEREST RATES IN THE 1980'S THAN SOME ECONOMISTS HAVE DONE JUST BY FLIPPING A COIN. Not only were almost all the economists wrong about the *direction* of rates, they were also wrong about the *speed* in which rates moved.

Why then was I able to correctly forecast both the direction and the speed of interest rate movements with such incredible accuracy? It is because I accepted the simple fact that *psychology had more to do with interest rates than did any decisions by the Federal Reserve System.* Indeed, Paul Volcker himself acknowledged that on most occasions he and the seven-member Federal Reserve Board (which sets the Fed's own discount rate) actually responded to free market rates... rather than trying to determine these rates!

When people sense inflation going sky-high, the savers ask for a bigger return and the borrowers willingly pay it. When inflation is seen as heading lower or even ending altogether, the process reverses. No mystery there. It seems clear to me that *as the reality of DEFLATION sinks in, people will go back to the interest rate levels that have been normal for more than 2000 years. Those rates call for earning 3% a year on your savings and paying 5% a year on your loans.* The 2% difference - known as the spread - is the money that banks and other money-lenders must use to cover their overhead, their losses and (if any is left over) their profit. Before the 1980's end - and maybe a lot sooner than that - the money market will *revert back* to traditional levels. This will take a lot of getting used to by everyone involved... lenders and borrowers alike. But the market is too powerful to resist. It will happen! When it does - and even during the time it takes shape - simply incredible changes will take place in the American economy!

CHAPTER EIGHT

Next Comes A New Boom In Rural Housing!

Many Americans have given up the hope and dream that they will ever own a home of their own. And many American parents have reluctantly *accepted* as a truth what they constantly read now in magazines or see on television news shows - namely that this will be the first generation in America's history to fall short of the standard of living they knew as children in their parents' home. *It is disturbing. Even depressing.* The expectation of owning one's own home has been perhaps the strongest single personal ambition shared by Americans from the very day that the Puritan-Pilgrims set foot on Plymouth Rock during that bitterly cold winter of 1620 to '21. *I mean that!* The very first thing Pilgrim survivors did when Spring arrived in 1621 was to choose the locations for their own small cottages. And by the time Autumn arrived and they joined together for America's first Thanksgiving - sharing their harvest with friendly Indians who had taught them such New England tricks as placing a fish in each hole they scooped out to plant corn - these Pilgrims did indeed own and occupy their own homes. When the Mayflower returned to England with the news that there was open land and uncrowded spaces available in Massachusetts, a much larger gathering of English Puritans and their families slowly made plans to follow the original Pilgrims. In 1630, an impressively large convoy of ships brought many more Puritans to Massachusetts. They founded the town of Boston. And they quickly moved to lay out streets and *erect their own small private homes.*

As the years passed, the trickle of settlers from across the ocean grew into a flood. Some immigrants stayed near the coastlines. Others headed inland. When they did, their first and sometimes only thought was to get a small *piece of land they could call their own...* and to build on that land (sometimes by themselves and often with help from their neighbors) a dwelling that they could also call their own. *No matter how humble that home, it was the proudest possession a family would own.* And should hardships of any kind threaten a family with the loss of that home, it was seen as a tragedy just as real and as intense as the loss of loved one. It is no wonder that even today - after a decade of rapid construction of apartment

In early America people wanted enough private space so that they could not hear their neighbors!

buildings and condominiums - some two-thirds of Americans live in their very own single-family home! But, oh, how many more Americans in "other" one-third yearn to own their own home! *And my message here is that events already in motion make it likely that many of them will before 1995!*

In 370 years, America has come full cycle. We are back again to the same kind of *restless craving for a better life* that drove the Puritans who called themselves Pilgrims to pick up their roots, from exile in Holland, and cross a stormy ocean. We are virtually all immigrants or the descendants of immigrants in America. We are descended from people who did not stay and endure misery in the place of their birth. Instead, those with "get up and go" simply *got up and came.* There was a saying in early America that when your nearest neighbor was so close that you could hear his axe in the forest, it was time to think about *moving on,* further West. *Land... open space... privacy...* those were sweet words to Americans on the frontier. And whether we like it or not, we carry the blood-line and the genes of those hardy pioneers in us!

The major reasons preventing Americans from owning their own single-family homes in America today have to do with land and interest rates. In the suburbs developed after World War II, *land is now scarce and expensive.* In many suburban cities and towns, taxpayers have erected anti-growth barriers to land use and development. Artificial scarcity has driven up the cost of open lots to the point where hardly anyone can afford to build on them. Then, too, lower tax rates has reduced the value of mortgage interest deductions, making *after-tax* monthly payments so high in relation to incomes that even if the total price of home and land does not scare first time buyers away, the monthly costs of ownership will.

But just when a whole generation of Americans had started to think they would never get a chance to own a home of their own, several lines are converging that say they now can! To begin with, lots of open land is going at low prices in farm communities... just waiting for developers to come in and buy it up. Second: the price of lumber has fallen from earlier highs, and the makings of a good home are now within reach. Third: interest rates are down and will go even lower. Fourth: after years of practice on a smallish scale, American industry has learned how to make real homes at lower costs in factories. Not just mobile homes, but actual *solid houses.* They are being built in sections - just as good quality as on-site homes - and trucked to building sites. Cranes put them together in a single day. It may be the *biggest development in America* since Henry Ford produced his first factory-made auto. Finally, manufacturing and service companies are moving operations out into rural towns and states - *opening up jobs* for those who are willing to pick up and move. It is all starting to come together. And I believe that during the early 1990's it will prove to be the mightiest force unleashed since the G.I.'s came home from World War II. Money will be made by investors *alert* enough to see the trend in advance and capitalize on it.

The market for real estate in America has *up to now* been considered a local market. That is, as you know, the cliche you hear most often... that real estate value is a matter of what street your property is on, what neighborhood you are in and what town or city your property is in.

But now I am seeing clear signs that real estate is increasingly becoming a regional or even a national market. A family looking for a new or pre-owned home is more willing than were their parents some years back to pick up their roots and move to a whole new environment. The concept of commuting is expanding. Now people cross state lines to their job as readily as folks crossed city or town lines twenty-five years ago.

Children who get out of college or even high school and find they cannot afford to live in the neighborhood or community where they grew up now think of jumping hundreds or even thousands of miles to get a new start in life. The same goes for families who are driven off the farm or forced to seek new employment opportunities far away when a company or industry falls on hard times. *One reason why it is possible now to change a place of residence so easily is that real estate is increasingly national in both its marketing and financing!* It is possible to buy a home in another area (even another state) making maximum use of the modern sales networking now in place.

But *even more remarkable is the growth of a truly national mortgage market.* Banks and Savings & Loans no longer have to depend on purely *local* savings for their money. Today many mortgages are sold and end up bundled with a lot of other mortgages to be used as *backing for bonds.* Thus the real estate market can find money (at some price) even when money is tight.

The final element in creating a national market for real estate has to be buyers who are looking for value... and are open to property anywhere in the nation. The new real estate mutual funds certainly fill that bill. So too does Japan Inc.

Japanese real estate investors such as Kumagi Gumi Company, Mitsui Fudosan, Mitsubishi Jisho, Nikko, Shuwa, Sumitomo Life & Realty, DaiIchi Insurance, C. Itoh & Company, Nippon Life and its subsidiary Nissei Realty Inc., Kajima and Fuji Bank have *gained fame for buying up choice office buildings in the U.S.*

Hawaii is clearly the place where Japan Inc. has had the greatest impact on U.S. real estate. It is "only" 3,800 miles from Japan. *In five years Japanese investors have sunk one billion dollars into Hawaii. This money has given Japan Inc. the titles to nine of the twelve major luxury hotels along Waikiki Beach.* In addition, Japanese investors have bought some 50% of the downtown office buildings in Honolulu and a significant number of million-dollar and up *homes* at places like Diamond Head. Some professionals now say that Japanese investors are bidding only against each other... having knocked most of the local investors out of the game. (Hardly anyone seems to object. *The Japanese hotel investments have apparently made tourists from Japan feel welcome on the islands, and last year one million Japanese visitors left money behind when they went home.*)

But Japan Inc. has developed a national view of U.S. real estate. They have the advantage of *seeing America as a whole...* since they are on the outside looking in. Thus investors from Japan have clearly jumped to the mainland. The headlines, of course, come when they buy a New York office building such as 666 Fifth Avenue. *Sumitomo Realty paid $500,000,000 (a half-billion dollars) for this forty-one story building located just north of Rockefeller Center.*

Replacement cost for prime Manhattan office buildings currently runs at $300 per square foot. In this case, Japanese investors paid $443.83 per square foot. *There is a certain amount of resentment building among U.S. investors forced to bid against Japanese investors willing to pay prices like that.* Average gross rents in the building are $28 per square foot - about $18 net. At this price the building returns 4% free and clear. Why would Japan Inc. pay so much? Why are they paying what others

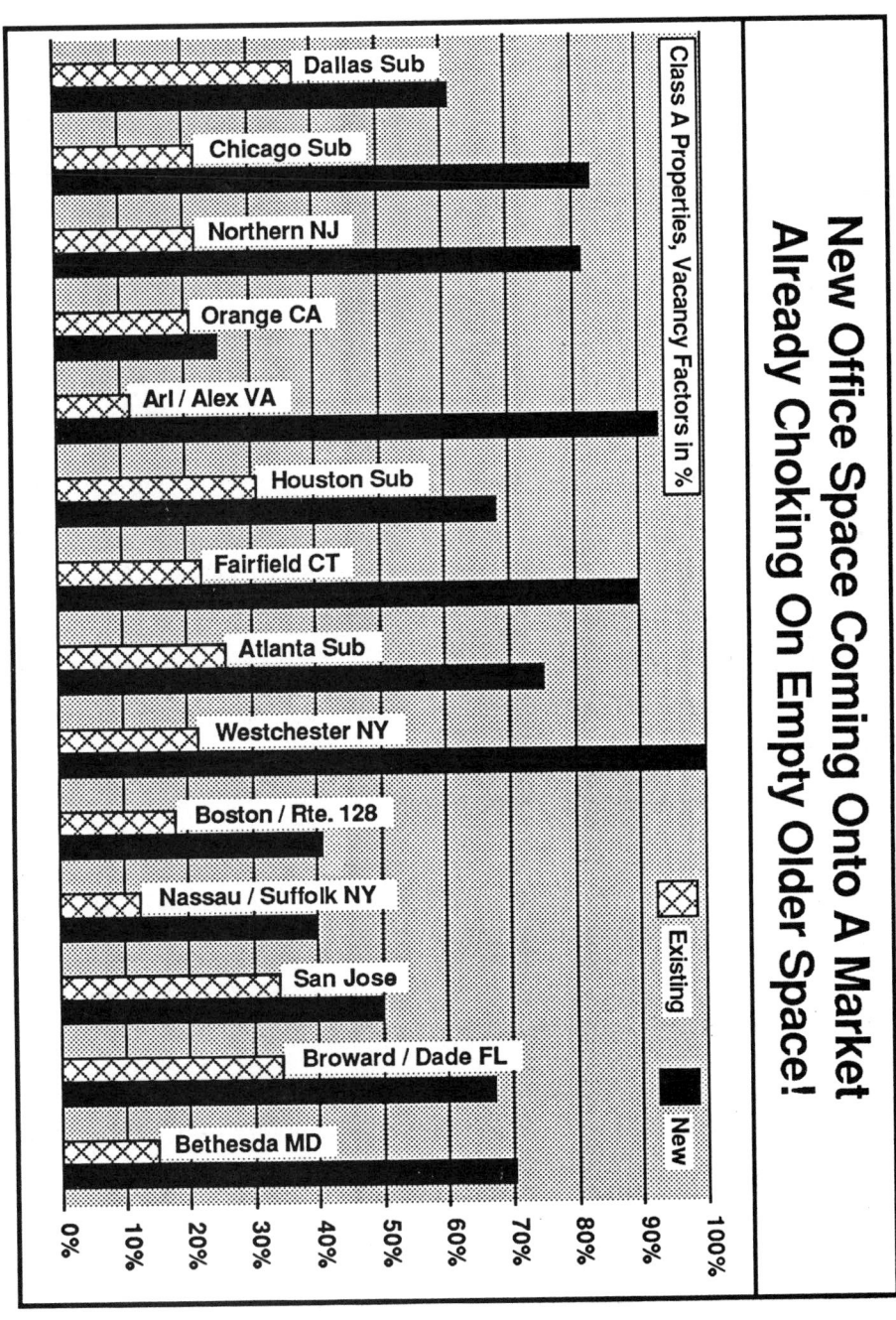

New Office Space Coming Onto A Market Already Choking On Empty Older Space!

Class A Properties, Vacancy Factors in %

Dallas Sub, Chicago Sub, Northern NJ, Orange CA, Arl / Alex VA, Houston Sub, Fairfield CT, Atlanta Sub, Westchester NY, Boston / Rte. 128, Nassau / Suffolk NY, San Jose, Broward / Dade FL, Bethesda MD

Existing, New

say is *way over market price* for buildings they select? The only reason I heard was that: *"They only overpaid in our terms.* But if you look at their cost of funds and the arbitrage of the yen over the dollar, they have not overpaid." *DOUBLETALK! That is what I think of that remark.* But listen to the rest of the "excuse" for their overpaying: "Sumitomo is *converting yen into dollars,* and protecting itself against a drop in the yen."

But what about these words, justifying such a high price for 666 Fifth Avenue: "In terms of *where the yen was before* it made its big move against the dollar (in the first quarter of 1985), they paid only 55¢ on the dollar, or $244.66 per square foot (below the going rate of $300 per square foot)." CAN YOU IMAGINE A REMARK LIKE THAT? *Buying real estate is not something you do using historic values. The fact is that in two years or less, the building at 666 Fifth Avenue might be in a declining American commercial market.*

Meanwhile, it is a fact that Japan Inc. is now trying to *diversify its U.S. real estate holdings.*

CHANGES AHEAD

Today it is normal to simply feed data - for the last two to ten years - into a computer and ask it to predict the future. No computer I know of is as yet smart enough to feel or sense subtle CHANGES lying below the surface. Instead, a computer simply draws a straight line out into the future and projects out recent trends... in effect saying that tomorrow will be like today. It is usually assumed that 40,000 people will keep on moving to California each month. But is that really likely? Will families and individuals continue to move where they are not wanted? Or will they move to where jobs are being created... and where real estate is now cheap and plentifully available? I think they will go where they are wanted... and may already be doing so! TAKE HOUSTON, TEXAS, for example. It has a lot to offer. One of Houston's greatest assets is ironically the single feature that currently causes it the most pain and suffering... *its surplus of empty housing and empty business space.* In recent years, Houston has been plagued by foreclosures... *and there is an inventory of such housing just begging to be bought at prices far below California or New York prices. Until very recently, a lack of realism prevented Houston from cashing in on its real estate assets. Everyone it seems, was waiting for high oil prices to come back.* (They will not, at least not in the foreseeable future. The price they have been waiting for was unrealistically high. The current price is more in keeping with worldwide supply and demand.) *Now owners of office buildings in Houston have stopped pretending that the current market price for rentals is artificially low. They have given up the fiction and have cut rents by 40%...* instead of asking too-high rents but giving the first two years free on a five-year lease. (They did so after being burned by tenants who took the two free years and then *skipped out* when it came time to start paying rent!) *The lower real rental rate is*

LAND VALUES CAN FALL!

See how Farm Land has fallen in price since 1981. This can happen to residential land!

Index, 1972 = 1.0

Year	Index
4.0	
3.5	
3.0	
2.5	
2.0	
1.5	
1.0	

73 74 75 76 77 78 79 80 81 82 83 84 85 86

Source: Federal Reserve Bank of St. Louis

already attracting businesses from outside Texas. (Corporations are jumping all the way from New York City to Texas, seeking lower costs.) As this trend becomes visible, *Houston will be seen again as a good place to live, work and play.* NOR IS HOUSTON THE ONLY CITY OR STATE FACING A COMEBACK. The rebirth of industry in America promises *better days to Midwestern cities.* And the trend of industry and people to move to rural areas is turning states such as New Hampshire and Maine into gigantic construction states... even though they are lands of snow and ice - not sunshine - in the the winter. *America is still a flexible, strong nation. Real estate will reflect this by 1989!*

PRICE RESISTANCE

IN BOTH THE EAST AND WEST COASTS OF AMERICA RESISTANCE IS GROWING TO THE PRICES BEING ASKED FOR BOTH LAND AND BUILDINGS.

There are signs - not clear and definite by any means as yet by certainly worth noting - *that a "Buyer's Strike" may be impacting new residential property already and forcing builders to drop the asking price on homes!*

NEW HOME PRICES have clearly climbed at a rate that places them *too high* relative to the low general rate of inflation. In 1986 for example, the median (middle of listing) price for all new homes rose at a rate five times the increase in the cost of living. And that was a national average. It included the areas where virtually no price increases in new homes took place. *In New England there were instances of new home prices going up at ten times the rate of inflation. More BIG homes were built along with fewer SMALL homes, so the median price slid up* even more than prices of individual homes in each catagory. It is clear however, that prices are at last *turning flat* in those markets that have in recent years seen the biggest and fastest price gains in new homes.

This does not surprise me. *The severe restiction of money growth during 1987 simply had to impact an industry as sensitive to the availability of money as is housing! But I sense a bigger factor* in the 1987 slide in new homes sales. And that factor is the escalation of prices. *Homes were being listed at prices people began refusing to pay!*

Incredibly large number of *"For Sale"* signs are up everywhere in greater Boston on single-family homes. It is as if homeowners, who have seen their equity swell, instinctively feel that a top is here... and they put their house on the market to "test the water." *(Despite the big increase in listings for existing homes, the number of "used" homes sold are running at just a tiny bit over year-ago levels.)*

Builders are amongst the most astute entrepreneurs in America. They keep tabs on what is going on in their area. And they know it is *taking a lot longer to move their product today.* WHERE A YEAR AGO A BUILDER MIGHT HAVE ADVANCE ORDERS FOR EVERY HOUSE HE PUT UP, IT IS NOT AT ALL UNCOMMON TODAY FOR A NEW HOME TO *STAY ON THE MARKET FOR MONTHS* AFTER IT HAS BEEN COMPLETED.

So builders do what logic and common sense tell them they must do: *They cut back on new starts.* In January of 1986, new homes were being started at an annual rate of *two million.* But that start rate skidded downhill more or less steadily for two years!

Builders tried to make up for the income lost when they cut back on starts. They read in the newspapers about inflation accelerating in America. *Most of them do not know that inflation is doing no such thing!* Wholesale (producer) prices have been falling to slightly under zero growth. *We may have begun a time of mild deflation, brought on by a full year of virtually zero money growth in the U.S.*

It is perfectly understandable for builders to have boosted their median new home price some 15% from $94,100 to $107,000. To some degree this is a result of builders moving up to larger homes in an effort to tap the "Money Crowd." You are now seeing the same process going on among Japanese car makers. They originally got a piece of the U.S. auto market by making tiny cars that U.S.

companies seemed unable or unwilling to build. But now Japanese car makers are "moving up" to big luxury cars loaded with extras. Unfortunately the market for such cars is getting to be glutted. *The same thing is happening in the housing industry... too many builders putting up large, expensive homes and competing for a pool of potential buyers that shrinks each time the price of homes is marked up.* (More and more people are finding they cannot hope to live on a housing scale similar to the one they enjoyed in their parent's home.)

CLASS A OFFICE PROPERTY: You hear a lot today about *the housing and office recession in Houston. And there is no denying that the oil-producing states have endured more than their share of real estate woes during the past five years. But the oil states may now be coming into better days. Considerable property is finally moving through foreclosure proceedings, into the hands of lenders such as banks and big insurance companies.*

Now the depressed oil cities are becoming *magnets, drawing prospective tenants* from as far away as Los Angeles and even Manhattan, where rents and operating expenses are skyhigh and climbing!

DENVER is one oil city that reflects this new turnaround in real estate activity! *In 1986 some 700,000 square feet of excess space in new office buildings came onto the market in Denver.* But new low rents - as low as $10 per square foot - began attracting new tenants, some of them brought in from outside Colorado through the aggressive marketing of such major landlords as Prudential Property Inc. (Prudential holds 500,000 square feet of space in Denver proper and another 500,000 square feet in the suburbs of Denver.) *Some shrewd real estate investors are moving into the Denver market as a result of the changed real estate circumstances there.*

But one city does not a national office Boom make! In fact, what Denver getteth, other cities giveth away! The growth of office space in use nationwide has slowed way down. Some of this reflects *a new determination on the part of business management to cut back on office personel every way they can.* You are familiar with the way middle management jobs - and their supporting staff - are now being replaced by computers! Another cause of reduced office needs is the merger wave, which makes thousands of office workers redundant! (Some of this change is gradual and is accomplished through attrition, but a gradual tightening-up of office staff *still means a slow or even zero rate of absorption for new office space.)*

This reduced growth rate for office space demand has come just as *a glut of new space has also come onto the market.* (The binge in building marked efforts to get properties up before the Tax Laws changed.)

Put the two factors together (big new supply plus small new demand) and you will get results such as this: *100%*

of the brand new Class A Property in Westchester County, New York - 400,000 square feet - recently stood empty. Other cities and suburbs are nearly as bad.

SO WHAT IS HOLDING CLASS A PROPERTIES UP TODAY? *Just this year alone, foreign buyers have snapped up more than $7 billion worth of business property in New York. The foreign buyers now own 12% of all New York business property.*

In Los Angeles almost half of the city's business property is already owned by foreign investors.

Foreign buyers have traditionally been a part of the American business scene. *The Canadians and British, for example, own significant amounts of U.S. commercial property.* And now foreign institutions, banks, real estate firms and construction companies are *engaged in buying up American business landmarks* such as Arco Plaza in Los Angeles and the Exxon Building in New York City.

Japan Inc. is promoting the use of a sophisticated real estate financing technique called *Master Limited Partnership (MLP).* This will allow them to broaden U.S. real estate ownership out into *wealthy private Japanese investors! They are, in effect, buying up America with our own dollars... money we send over to import not only cars but industrial goods!*

AN INDUSTRIAL REBIRTH is clearly taking place in

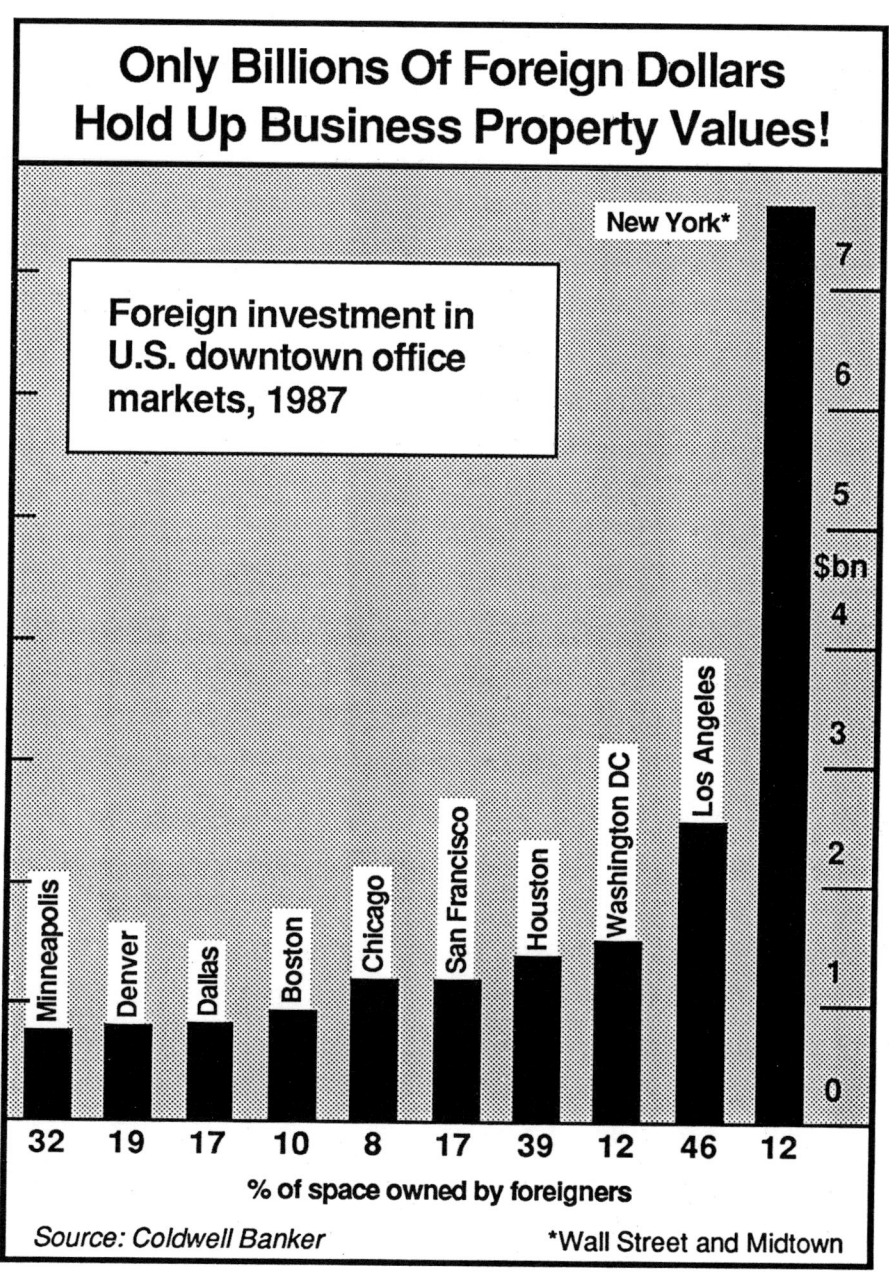

Only Billions Of Foreign Dollars Hold Up Business Property Values!

Foreign investment in U.S. downtown office markets, 1987

New York*

Minneapolis — 32
Denver — 19
Dallas — 17
Boston — 10
Chicago — 8
San Francisco — 17
Houston — 39
Washington DC — 12
Los Angeles — 46
New York — 12

% of space owned by foreigners

Source: Coldwell Banker

*Wall Street and Midtown

America. Robotics for example, appears to be emerging as *a new growth industry in the United States. The long industrial depression in the Midwest has left prices of land and business buildings relatively low there. All of these factors are important to a business planning to relocate.*

But a new study of how business executives rank states as a place to operate a business shows that the Midwest also has some *negative factors* working against its rebirth. It is widely known that workers in the Midwest will try to organize any new business that moves to the region and hires them. They instantly *seek to impose wages double the national average... while demanding work rules that would require only half as much output per hour* as say, Japanese and Koreans produce. In an age of international competition, this causes executives to rank the Midwest *dead last* as a region... and to rate Michigan lowest of any of the forty-eight contiguous states.

Executives rank the Southwestern States first as a group. That is no surprise. But what is *a real shocker to some is that the North Central States came in a close second. What is even more interesting, the top three states were all from the North Central region: (1) North Dakota, (2) Nebraska and (3) South Dakota. This backs up my prediction that in the new Boom to come in America, U.S. industry will move out to farm states to enlist the hard-working, well-educated and skilled farmers!*

MORTGAGE RATES AND REAL ESTATE: All you

now hear about mortgage rates is how realtors, developers, builders, savings banks and Savings & Loan associations are *worried that higher rates can seriously hurt the housing industry in the months to come.*

I think that most of these professionals in the fields of finance and real estate are missing the true point... *the matter of real interest rates. (That being the difference between the rate of inflation and the mortgage interest rate.)* The historic long-term real mortgage rate is 5%. You can see that going back 2,000 years or even further.

But I must caution you that real interest rates alone, as important as they are, cannot help you *plan ahead* correctly in real estate. That real rate of return interests folks who *loan* money... but it is not the key factor in the mind of those who *borrow it to buy real estate.* They are much more interested in comparing the rate of interest to market *prices for real property.* In the 1970's, U.S. farm property rose sharply in value... then it hit a plateau and *began to slide down.* Farmers who borrowed in the 1970's expected the value of farm land to keep rising. When it turned down, they were squeezed out. By the same token, *homebuyers in some parts of America are deeply concerned as they discover that the 20% a year jump in housing prices of the past two or three years has stopped! Prices in such "hot" markets may tumble 10% to 20% soon! So even low rates will have no appeal there!*

ONE TRILLION DOLLARS WORTH OF VALUE

Adrian Van Eck

SIMPLY EVAPORATED IN THE STOCK MARKET
BETWEEN THE MIDDLE OF AUGUST AND THE
END OF OCTOBER, 1987. *A SPECIAL EDITION OF
ABC TELEVISION'S "NIGHTLINE" HAD AN
INTRIGUING QUESTION ASKED ABOUT THAT
ONE TRILLION DOLLARS OF MISSING VALUE. IT
SEEMS TIMELY AND PERTINENT TO ANYONE
INVOLVED WITH REAL ESTATE. SO I SHARE IT
WITH YOU HERE, IN CASE YOU DID NOT SEE IT.*

The question was: "Where did the money go? Who has
it? Did someone get the money that I lost?" And, of
course, the answer was that no one had taken their money.
It was just gone! Up in a puff of smoke! One day it was
there... and a few days later it was gone... just like that.
*What had happened was that the market, meaning the
buyers, had changed its mind about what stocks were
worth. Where earlier they had been willing to pay $90
for a stock... now they were only willing to pay $60.*
Where they have paid $30... they were willing to pay only
$20 a share. It was simple. Just a matter of three minus
one equals two. The folks who owned shares were mostly
shocked. (Except those who subscribe to my Investment-
Planning Letter, who had been warned in mid-August -
with the Dow at 2700 - that the market would take a
"Time Out" and that the Dow would "test 2,000.") I am
personally surprised that men and women who own, buy,
sell, finance, broker, manage or design *real property*
seem so sure that this kind of down draft cannot and will
not take place in the real estate market! Just as was true

on Wall Street, *we have a whole generation of people now in real estate who have never seen prices go down... and do not believe they will ever go lower.* The prevailing belief in some professional East and West Coast real estate circles is that property values will be 10% higher next year... 20% higher the year after next... 30% higher the year after that!

Experience has taught me that words alone do not change people's minds. *Until they live through a decline in property values,* they usually will not believe me... no matter how much history I cite... and no matter how I seek to build a case by showing the way *farm land has already dropped in value.*

I could talk until blue in the face about the collapse in real estate values in Florida in 1927. Or the way the price of Chicago real estate soared much too high and then hit an air pocket in the 1800's. *That is then and there, comes the reply. This is here... and now!* Real estate values cannot go down. That is a conviction underlying just about every single decision made concerning real estate in America each and every day of each and every week. Well, *I am here to tell you now - just as I told common stock investors in August - when EVERYBODY knows a "FACT"... it probably is not so... at least it probably is not so any more if it was so before.* To put it bluntly... a lot of real estate in America is now on the market at prices too high for buyers to justify in the zero inflation, even DEFLATIONARY economy I see coming in the next seven years! *If you want to know what that means, look to Houston!*

Back in 1980, oil was selling as high as $40 a barrel. Many people were dreaming of $60 oil... even $80 oil. *(I tried to warn people that the bubble was close to bursting. I warned of hard times coming in Houston real estate when deflation arrived in The Oil Patch.* I can remember one irate subscriber calling us at the time from Houston... suggesting in strong language that I did not have any idea what I was talking about. I told this man to "call me back again in five years... and let us see who is right.") The price of oil turned down, just as I had predicted. It is now some 75% below the price "they" expected. *And a roaring INFLATIONARY BOOM IN HOUSTON REAL ESTATE gave way to unsold new homes, foreclosures and - more recently - bank failures as real estate developers and builders were unable to pay down loans taken out in days of soaring optimism.* If it can happen in Houston, Texas, it can happen anywhere in America. Just do not let it happen to you!

A lot of good men and women paid the price of believing that real estate in Texas could only go one way in price - up! Former Govenor John Connolly probably spoke for many of them recently when the auctioneer sold everything he and his wife had spent a lifetime accumulating. *"If it had only lasted a little longer, I could have pulled it all together,"* Connolly said. That is true. And we felt a great sadness to see the personal losses endured by this man and his wife. As a former Secretary of Treasury of the U.S. Government he probably knew everything there was to know about finance and the value of real estate in Texas except one small fact... *he did not know when the party was about to end! (And he may not have realized that real estate can go down in price even faster than it can go up!)*

WATER RUNS DOWN TO THE LOWEST LEVEL. SO DO REAL ESTATE PRICES! In Massachusetts *would-be homebuyers are fleeing Boston and its suburbs, choosing instead to buy homes in brand new subdivisions being carved out of farmland in Central Massachusetts.* This is just what I predicted would be happening. The rural towns in that area now seem like bargains to people who get "sticker shock" when they try to buy a home closer to Boston. Meanwhile, the number of listings at the Boston area real estate firms mount higher and higher. *It is only a matter of time, in my opinion, before the prices crack and desperate sellers slash their offering prices, here and in other states!*

Coming cuts in defense spending bode ill for Massachusetts... which along with California and New Jersey get the lion's share of U.S. defense contracts. It is clear that the very areas of America that will be impacted are the same ones that have seen real estate prices go sky high!

There are other straws in the wind. The industry

centered on Wall Street is laying off high-income employees. It is cutting back - and not just on Wall Street. It is doing so all over America. This means layoffs in the accounting, law and banking firms that serve Wall Street companies... hurting demand for *high priced housing.* It also means reduced demand for office space at the very time *it is already suffering from over-building and a GLUT!*

* * *

I have said here many times that the real estate industry in America - and that includes investors, property owners and real estate managers - has far more sensitivity to reality than any other industry. Maybe it is because money and power are so dispersed in real estate. But *people "feel" change faster in real estate.* They react quicker! So builders, developers, brokers, investors and property owners are already starting to take note of *the slide in NEW HOUSING STARTS and the dip in PERMITS.*

It is my contention that median and average housing prices are *increasingly misleading.* As home prices have continued to rise, fewer and fewer people can afford housing. They are apt to be people who already own a home - and want to trade up. They have a big equity and *plan to use that equity to put down on a bigger new home. The result is that builders tend to concentrate more and more on the bigger houses wanted by "trade-up" buyers.*

I have seen a lot of that in the Boston area in recent months. Depending on where you live, you may have seen a lot of it too.

But, of course, this process gets to resemble the old "pyramid club" concept... where the first people in end up rich and the *last ones in end up stuck!* As the pool of first-time buyers shrinks - because people cannot save up down payments as fast as the size of required down payments grow - *there are fewer and fewer new buyers in the market.*

Without first buyers, there simply are not enough SECOND-TIME buyers around to purchase the homes of THIRD-TIME buyers - *those who are ready to trade-up to big luxury homes. So everyone is frozen... locked-in to whatever home they already own... unable to move up the real estate ladder.* YOU ARE NOW SEEING THE WAY USED-HOME SALES REACT TO SUCH A FREEZE IN MOBILITY.

The next step in such a process is for builders to find that the new homes they put up in anticipation of making a nice profit are *simply not moving.* Even if the house was pre-sold, when it comes time for the buyer to take the title *he may have to forfeit the deposit and back out of the deal...* simply because the increasingly sluggish resale market prevents the sale of his "old" house. That is already starting to happen in "hot" real estate markets.

Views on the future course of mortgage rates vary widely. Some experts say rates will stay about where they are now. *I know of no one else who is saying what I am saying: You are about to experience one of the few huge drops in interest rates in this century!*

I expect to see thirty-year Treasury Bonds at a 6% yield before this coming decline runs its course. And that is my minimum expectation. I really believe T-Bond yields will slip and slide as low as 5.5%... even 5% before it ends. *Thirty-year mortgages will probably run a point or so higher... mostly because mortgage money increasingly comes from Wall Street rather than from local savings pools.*

Let us assume for the moment that I am correct about interest rates. The usual expectation in the real estate industry is for a Boom in housing, complete with fast rising home prices. Well, *I think you will see a Boom in housing, all right... even a SUPERBOOM. But I do not expect to see another wave of housing inflation.* Indeed, it is my belief that you will now begin to see two long-absent phenomina return to America: You will see *homes slowly lose their value as they get older... just as cars do and as homes used to do.* Instead of seeing "used" and new homes sell for more or less than the same price per square foot, you will see an increasingly wide gap open between new and "used" homes. *What will be even more shocking, the gap will be much wider for OLDER HOMES... those with problems in plumbing, electrical wiring, etc.* It is likely that real bargains will show up for buyers willing and able to modernize such an old home... and profits from doing so will be *larger* than is the case with today's relatively "flat" pricing spanning old and new housing. *The second shock will involve land prices. As more buyers flee to rural areas - where land is still cheap - the draining away of buying power from older suburbs and cities is likely to force down current land values in now-hot housing areas.* THIS WILL BE THE DOMINANT FORCE IN REAL ESTATE FROM NOW UNTIL THE MID-1990's. You must not take it lightly. Starting today, money will flow into rural areas. This will be just as big a revolution in real estate as America experienced after World War II, when the suburbs were carved out of farmland on the fringes of cities all over America. *It will be the latest in a series of migrations that date back to colonial days,* when early citizens pushed out past the mountains and the barrier lines that had been drawn on maps by the British Crown!

Americans are a restless people. We move to new areas whenever better economic opportunities beckon us. It is forgotten now, but the recent Economic Miracle of Massachusetts had its roots in cheap labor and cheap land. The old shoe and textile mills were moving out. Business was in the doldrums. But the newly emerging high-tech industry found the well-educated people of Massachusetts and New England just the kind of workers wanted to staff new plants and offices. *The same thing happened in Southern California and the New York / New Jersey area.*

Now the shoe is on the other foot. American industry is starting to build new factories as they pull manufacturing back from foreign locations. And once again *they are looking for cheap land and the right mix of worker experience, work ethic, local desire for industry and out of work labor.* They are finding everything they want in farm states, where people are used to working hard... where communities are anxious to attract jobs and tax revenue, where land is cheap and plentiful... and where farmers forced off the farms are *happy to find work close enough to their present homes so that they do not have to move away from their small towns that nurture them and their family.*

IT IS IN SUCH SMALL FARM TOWNS THAT THE NEW FACTORIES ARE BEING BUILT AND EQUIPPED. As farms disappear to make way for the factories, new housing has to be built. The first homes will be for the displaced farmers who will work in these plants. But then many *new workers will come to the towns to take additional jobs that open up, and more new homes will be built for them.*

To the extent that investors own or acquire land in the towns that seek and attract new plants, *there are profits waiting to be made in the reindustrialization Boom.* The same holds true for builders and developers who are close enough to such rural towns to *share in the prosperity.* But for those who do not see this shift coming, or who are too far away from such a town to share in it, the profits will

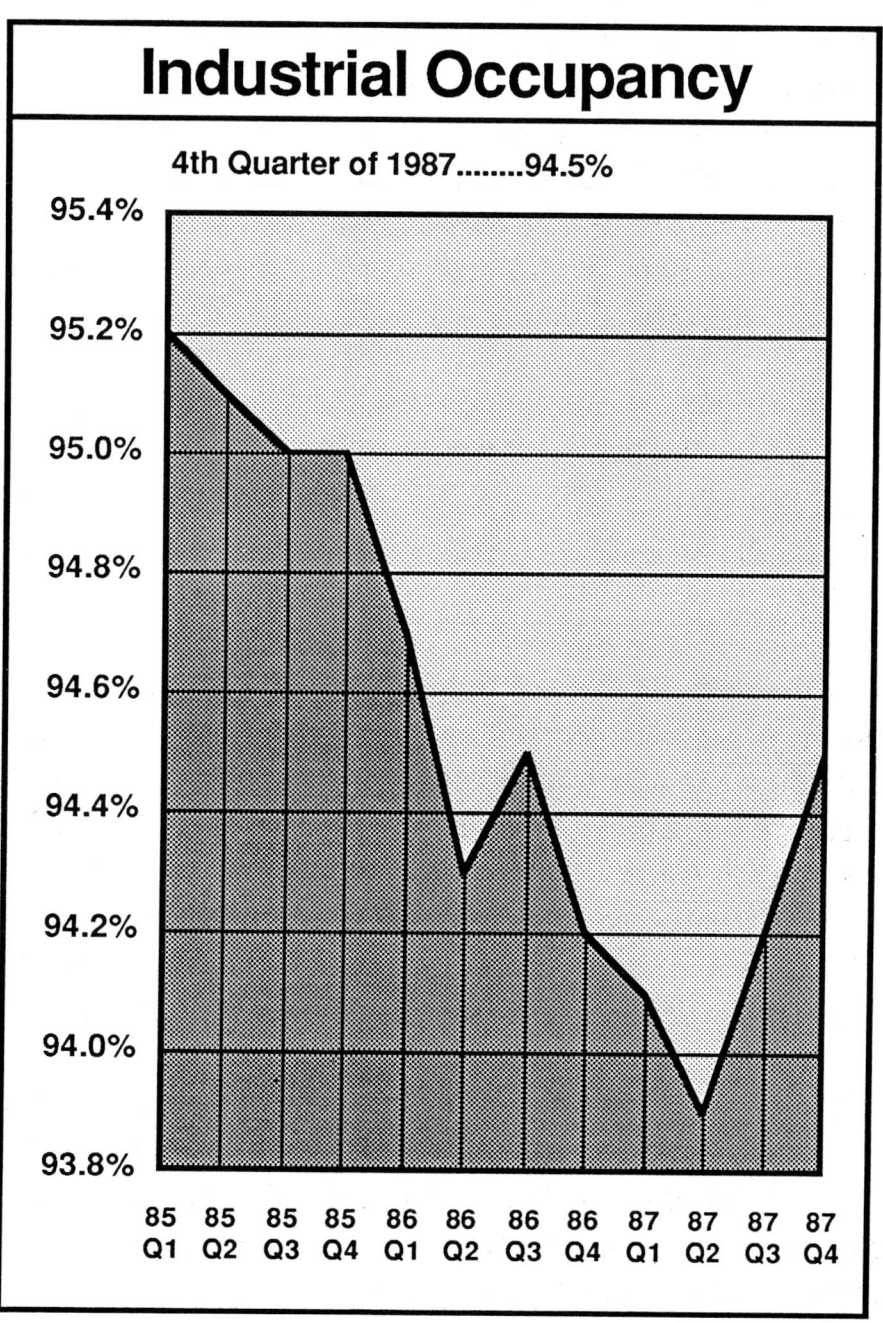

Industrial Occupancy

4th Quarter of 1987........94.5%

be harder to come by. *If you own property, sell property, broker property or finance property in one of the areas that will be losing people, it is a fact that values will start falling in your area. This is a warning!* And do not expect the Federal Government to bail you out. Within a year, Federal employees may face layoffs and pay freezes that will impact housing in some areas... especially suburbs of Washington D.C.

MOST PEOPLE WHO OWN, BUY, SELL, USE, MANAGE, BUILD, DESIGN OR FINANCE REAL ESTATE ARE NOT READY FOR THE WAY U.S. REINDUSTRIALIZATION WILL IMPACT PROPERTY!

Look ahead at all three of the factors above... and see how you can protect yourself against risks while placing yourself right to cash in on each of them. Start with deflation. Examine what happens when DEFLATION strikes real estate. First, to sort of set the stage in advance, look at the numbers when INFLATION AFFECTS real estate. Polls show that *most businessmen believe this will be the norm at least for the next decade.*

START WITH PROPERTY WORTH $100,000. Pay 20% down. Borrow $80,000 and purchase the property. Now let inflation strike. For the sake of simplicity, ignore such matters as depreciation charges or loan pay-down. *Just assume that prices in the same area go up 20%. Now your property is worth $120,000.* Your equity is up to some $40,000... one-third of the market value. It seems like a good investment. So you "let it ride." Now prices of similar properties sold nearby go up to $150,000. *Your equity jumps to $70,000.* Not bad! And then prices keep climbing to $200,000. (This certainly has happened here in the Boston area in recent years. It has also happened in Southern California, Greater New York and a few other areas around America.) *So a $20,000 outlay is now worth $120,000. (And that is a minimum.* It is likely that some reduction of mortgage principal has taken place, expanding net equity even more!) You are happy. Your banker is happy. *And you are getting advice from every quarter to borrow against your equity... to expand your real estate holdings. You are now being told that your $120,000 equity will allow you to buy two more identical pieces of property for $200,000 each... bringing your new total real estate holdings to $600,000 in current market terms.* Just think how rich you could be by the year 1999 if you pyramid your real estate holdings by buying up to the hilt today. (Again, for the sake of simplicity, ignore chances you are being told you will have to borrow still more money in the years to come, and constantly expand your real estate holdings.)

According to a new forecast by the National Association of Realtors, prices will climb steadily for the rest of this century at an average annual rate of 6.5%. (The Association assumes that incomes and the general inflation rate will climb at the same 6.5% per year rate until the year 2000.) *I ran the 6.5% a year compound-inflation in real estate out to just the year 1999, and I found that it would double the $600,000 value of the real estate holdings you are being told you can purchase now by borrowing all you can on a presumed $120,000 equity.* If the National Association of Realtors is correct, you would be holding *$1,200,000* worth of property by 1999. *And you could presumably borrow a total of $2,880,000 in 1999 against your presumed $720,000 equity and an additional $2,400,000 worth of property you could acquire in that year.*

It does not take too much imagination to compute that if you increase your borrowing each year up to the limit allowed by a 6.5% a year average (compound) inflation in real estate, *you could - according to the projections from the National Association of Realtors - increase your net worth in just this property from an original $20,000... to $120,000 today... and on up from there to some $1,000,000 by the year 2000.* (That is only a dozen years from now. You should start getting used to saying 2000. It is no longer WAY in the future!)

Numbers like that... $20,000 into $1,000,000 in real estate... are waved in front of your face just about every month... maybe even more often in real estate "seminars." *I am willing to admit that some shrewd investors have probably achieved such profits during the last forty-three years.* If that were not so, it would not be possible to get so many real estate investors convinced so easily today that it can and will happen to them starting now. *FORTUNES CAN STILL BE MADE IN REAL ESTATE. BUT YOU CAN NO LONGER COUNT ON SIMPLE INFLATION TO DO THE JOB FOR YOU.* If I am right - and I have done my historical and current research - *deflation will be the dominant factor in real estate beginning in 1988. Just look at what this means:*

Go back to the $200,000 property value with $120,000 equity. Deflation could not do much harm to the person or company that holds property today with such a high ratio of net worth. A 10% decline in values would still leave the property worth $180,000 with $100,000 in equity. A 20% decline in values would reduce the market price to $160,000 and cut the equity back to $80,000... still a 50% net worth. *Fifty percent equity is a comfortable ratio. And carrying costs for a loan would be low enough so that if the property in question were rental property, the owner could easily handle a rent-war and a battle for tenants in the open market.* But look at what happens if the owner decides to buy two more identical pieces of property, using borrowed money. Now we go to $600,000 in value with *$480,000 in loans.* A 10% decline in market prices cuts equity to $60,000. *A 20% decline in prices would completely destroy the owner's net worth... wipe it out... cut it to zero. I can easily visualize real estate prices in "hot" markets cooling down and falling 10%... or 20%. Experiences in farm states and oil states since 1980 show exactly what happens when sudden, unexpected real estate deflation hits* *property owners who are borrowed right up to the legal limit.* If it is rental property, falling rates will leave such owners unable to cover taxes and bank payments. And if they try to hold rent up, vacancies drive them into foreclosure. THE USUAL CRY BY A REAL ESTATE OWNER WHO IS HIT BY DEFLATION GOES LIKE THIS: "I JUST NEEDED *ONE MORE YEAR...* AND I COULD HAVE DONE IT." What they mean is one more year of rising real estate prices would have let them bail out with a profit. But when you examine the individual owners, you often find that in most cases they have been leveraging up to higher and higher levels of debt, adding more and more properties. *Chances are good that if the inflation had continued for another year, they would have been deeper in debt at the top.* (A study in history - and there have been a dozen inflationary real estate Booms in America's past - shows that buyers of real estate were convinced at every single top that *prices would go on rising for six or more months.* They had been confident that they would see the top forming and get out before it hit. But, of course, it is the nature of tops that investors get over-optimistic about how long it will last and how high prices will go. You saw an example of this kind of thinking in August, September and early October, 1987, in the stock market... as buyers bought options with borrowed money even while the Dow was sliding its first 500 points!)

I see a sharp drop coming in mortgage interest rates, making debt seem more attractive! So beware! Resist the temptation to leverage your real estate investments... particularly in those areas that have been "hot" for years and are *now over-priced.* Location will be the decisive factor now... more than at any time in recent years. *Without general real estate inflation to "bail you out," you must take particular care to pick your spots!*

REINDUSTRIALIZATION will not only change the real estate face of America, it will change our Way of Life... our Way of Living if you prefer. *I estimate that America's standard of living will improve by some 25% on an average per capita basis within a decade, and possibly by 1995.* Some of this higher standard of living will be taken in the form of increased leisure. You may begin to see Fridays become a five hour day, to allow workers to get an early jump on weekends. This will lead to the *expanded use of weekend "homes away from home."* That is already a feature in the lifestyles of the upper middle class in America. The trickle-down effect will spread this new concept of living down deeper into the middle class. I see a tremendous increase in demand for smaller homes in vacation areas... since second homes usually feature simple lifestyles.

But I am getting ahead of my story here. These will be the fruits of REINDUSTRIALIZATION and as such are down the road a bit. *What about right now? Where will the new plants go? Most executives responsible for placing new plants now favor brand new areas... untouched by old factory attitudes. This points to rural sites.* SOME OF THE FAVORED SITES WILL BE JUST OUTSIDE TODAY'S SUBURBS. SOME WILL BE IN THE OPEN-GAP AREAS BETWEEN BIG CITIES. (These areas are clearly visible from the air... and executives who make siting decisions often travel a lot. *You have probably witnessed some of them in your own travels.*) When you look back on FORTUNES MADE IN REAL ESTATE seven or ten years from now, you will most likely find most of them taking place in the areas attracting AMERICA'S REINDUSTRIAL-IZATION. Incidentally, much of big business is now so loaded with debt from mergers that *many of the new plants will be built for entrepreneurs... or for Japanese companies moving their production for the American market to America.*

The coming of a new Boom in factory-building will change the pace and location of America's housing action to low-cost areas! BUSINESS WILL LOCATE WHERE WORKERS CAN LIVE CHEAPLY, SO PRICES OF PRODUCTS CAN BE KEPT DOWN.

CHAPTER NINE

The Road For Gold Leads Nowhere!

For more than ten years Americans have been conditioned to think of a GOLD BOOM instantly whenever they hear the phrase HOUSING BOOM. That is because during the 1970's, *a Housing Boom meant a Boom in housing prices.* The Government created more money. THAT MONEY FOUND ITS WAY INTO THE BANKS. And the banks loaned it out to people who wanted to buy houses. But it did not produce any increase in the *rate of home building.* Instead it flowed directly into rising home prices. *Pure inflation.* That is what it produced. And inflation led directly to higher prices for gold. A lot of people came to believe that the link between a good year for housing and *a good year for gold* could not be broken. They still think that. Well, you are about to see that link snapped. So beware. Do not let yourself get caught up in hysteria sure to be generated by *promoters of precious metals.* You will lose money if you do! THIS TIME THE BOOM IN HOUSING WILL ACTUALLY PRODUCE A SUBSTANTIAL IN-CREASE IN THE RATE OF HOME BUILDING!

Now you will see what happens when the supply of homes increases just as fast as the supply of money available for housing. Or even more likely, you will see what happens when the number of new homes increases *even faster* than the number of dollars flowing into home loans. Just the reverse of the 1970's will now take place. Too many houses chasing the available dollars. *That spells the end of inflation!* A shocker. *Gold-bugs will refuse to believe it at first.* When they see the statistics printed in their favorite financial section or publication, they will rub their eyes and wonder if it is a misprint. Imagine a Housing Boom... with the price of homes in America's East and West actually declining! But it will not be a misprint. And it will not be your imagination. It will merely be capitalism at work. Instead of artificial barriers erected by suburban communities trying to *keep out* new home buyers, you will see competition by rural towns anxious to attract new residents and new businesses.

For these new people will allow farmers and their communities to survive. It will mean change. America may even change its definition of just what *is* a farmer, as men and women work their fields evenings and weekends, while holding down full-time jobs in offices and plants. But the result will be satisfying.

As for gold... it will cease to be a grand passion for speculators. It will seek its own fair level as a long-term store of value... exactly the same role it has enjoyed for hundreds and even thousands of years around the world. *My own best estimate is that gold will settle somewhere close to $300 an ounce.* I arrive at that level by a crude but effective calculation. Sixty years ago, gold was worth *$20 an ounce.* At that time you could take twenty one ounce gold coins and exchange them for one of Henry Ford's new automobiles. Not for one of the many fancy luxury cars on the market then, I hasten to point out. Just for the simple transportation-on-wheels introduced by America's master of low cost mass production.

Today you can still buy some newly introduced autos for a price around fifteen times that of sixty years ago (around $6,000). I regard this as a *fair measure of inflation* since then. So I get a current real value of some $300 an ounce. THAT IS THE LEVEL I BELIEVE GOLD WILL SETTLE DOWN TO WHEN SPECULATORS FINALLY GET IT STRAIGHT IN THEIR HEADS THAT INFLATION IN AMERICA WILL NOW BE REMARKABLY LOW. (Markets often overshoot targets temporarily at the end of a major decline. So I accept the very real possibility that gold may at least drop for a while *below $300* an ounce. But that is the level I see as the final target, when all is said and done.) At that price - $300 - gold will be attractively priced for what has long been its major attraction. I mean its physical beauty. *Gold jewelry* is likely to become more popular again as it becomes more affordable. And since there are some U.S. gold mines with rich veins close enough to the surface to permit gold extraction at just over $200 an ounce, and there are new low-cost production techniques bringing old mines back to life, *there will still be some profitable investments made in U.S. gold mines.* So you might as well adjust and prepare for it, in your own best interest, because this is the way things will be for gold during the next seven years!

* * *

By way of background information, here are some comments I made recently Please read these remarks. They are timely, and will help prepare you for what is coming in gold.

From the FRC Investment-Planning Letter - August 20, 1987:

"We Would Rather Be Early In Gold!

"We have never made a secret of the fact that our forecasting record is one long, continuous tale of *getting you in soon... then getting you out early.* We would rather be early than late... and we hope you feel the same way! WE KNOW MONEY DOMINATES MARKETS. ALL THE POLITICAL PUBLIC RELATIONS HOOPLA CANNOT STOP MONEY FROM HAVING ITS WAY. *We watch money. You must do it too!*

"Our recent (September) Forecast Letter has an M-1 chart. It shows M-1 reaching a peak in late April, dipping a bit, then going back up to the same *peak in late May.* Stocks hit a double-bottom on the same days that money hit a double-peak. When Volcker and the Fed began to actually SHRINK M-1 (May 20), stocks began to rise. *But that is not all that happened on the day Volcker and the Fed started to squeeze the financial markets hard. GOLD ALSO STOPPED MAKING NEW HIGHS. That's true. Gold has not reached the price it had attained on the day M-1 began to shrink! Coincidence? Not on your life! Our recent Forecast Letter had another chart showing money (M-1) slowing down in its growth all during 1984. Gold started down in price when the slowdown of M-1 began. It kept on going down until the Fed eased up on money! The correlation was darn near 100% precise!* THERE IS NO WAY GOLD CAN GO UP IN THE TIGHT MONEY SLOWDOWN AHEAD. Those who foolishly see inflation ahead will be *burned.* Those who are buying gold because they think it will go up in a stock crash will be *doubly-burned.* Gold will fall when stocks fall. But stocks will only fall until recent excesses disappear. Gold is heading for a *destructive collapse. One hundred dollars an ounce to start with.* Then probably more later!

"THIS MAY BE YOUR LAST WARNING: GOLD WILL COST PEOPLE A LOT OF MONEY." (End quote, August 20, 1987.)

From the FRC Investment-Planning Letter - September 17, 1987:

"GOLD: The Federal Government is at war with itself over *the price of gold*. For now the outcome looks like something of a near-term standoff. But any day now the Federal Reserve Board's tight money policy will defeat the Administration's inflationary Populist fiscal program. *Then gold will suddenly be seen by investors for just what it is: An overpriced metal facing incredibly large new increases to the world supply just as demand fades away to a shadow of its old self. That is a prescription for the collapse in gold prices...* or nothing that we have read about gold since the dawn of recorded history has any meaning today. (A notion actually held by many promoters of gold!)

"THERE IS A WIDESPREAD BELIEF THAT AMERICA IS HEADED FOR A MAJOR DEPRESSION... AFTER A "BLOW OFF." IT IS USUALLY SAID BY SUCH SINCERE FOLKS - AND WE DO NOT QUESTION THEIR SINCERITY OR THEIR INTEGRITY - *THAT GOLD WILL SOME-HOW, STRANGELY PROTECT YOU AGAINST DEFLATION DURING THE BAD TIMES THEY THINK WILL HIT AMERICA IN 1989 OR 1990.* AS

YOU KNOW, WE SAY THEY ARE WRONG TO EXPECT A DEPRESSION. SO LET'S GO RIGHT TO THE SECOND PART OF THEIR BELIEF - THAT GOLD WILL PROTECT YOU AGAINST *DEFLATION*.

"The reason some think that gold does well in a depression is because they appreciate history. (A most commendable trait!) *And in the FDR depression era gold went up in price. But that was a deliberate policy of FDR. His administration wanted to call in all the gold then in private hands.* He knew people would bury it in their back yards if he tried to swap it *even-up for the paper money FDR was determined to print in huge quantities.* It would be seen as the equivalent of confiscation. So, to flush that private gold out of hiding, *FDR got Congress to raise the official U.S. price for gold to some 175% of the world's free market price.* Most people flocked to turn in their gold. Then the Federal government locked it up, removed it from circulation, *and went on a rampage of money creation that failed to create new prosperity.*

"A few years ago, we told you about a paper circulating in the White House calling for *a rigged $500 per ounce price for gold. It was stated that this would create a new Boom in America.* We said then it was a bad idea. But the White House got Congress to pass a law ordering the U.S. Treasury to *buy all gold mined in America.* The idea was to mint new U.S gold coins. This appealed to those who wanted gold money back. But it also appealed to another

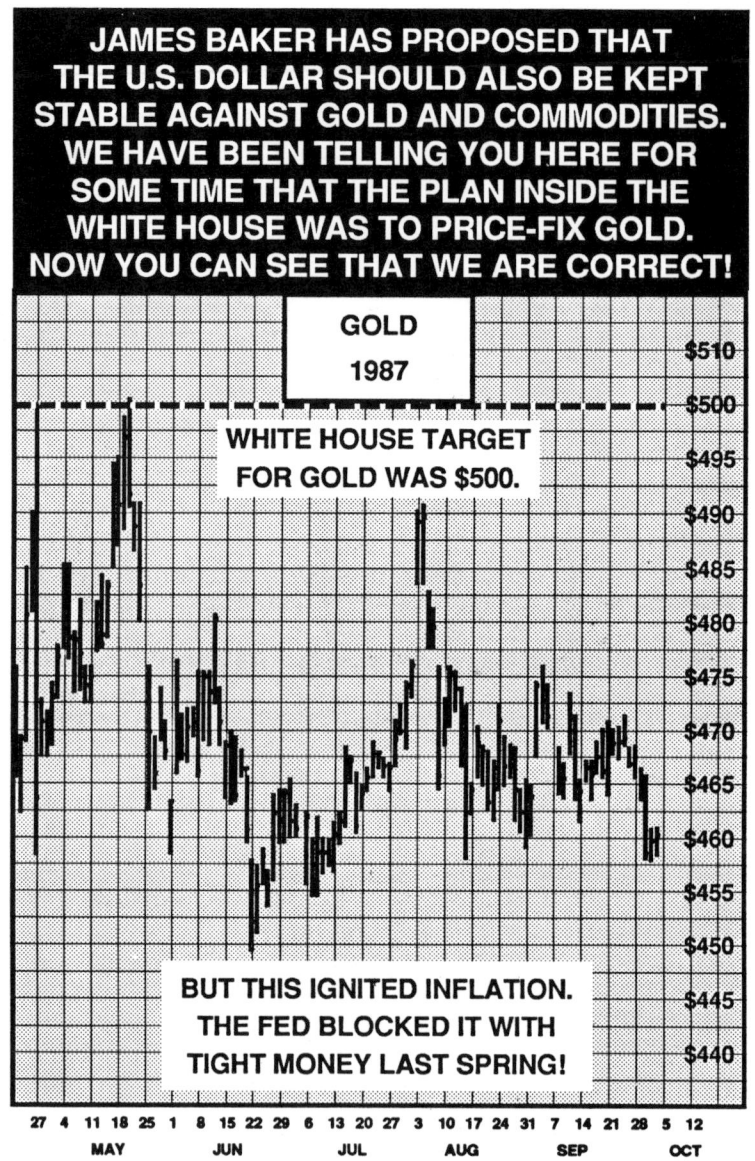

Here is a chart on gold, with comments, from my October 15, 1987, Investment-Planning Letter.

facet of Reagan's complex personality. He proudly admits he voted for FDR four times. *He obviously - as we warned you months ago - has bought the idea of pushing gold to $500, thus emulating FDR.* So gold is selling at twice the cost of production now. *This is stimulating a fantastic expansion of new gold mining. A glut of gold is pouring onto the market.* BUT REAGAN DID NOT GET THE OTHER PART OF HIS FDR-TYPE PLAN, FOR THE FED HAS *CRUNCHED DOWN ON MONEY GROWTH.* This has effectively stopped inflation, although the market fears its invisible ghost. *AS TIGHT MONEY BUSTS FALSE HOPES FOR INFLATION, JUST AS REAGAN ENTERS HIS LAST YEAR, GOLD IS SURE TO FACE REALITY AND DROP FAST IN PRICE!"* (End quote, September 17, 1987.)

And finally, here are some comments from the July 16, 1987, Investment-Planning Letter. They still seem timely to me:

"THE ENTIRE 1987 RUN-UP IN PRICES FOR BOTH GOLD AND SILVER HAS BEEN BASED ON A *MISTAKEN NOTION* THAT THE FALLING DOLLAR WOULD BRING 10%-A-YEAR OR MORE INFLATION TO THE U.S. IT IS OUR FIRM BELIEF THAT *AS THESE MISGUIDED IDEAS ABOUT THE RETURN OF INFLATION EVAPORATE, SO WILL ALL OF THE 1987 PRICE GAINS IN GOLD AND SILVER!*

"Please take very, very, very seriously what is really going on in the realm of money creation *(zero growth since New Year's Day, 1987, in M-1)* and in the matter of oil (likely to *go down 10%)*. You will have trouble anticipating the shock these two facts will *cause the market* as events reveal them soon. It will be like walking through a door and having a pail of ice water poured onto your head. It will help a lot if *you at least know it is coming.* You can get as ready as possible. (For others, it will be an experience similar to a high-speed crash!)

"And you know, it is not really enough to say that buying gold or silver as a hedge against inflation will prove *dangerous to your personal wealth in an age of price stability or even DEFLATION.* That only covers half the story... the half dealing with DEMAND for gold or silver. There is another side too. It is that of *SUPPLY.* And here the case against putting your dollars into gold or silver is even more convincing. *We see a gold / silver GLUT ahead!*

"Always keep in the front of your mind that the Federal Government of the U.S. is now bound by law to purchase all new gold mined in the U.S. BUT THERE IS NO PRICE MENTIONED IN THAT LAW! In it, Congress directed the Administration to pay the *world price at the moment.* There are many promoters running around predicting (as they have in each of the last four years) that the world price will go to $600 or more. *But if we get the kind of economic / financial policies we are looking for*

under new Fed Chairman Alan Greenspan, we probably will go back to our gold price target of $300 an ounce. As for silver, the law does not require purchase of silver by the Government (as it once did, in the late Nineteenth Century).

"And as for gold, some say it will be in short supply. *They are pipe-dreaming.* It is well known that new gold mines now being opened up in America, Canada, Australia and Brazil are going to *flood the world market with tons of new gold within a year or two.* Australia alone is spending $165 million (Aus.) this year to open new mines. Gold output is expected to reach *90 tons there for all of 1987, up from only 18 tons* just six short years ago. Canada is expected to produce *120 tons of gold this year, up from 52 tons* in 1981. America is expected to produce 144 tons of gold this year, up from 43 tons in 1981. Within a decade that U.S. total is projected to hit *200 tons a year.* And the fastest expansion of all may be coming in Papua, New Guinea. *The Ok Tedi mine there is producing 43 tons of gold this year. And a new mine (the Porgera) is yielding ten times as much gold per ton of ore as South Africa's richest mine.* Output is planned at 200 tons a year by 2000. And remember, as much as *six ounces of silver are produced along with EACH gold ounce! You are looking at a NASTY GLUT!"* (End quote, July 16, 1987.)

CHAPTER TEN

Silver - A Way To Lose Money In A Hurry!

I received a letter some months ago from a reader who was angry that I had said: *"Do not buy silver!"* She said I had kept her out of silver when it shot up in price to $11 an ounce. Soon after she mailed the letter, silver hit a speculative peak and fell 40%, wiping out the savings of many small investors! This is precisely the kind of subscriber communication I receive when I say not to buy silver. But I stand by this advice.

When I began in the investment advisory business way

Here is a prophetic chart from my September 17, 1987, Investment-Planning Letter.

back in 1955, I was lucky enough to become the protege of a man named George Danforth in the college town of Wellesley, Massachusetts. He had already distinguished himself over many years. (He was a deep student of business and history and was *without any doubt in my mind the greatest forecaster America had produced in twenty years.*) He taught me a great deal about the Booms and Busts of history. In every case, people were skeptical during most of the long Boom... but lost all fear and had incredibly overblown hopes for profit just before the Boom exploded into a Bust! I never forgot those lessons. He burned them in my mind. The lessons of history were reinforced right in front of my eyes in early 1961 when science stocks shot up to prices as much as 150 times earnings. Subscribers wrote in disbelief and anger when the advisory firm I was with then sent out telegrams urging the sale of all science stocks. But within four weeks the Boom ended in a collapse. I will never forget a tear-streaked letter from one subscriber who said he had gambled everything on that Boom - and lost. Now his house was going to have to go, and he had to phone his son and tell him he would have to leave college! *WHEN I SAY AVOID SILVER, I DO SO TO HELP YOU SAVE AND PROTECT YOUR HARD-EARNED MONEY FOR MORE REWARDING INVESTMENTS.*

Silver is often called a "Poor Man's Gold." *A more accurate name for this white metal today would be an "Upper-Middle Class Men's and Women's Fools Gold."* Day after day promotion pieces come onto my desk that speak in glowing terms of the profit outlook in silver. *It is no longer an event of note when I see or hear some promoter of silver's alleged virtues promise $15 silver... $20 silver... $25 silver... even a return to $50 silver.* Do you see and hear the same promotion claims? If so I urge you to do exactly as I do with them: date-stamp them and carefully file them away for future reference. I have been doing this for years. *Now I have a file that helps me evaluate a claim better... by looking at how often the person making the promise has made the same or similar promises before... only to come up with some excuse as to why silver fell short of such hopes and dreams.* THE U.S. GOVERNMENT HAS DUMPED ITS SILVER RESERVES AND REFUSES TO BUY MORE. MINES IN LATIN AMERICA HAVE BEEN SHUT DOWN BECAUSE *THE MARKET PRICE IS BELOW THE COST OF PRODUCING THE METAL.* WHEN YOU CONSIDER HOW DESPERATE THESE NATIONS ARE FOR DOLLARS AND HOW WILLING *THEY ARE TO SUBSIDIZE A MINING INDUSTRY, THE LATIN AMERICA DISCOURAGEMENT IS CER-TAINLY A TELLING FACT. One of the favorite tricks and gimmicks of silver promoters is to compare mining figures with annual consumption and project a shortage. But that ignores silver scrap, a powerful, decisive element* in supply and demand for silver! I constantly have to warn callers that silver will fall to $4 an ounce. The metal is uncommonly volatile, rising and falling 5% on some days. But it is trending down. *IF YOU ARE STILL IN SILVER NOW, GET OUT!*

CHAPTER ELEVEN

A Warning And A Promise About Stocks And Funds!

The biggest gains tend to show up in the *middle* stages of a very long bull market. *(And that is where I see us as entering next!)* Unfortunately, these gains scare the living daylights out of most investors. Instead of sharing in them and profiting from them, the average American investor shies away from them... *even runs from them.* He or she is usually licking deep emotional wounds from the correction that comes after the first stage of the bull market. What so very often happens is that Mr. or Ms. average investor has *waited until late in the game* to get into the market in stage one. In fact, the historic norm is for them to stay on the sidelines all the way up - no matter how long that takes - because they cannot believe what they are seeing. Then, right at the *very top* (and in more than a few cases just on the other side of the top, as stocks begin their correction and are being touted as *"bargains"* by so many of the investment advisory services) the investors rush in and BUY.

The usual pattern is to hold the stocks all the way down. Not just to the bottom... but for a few weeks after the bottom. They wait until the second or middle stage has begun... until their stocks have begun to move up again. *Then they SELL!* At first they are quite proud of themselves. They mistakenly believe that they have shrewdly gotten out of their stocks at or near the peak of a brief and temporary rally in what they have convinced themselves is a new bear market. Only later do they realize that they were wrong again in their timing... and that stocks, including the stocks they bought near the top of stage one and sold near the bottom of stage two, *are still going up. At first they are just surprised. Possibly even amused. But then the stocks climb back to the level at which they bought them originally... the level that would have let them get out even. And by now they are no longer amused. They are angry!* Angry first at themselves. And then angry at the market itself. At first they vow never to get back in the stock market again. But as stocks continue to go up they relent a little and decide to move some of their money out of the money market account where they are hoarding it. But this time they are cautious. They move the money into a bond fund. As time goes on and stocks still keep on climbing - which they are apt to do in the often long running second or middle leg of a giant bull market - the investors grow *a little bolder still* and move some of their money into equity mutual funds and individual stocks. *(I believe you will begin to see this happen soon - as investors realize October 19, 1987, was certainly not the end of the great bull market of 1982 to '95!)*

If you are going to get involved in this bull market at all it is important to you, your money, your family, your security and your peace of mind that *you maintain your perspective at all times.* Unless you resist your own emotions... whether they be fear during much of the upswing or greed near the top of each move... your chances of making and keeping money in this bull market are going to be somewhere between slim and none. THE FACT IS THAT REMARKABLY FEW INVESTORS MAKE MUCH MONEY DURING BULL MARKETS. Most people react to events late in the game. The secret of making money is to *anticipate* events, rather than react to them.

By and large, in my own Letters I prefer to be a little *early* in all of my moves, whether buying or selling. What this often brings me is notes from subscribers telling me that they are (1) amazed at how right I have been until now and (2) sorry that I am so wrong "this time." I do not *argue* with my subscribers. It is their money. I tell them what is going on and what is coming next. Usually after they have gone against my view of the economy and the market once or twice *they are more disposed to listen to me.* Then I start getting notes from them saying how pleased they are at their results, how happy they are to know and understand what is really going on for the first time, and often how amazed their friends and relatives are at their insight into coming market moves. *The real test, of course, will come years from now - when I tell them to get out of the market during the frothy, emotional final run-up of stage three...* usually a time when investors throw all caution to the wind and invest every penny they own or can borrow. If they listen to me then, I will feel that I have *really* helped them!

Adrian Van Eck

CHAPTER TWELVE

Must We Live Through "Another 1929?"

NO! That is the answer to the question above. No, we do not have to live through "Another 1929!" It is possible that we will, of course. If not in the 1990's then some other time... *maybe thirty years from now.* But saying it is possible under certain sets of circumstances is a very long way from saying it must happen. The very same fears (of Another 1929) were expressed back in the 1950's. *People tend to forget today just how frightened Wall Street was in 1949. Talk was everywhere that the Great Depression was about to return.* Instead, during the early 1950's as the Dow Jones Industrial Average broke free from a long plateau under the 200 level and doubled in just four years. It got back to the previously unthinkable level (near 400) that had marked the 1929 top! You would have thought the end of the world was at hand to listen to some of the fearful types on the media.

But stocks rose right through 400 to 500. And again there was in the air talk of "Another 1929." But it did not happen. Then 600 was reached. A correction... but still no collapse. 700 was next. Then 800. *Incredible!* The stock market had doubled and doubled again by *1959!* The same 300% gain that had marked the end of the bull market, the end of the Boom... almost the end of Western Civilization in 1929! It was thirty years after 1929... and "experts" loudly predicted an imminent crash and depression. Yet there was no *real* speculative excess. Inflation was very low. Business was a long way from being over-expanded. Debt totals were under control (partly because Ike actually encouraged periodic recessions and stock market corrections).

John F. Kennedy replaced Eisenhower in the White House. To the surprise of IKE himself (and many others), *JFK maintained the same strict control over inflation that had marked the 1950's.* The market dipped, then moved up to 900. During LBJ's Presidency (1966) it flicked at the 1000 level for the first time. And do not think 1000 did not scare the bejeebers out of Wall Street. *1000! That is ten times the 100 level that the Dow had touched on the downside just twenty-four years earlier* (right after Pearl Harbor). Ten times! Surely *this* was "Another 1929"... that is what many people said. They were wrong. It is true that the market could not really break much above that 1000 level until 1983 - *seventeen years later!* But neither did the market's corrections fall back anything like the 90% that had made 1929 to 1933 such an unpleasant time-period to live through. During the five full years ending in 1983 for example, the Dow moved up and down like a yo-yo in a band marked by 740 on the bottom and 1040 on the top... just 150 points above and below an implied 890 midpoint.

One of the reasons we did not have "Another 1929" at the end of the 1950's, at least in my humble opinion, is precisely because so many people had been so worried about "Another 1929" all during the 1950's. They never did lose their fear of speculation! *And so they avoided the very kinds of excesses that had caused the crash in 1929.*

Now, I have to tell you that at least until this point in the 1980's, there has been enough genuine fear of "Another 1929" floating loose on Wall Street and indeed all over America (and Canada) so that - once again - the really serious excesses that led to 1929 have been avoided. *Let me prove that to you.*

The stock market today is selling at only 60% of its 1966 level after you adjust out inflation. *Think about that!* Yet a lot of people are worried out of their sleep because there is talk that the Dow has doubled during a long period when prices in general more than tripled. *When you adjust for inflation the doubling is gone. At 2000 on the*

Dow, the stock market had regained less than half of its loss to inflation since 1966. That does not account for any of the REAL growth and expansion in population, production and profit since 1966. To reflect that would require the Dow going even higher... say 4000 or more. And I think that before this great bull market finally ends, it will hit that number - 4000! *It may even go higher than that!* (Note: To equal either the bull market of the 1920's or the stretched-out bull market of 1949 to '68, the Dow would have to rise to a level *over 5000 on the Dow!)*

HAVING SAID ALL THIS, I SUGGEST THAT YOU KEEP YOUR PERSPECTIVE AS WE MOVE INTO THE 1990'S IN THIS BULL MARKET. Remember, the *safest* gains probably come in the first stage. That is behind us now. The *biggest and longest-running* gains usually come in the second stage. (And I believe we are now entering that middle stage.) The *hottest-burning* gains tend to come in the third stage. And that is still well ahead of us.

Adrian Van Eck

CHAPTER THIRTEEN

America's Puritan Ethic!

One of the scenes of history that I have always seen as an example of candor was when the Puritan protector of England - Oliver Cromwell - called in a portrait painter to leave a permanent likeness of his face for posterity. As you may recall, Cromwell and Parliament had won a long and bloody Civil War against the King and his Cavaliers. Cromwell was a proud man. Yet he told the artist to paint him just as he really was... "warts and all!" This came to be a symbol of Puritan thinking: hard, practical and no-nonsense. As the Puritans crossed the ocean in ever larger numbers to New England, they took this kind of thinking with them. It was to spread across America... and became the American way of looking at life. "Don't beat around the bush... don't sugar-coat it... give it to me straight... I can take it!" That has been America since the days (1620 to '30) when the Puritans first settled.

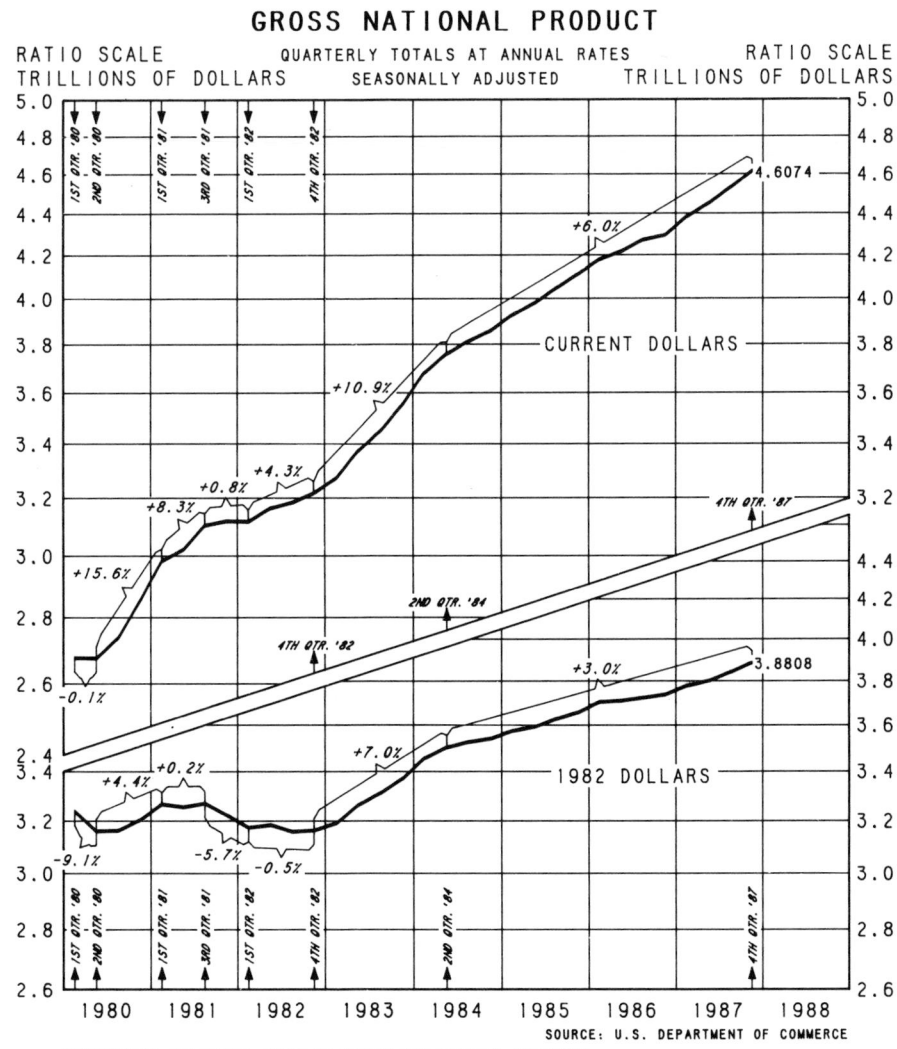

GROSS NATIONAL PRODUCT

RATIO SCALE — QUARTERLY TOTALS AT ANNUAL RATES — RATIO SCALE
TRILLIONS OF DOLLARS — SEASONALLY ADJUSTED — TRILLIONS OF DOLLARS

SOURCE: U.S. DEPARTMENT OF COMMERCE

PERCENTAGES ARE ANNUAL RATES OF CHANGE FOR PERIODS INDICATED.

To suggest that the economy is due for a depression is to claim that we are topping out from an overheated boom. *The bottom GNP, adjusted for inflation, reveals no such frenzy since 1979!!*

But sometimes Americans can get carried away by the belief that the only news they can trust is bad news. "Warts and all" has come to mean "I cannot believe anything that is positive." Too bad! Because sometimes the truth is NOT ugly! When Winston Churchill told the people of Europe by radio in 1943 that HELP WAS ON THE WAY, he was being candid. It was true... but it was good news! *(The Americans were coming!)*

The problem with good news today is that Wall Street (and investors across the country) treat it with suspicion. Bad news on the other hand, no matter how fanciful and far out, is readily accepted. In fact, bad news seems to be "in" today in the world of business and finance. A speaker who predicts the end of the world is at hand can count on a large and appreciative audience. Bearish pessimists who have failed to accurately predict the future in 1959, 1969 and 1979 are suddenly finding the spotlight on them again as the media seeks them out and says, in effect, "Say something bad about 1989... the worse you say, the surer you are of getting on the evening news."

There will come a day - perhaps in the mid-1990's - when I will again be warning of REALLY BAD NEWS ahead. But right now I am bullish. And I will continue to stay bullish as long as I can see good days ahead - whether bullishness is popular or not!

CHAPTER FOURTEEN

4,000 On The Dow By 1995!!

As you well know, I took no part in the display of public panic that swept through much of the business and investment community in late-1987. When subscribers phoned to ask if I was worried, I told them to buy more long-term bonds at bargain prices and to prepare for a resumption of stock gains - especially in selected Special Situations. My favorite maxim at a time like early October, 1987, when so many serious-minded folks are worried about "losing so much money", is simply this: So long as you do not sell a stock or bond at a loss... and you can define that as you wish, either a loss below your actual purchase price or a loss below the peak market price... and as long as that stock or bond recovers and goes to a new high within a reasonable time, then you do not have a loss in fact!!

The question then arises (and quite properly so) just how can I be so absolutely convinced that higher prices for stocks and bonds still lie in the reasonably close future. The answer is that a growth movement will not end until it has run its course. So long as the reason for the long-run growth trend is still in place... still going strong no matter how many years it has been running along... then you can be sure, just as I am certain, that still higher peaks are in the future for carefully chosen investments. (I mean that *carefully chosen* bit. Just because I am all-out bullish on thirty-year T-Bonds does not mean that I am bullish on junk bonds.)

If you are going to succeed at managing your money or your business in this seemingly chaotic age, you have to keep a sense of historical perspective at all times. That is not easy and will not be easy. Not many people have it. So they will try to tell you that you are wrong even when you are right. Keep your own mental compass at all times! And use the financial equivalent of a map. Be aware at all times where you are now... where you have come from... and where you want to go. That is a bit general, I know. But it is a valid framework. Ignore it at your peril. FOR EXAMPLE: Never, never lose sight of the fact that the Dow Jones Industrial Average hit the 1,000 mark for the first time in February, 1966. That is hardly yesterday. It is over twenty-two years ago. Think of that for a moment. Can you remember what you were doing in February, 1966. Do you realize just how long twenty-two years is in terms of the stock market?

Permit me to give you a few examples, by way of perspective: It is the equivalent of the years from the start of the Post Civil War Boom up to 1887. That was just about the time America's Boom (already being written off by some as long in the tooth) really began to hit its true stride. As Edison's electricity and Bell's telephone combined with inventions like McCormack's reaper, America exploded in a frenzy of new productivity. The expansion of America's railroads and steel mills, which had long powered the growth trend, surged anew in a climactic seven year Boom that created enormous new wealth in the United States. It was to become a time of mansions with real gold plumbing. In many ways, the seven years from 1887 to '94 showed what America could really do in business and finance. The fact to remember is that this seven-year Boom began at a time twenty-two years after the economic Boom had peaked... and years after the postwar growth had begun. In short... no one expected it when it came. (A point to remember is that by the time it ended in 1894 almost no one was afraid of it ever ending.) Now look at another twenty-two year period in U.S. history:

Back in 1922, many people in America thought the long Boom that had begun around the turn of the century was collapsing. But the growth forces that had dominated the first two decades of this century - the mass-production of the automobile, the building of roads and the spread of people out of the inner cities - were just about to explode into high gear. Deflation had forced Henry Ford to produce a car that was so cheap it all but forced every family to buy one. (And he began installment payments, to make that possible.) Soon new roads were pushed out to Florida and a whole generation took to wheels. Growth became a national obsession. The radio was introduced and joined the auto in opening up a faster way of life. Common stocks reflected this growth craze. In seven years, from 1922 to '29, stocks zoomed more than 500%. Remember this (and the fact that the Boom was about twenty-two years old when the real stock market Boom began) the next time you hear or see that the Dow (up only about 100% since early 1966) is too high. Is this 1929 again? *Not a chance!*

The forces that have been driving America's growth are not exhausted yet. Computer controls are right on the edge of transforming America into the NEW LOW-COST WORLD PRODUCER. This Boom is entering its hottest phase. It is likely *growth* will become a national obsession again as in 1886 to '93 and in 1922 to '29. My target for the Dow is 4,000 by 1995. (If that sounds unreasonably high to you, please consider that back in 1949 both the American and Japanese stock market averages were at the same level. Today, Japanese stocks are ten times as high as U.S. stocks.) Keep your perspective. See today as it is: The leading edge of a *long-term* growth trend. Be bullish!!

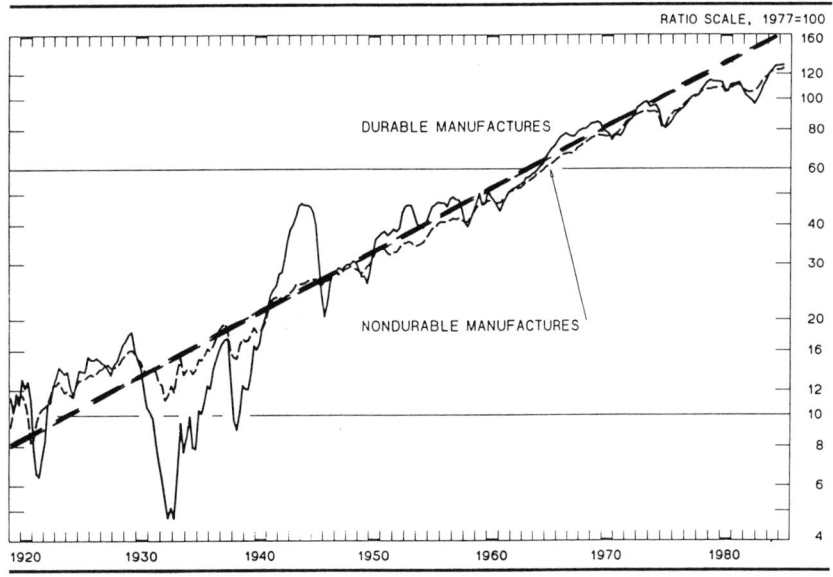

There is a definite, clear, long-term trend line (broken line) for U.S. manufacturing. In the 1920's output went too far above the line and we had a crash. *In the 1950's and 1960's, output grew along the line as if it were tied to it.* Since the early 1970's U.S. output has been almost flat, while the line keeps going up. As you can see on the chart, when this has happened in the past *output has put on a growth spurt to catch up to the trend line!!*

Adrian Van Eck

CHAPTER FIFTEEN

New Growth In The 1990's.

I sincerely request that you give full consideration to the the now mounting facts that suggest a bit urgently that an American *Boom without inflation* is a virtual certainty in the fairly near future!

I felt guilty in late-1987 as phone calls and letters poured in demanding to know if it was "all over." I paced the floor and asked out loud to no one in particular... "Where did I go wrong?" How have I failed to educate, enlighten and persuade so many of my readers that it is nowhere near the end of this bull market move... and that the 1990 to '95 period may possibly be the greatest time of economic growth that America has ever seen!

I am talking here about economic growth so powerful it will change almost everything we take for granted and hold familiar in the United States of America. Our companies. Our investments. Our standard of living and our family's security. Our comforts and our leisure. Our place in the world of nations! Our saving and our borrowing. Yes, our very sense of being... who we are and where we are going! Our hopes for our children and our grandchildren! All of this and more! And the changes will almost all be positive... better than we dare hope or dream today!

You know, I think the market itself has now either caught a glimpse of The New Promised Land waiting on the other side of the next hill in front of us... or has at least sensed what is there. Because I do not fear this market any longer.

I can now see clearly - standing at the top of this hill - just what it is that the market got itself so worked up about in 1986 and most of 1987. Oh, my goodness it is a glorious sight to behold! It is enough to make the blood pound in your temples. The market is all-wise, all-seeing, omnipotent! It is the individuals who trade in the market who often lack the vision to see and understand where we have been, where we are now... and where we surely are going!

Subscribers constantly ask me: "Will you tell us then, when it is finally almost over?" And my answer, clear as a bell without any hesitation or hedging or fudging is this: "If you have been with me for years (and many of my

The 1920's And The 1980's

Back in 1980, we forecast that the 1980's would be a replay of the 1920's. By and large, events have proven us correct. But the biggest part of the Boom lies ahead of us. Our belief since early 1987 is that the Fed is going to slow this portion down, and stretch it out - safely - to 1995!

Monthly close of the Dow Jones Industrial Average; 1920's indexed, 100 = 1000.

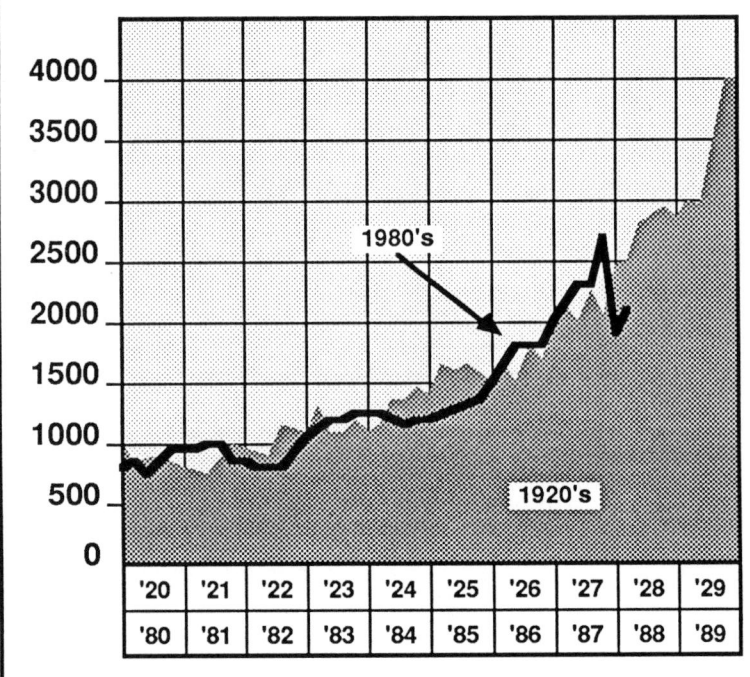

The growth of service industries has allowed per capita GNP to continue to grow in America, despite the slowdown in industrial growth. *This is what made so many people believe wrongly that we have now entered a Post-Industrial Age.*

readers have!) then you know I always tell you in advance when you should get in or out!

I do not pretend to be good at fine tuning my timing advice. I can see into the future but it is so clear to me that it always seems to be closer in time than it proves to be. So I promise only to warn you EARLY... in advance of any major turn. And note that I said MAJOR turn. I have no real interest here in catching very short-term trading blips. (Others can do that, and I tip my hat to them.) My own talent, if I have one, is to sense instinctively when a major shift is coming. Sort of like what a weather barometer will do for you... warning of a storm or of clear skies. (I did that for readers in August and September of 1987, for example. And I flashed an "all clear" signal in late-November, 1987.) When the FINAL top comes, years from now, I expect to see it coming EARLY and warn you in time to get out. Meanwhile, enjoy the Boom!

Adrian Van Eck

CHAPTER SIXTEEN

Computers Will Save America!

Most investors know that Japan Inc. benefits from research programs coordinated and paid for by the Japanese Government. Yet almost no one seems to be aware that the United States has an even bigger and thus far more productive research program coordinated and paid for by our own Federal Government. It is not a secret or classified program. It is just overlooked and ignored by Wall Street. Too bad for them. For this Federally sponsored research is paying off big right now. And you will have an edge over most other investors because you will know about it. If you are standing up, sit down. And if you are sitting down, pull your chair up closer and hear what I am about to tell you. There is money to be made from this knowledge!

Back in 1958 - thirty years ago - the Soviet Union stunned America by launching the world's first man-made object into an orbit around the Earth. The Eisenhower Administration and Congress moved on two fronts to compete with the Soviets. The first front was a little-known agency inside the Department of Defense. It was called ARPA (Advanced Research Projects Agency). Later this was to become DARPA, as Defense was added to the front of its name. The second front was called NASA (National Aeronautics and Space Administration.) This was soon the darling of the media. It put John Glenn (later to be Senator Glenn) into orbit. Then it sent men to the moon. More recently it has launched space shuttles. But while all this was going on, DARPA was stimulating basic and applied research in America on a scale so ambitious it leaves the Manhattan Project of World War II (which created the A-Bomb) far behind in size and scope.

The beauty of DARPA has been the way it operates. It hands out money to colleges and corporations and gives them tremendous flexibility and leeway in exactly what projects to pursue and how to go about their research - within broad guidelines, of course. Very little of the applied research and virtually none of the basic research has been classified. It is available for license. The laboratories that do the research and come up with the breakthroughs - and there have been and continue to be many - are encouraged to use their own intimate expert knowledge of their research to spawn commercial by-products... which they have done and are doing! It is DARPA that has been credited with developing technologies that include phased-array radar, composite materials, laser holography and forward-swept wing aircraft designs.

But fortunately for America today DARPA, under President John F. Kennedy, recognized the importance of the then still embroyonic field of COMPUTER SCIENCE. A subsidiary program was formed and funded to concentrate just on computers and their applications. It was named IPTO, for Information Processing Techniques Office. It was to be IPTO that funded the development of virtually all of what we now know as computer science! Yet, amazingly, it is all but unknown.

So powerful has been the thrust of DARPA into the field of computer science that breath-taking new discoveries and inventions now come right on the heels of each other. DARPA in recent years has been pressing hard for new achievements in ARTIFICIAL INTELLIGENCE. Using laser beams and color television cameras as eyes - usually together to provide in-depth ability to see objects - DARPA has forced the early evolution of computer-guided, unmanned vehicles that can follow a winding roadway through a twelve-mile-long test course. It was only one small step from there to computer and laser controlled machine tools that can not only take over complex assignments on assembly lines from human workers but do them perfectly, without errors of flaws, twenty-four hours a day... thus paying for themselves in as little as two years! NO CHEAP FOREIGN LABOR CAN MATCH THE LOW-COST OR HIGH-QUALITY!

When I say that America's computer technology is ready at last to bring about a new capital goods Boom in America, I know what I am talking about. This new American economic Boom is not coming about by accident. It was planned! I know the phrase "economic planning" offends a lot of readers, including perhaps yourself. It offends me too. Nevertheless, this Boom has been planned. That is a fact, not a fantasy! Back in 1983, the Reagan Administration saw the new fifth generation computer program announced by the Japanese Government as the modern equivalent of Russia's Sputnik - a severe challenge to U.S. leadership in the world. And so the Reagan Defense Department asked Congress to create and fund a brand new program called the Strategic Computing Initiative. $600,000,000 was voted to pay for the first four years. $600 million!

Although this program was placed under DARPA, it was clear from the start that its reason for being went far beyond the needs of the military. And this was by design! Two of the world's top heavyweight computer geniuses (Professor Dertouzos of M.I.T. and Professor Feigenbaum of Stanford) saw the threat behind Japan

Inc.'s FIFTH GENERATION COMPUTER PROGRAM. They used their influence (which was considerable) with Congress. And the Reagan Administration went right along with the professors in pointing out commercial and civilian benefits from such a program. Indeed, the 1983 Reagan proposal for the creation of SCI (Strategic Computing Initiative) featured a section headlined: "SPINOFFS FROM THE TECHNOLOGY BASE CAN STIMULATE NATIONAL ECONOMY." In this section, the Administration told Congress: "The Strategic Computing Program promises the production of machine intelligence technology will enable ANOTHER MAJOR CYCLE OF NEW ECONOMIC ACTIVITY IN THE COMPUTER AND ELECTRONICS INDUSTRY... spinoffs from a successful strategic computing program will surge into our industrial community... the United States stands to profit greatly both in national security and economic strength by its determination to exploit this new technology." Not everyone was thrilled by this Reagan Administration push for Federal funding of such advanced computer research and its implied goal of "ANOTHER MAJOR CYCLE OF NEW ECONOMIC ACTIVITY."

The four-year program conceived in 1983 (Strategic Computing Initiative) has gone beyond even the wildest hopes of its sponsors. In the world of industry and commerce it is now exploding in a host of hardware and software breakthroughs that permit incredible advances in controlling machines and managing factories.

CHAPTER SEVENTEEN

Watch The Factories Come Home To The U.S.A.!

America has avoided new capital investment in machines and factories for twenty-two years. It has imported its manufactured goods to a degree never before contemplated or tolerated. Now that time is ending. And a new time is in the process of being born... a time of manufacturing products in the United States again. It is clear this time is coming whether the U.S. producers want it to or not. Indeed, many of the brand name companies in America clearly do not want to see this new time come. They like to import their products - slapping their own label on the imports. They will be dragged kicking and screaming into the new time... and they will be forced to build or modernize factories in order to compete and hold their share of markets. The surprise... I should say the shock... will come when they discover that by using new computer controlled machines and new computer assisted management techniques they can now produce higher-quality products at lower costs than they can import. What is more, they will make more profit. And they will protect themselves against the ever-present danger of their foreign suppliers turning on them and producing identical products under their own name and taking away the U.S. and foreign markets from the U.S. brand name companies.

You know, the thing that strikes me in today's situation is that I should not have to discuss this with you at all. In earlier years... earlier decades... earlier centuries... what I am saying here would be such common knowledge that it simply went without saying. But now? Well now it has largely been forgotten. I am amazed to see how few people understand that you cannot have a recession until you have a genuine capital investment Boom first. They go together... sort of like salt and pepper... day and night... rich and poor. It is an iron law of nature that you cannot have a recession until you have a Boom first. And I do believe in iron laws of nature. There is a balance in nature that is always there, whether or not we recognize it! (I have always known and believed that. And every once in a while I see a fact that proves it again. For example, I was reading about the terrible drought of 1887. Farmers in the U.S. Northeast saw crops wither and die in the dry fields. It was the final, bitter end for the majority of Northeast farmers. They had been struggling to meet price competition from the lower-cost new farms of America's new Bread Basket further West. They quit trying and let many an old farm revert back to forest land. Yet in 1987 it rained so much and so hard and so long that people were joking about building an ark! Water was everywhere... spilling far over the normal banks of rivers, even flooding the residential and commercial shopping centers of communities that must have been burned dry in the Great Drought of 1887. I did not see a single newspaper story calling attention to that super-dry year exactly 100 years ago. No one knew anything about it. There is no longer a real sense of history even in one of America's most historic regions. So be it. My point is that whether anybody is aware of the fact that nature has balanced the books or not, it has still done so. It is a fact. And facts will always win out over fantasies.)

President Abraham Lincoln endured the agony of a great many political and military fantasies in his years in the White House. On all sides he was besieged by critics who demanded to know why the North could not simply sweep the South from the battlefield and win the Civil War. Lincoln however, deeply appreciated the valor and stubborn courage of Southern officers and men. He cried inwardly at the loss of so many fine men on both sides.

And he winced at the false beliefs of so many in the North, who had expectations of a quick, easy victory. Abe Lincoln had a clear view of reality, even when those around him did not. He tried hard to help those whom he served as President see and appreciate what he could see so vividly. He was fond of telling little anecdotes as a way of making his point. For example, he would ask: "IF YOU CALL A DOG'S TAIL A LEG, HOW MANY LEGS DOES A DOG HAVE?" Some of the folks who heard this tale thought it was a trick question, and asked him if the dog had been hurt and lost one of his "other" legs. The frustrated Lincoln would blurt out: "The answer is four. Only four. Never more than four. It matters not whether you CALL the dog's tail a leg. The fact is it is a tail and not a leg and so the dog will only have no more than four legs!"

By the same token, it matters not what some in Washington or on Wall Street call the economy of the 1980's to date... or the economy of the 1970's. The FACT is that we have not had a capital investment Boom in twenty-two years. We had a long period of inflation when U.S. factories raised prices to seek profits, instead of investing in new machinery and factories. And more recently we had a period when U.S. companies closed down their old factories and imported their products. As I said, many if not most brand name U.S. companies like things just the way they are. So, if these managers were left to their own devices the chances of a capital investment Boom would be close to zero. My long-range studies tell me that the period of heavy imports was merely a transition from the old to the new. First companies had to shut down antiquated plants. They did this. Now they will have to open new ones. And they are doing so. Japan Inc. is leading the way here. In New York City the Japanese took over a plant closed down as unprofitable by a big U.S. company, stuffed it full of new machines from Japan, hired hundreds of local American workers and are going full blast with the only plant of its kind in the U.S. refurbishing subway cars!

There is a widespread belief that capital investment can only be justified when companies want to rapidly expand their output to meet big new demand. That is why the thinking is that an economic Boom must start first with consumer buying. Wrong! This is upside down! A *real* Boom must begin with capital goods investment. The history of American capitalism shows that such investment comes when there is a glut of goods already available. Manufacturers invest in labor-saving machinery in order to get their own costs and prices down lower, so they can win or keep a chunk of the market and survive even if others go broke. That surely is today! The multiplier effect takes hold after capital investment. This magnifies and spreads the Boom. That is what I see coming fast!

Adrian Van Eck

CHAPTER EIGHTEEN

The Next President Will *Have To* Be Pro-Business!

Once upon a time there was a war. And America fought in the war. And the war was expensive. But the politicians did not want to tax the people for the full cost of the war because they were afraid that would make them less popular... and no politician wants to be less popular. So they printed lots and lots of new money to help pay for the war. And that money competed for goods and services already available. And it caused prices to go up. The politicians did not want to admit that they were the ones who had caused and were causing the inflation. So they blamed businessmen. They said greedy businessmen were pushing up prices to make lots and lots of profit. The businessmen scratched their heads when they heard this talk by politicians. They knew it was not so. For they were not really making a lot of profit. They had to pay more money to workers for wages. And their taxes were up. So was the cost of everything they had to buy in order to operate their business, from the parts and supplies to the rent and electricity. Each year they had to raise prices just to stay even. It was very frustrating. And not much fun at all!

And then one day the politicians decided that it was not enough to blame the businessmen. It was time to actually do something about the way prices were rising faster and faster. For people were starting to grumble... and to blame the politicians... and that was not good to hear. Because politicians do not want to be blamed for anything, even when it is their fault. So the politicians looked around and they found someone new to blame. They would blame it on the central bank... the Federal Reserve Bank... even though for years the same politicians had been begging that bank to be "good," meaning to print lots of new money! It was necessary, in order to convince the public that the bank itself was the culprit, to hire a new boss for the bank. And so the politicians did exactly that. They selected a man with a reputation for toughness. A stingy man. A shrewd and even mean man.

Adrian Van Eck

And that new Chairman of the Fed shut down most of the printing presses turning out money... allowing only enough money to handle population growth and real growth in the economy. And since almost no one in America understood or even knew what he was up to, they continued to raise prices... because by now that had become a way of life. Indeed, some businessmen had grown so accustomed to inflation that they counted on it to let them give automatic raises to their workers each year ("to keep them happy") and to let them report 10% growth in sales each year to their shareholders ("to keep them happy"). But now when they raised prices, a strange thing happened. People stopped buying! For now money was tight. And people could not afford the higher prices. A shock spread over America. The companies told the workers they could not afford any new raises. And the workers did not believe them... for raises had become automatic even for bad and lazy workers... so long as they just showed up for work most of the time. And so the workers went on strike. And the big bosses of the unions ran to the White House and said: "Quick. Fix it for us. Tell those awful businessmen that they have to give us 10% raises or you will punish them!" But the response from the White House was not what they had expected. The President glared at them and said: "You are being paid enough already. Shut up and go back to work!" And since there seemed to be no other choice, they did so. And the businessmen could run their companies again.

But then the shareholders in turn could not see why sales

were no longer shooting upward automatically. And so they pushed directors to buy or merge with other companies... to get bigger numbers. This was done. But multi-billion-dollar debts resulted. This forced companies to sell off some divisions to get money. And it caused them to let many middle managers go for no reason other than to pare costs. One remarkable result of all this was that some of the sold divisions "went private," being bought by managers and investors. And some of the "fired" middle managers started their own small companies. These new operations were often a joy to behold... lean and streamlined, like a racing boat... yet keen and alert to new ideas for productivity, new products, new markets and new ways to distribute goods and services!

The stock market saw what was happening, and stocks began to rise. As more and more investors were attracted, they went higher and higher... and their moves grew faster and faster. Yet there were many skeptics who could not believe what they were seeing... and kept warning that it must end quickly... and badly.

The story above has happened not just once or even twice but three times... after World War I (under Coolidge)... after World War II (under Truman and Eisenhower)... and after the war in Vietnam (under Reagan). After Coolidge came Hoover, who did not share or continue the Coolidge Prosperity Plan. Unlike Coolidge, Hoover was a meddler in the economy... a statist. (FDR actually called him a socialist when he ran against Hoover in 1932... something today's liberal media will never tell you.) There was indeed a depression in 1930. But it is just as important to see that there was not a depression (as had been predicted) in 1960. Nor will there be one (as I see it now) in 1990!

Just as John F. Kennedy continued Ike's low inflation policies during his 1000 days in 1961 to '63, forcing business to modernize and actually improving an already good economy, so is it likely that the President who takes office in 1989 will have to be pro-business, pro-growth, pro-profit, pro-innovation and pro-modernization... yes, Pro-Boom.

CHAPTER NINETEEN

What Japan Inc. Knows About Us That *We* Should Know!

There is general agreement today in American business and investment circles that Japan is a very smart, very aggressive and very determined competitor. This agreement leads to fear on the part of many... fear that Japan Inc. is such a formidable competitor that we in America have no hope whatsoever of surviving as an industrial power. The fear is that with the passage of time, Japan will take over the manufacture of everything we make in America. We will be left only such tasks as setting up domestic sales agencies to handle their products, transporting their products into our own American local markets, financing the purchase of their products by American citizens... and then perpetually borrowing our own money back to finance our seemingly chronic Federal deficits. You have heard such fears expressed yourself, have you not? And maybe on days when things were not going as well for you as you would like and you were in a "down" mood you had a few moments alone with your own thoughts when you wondered if perhaps some of it may not be coming true... maybe even all of it about to happen? When you read recently that American auto workers take twice as many men (and women) and hours to make each car as the Japanese do, did you not wonder if there is any way at all we can compete with them... or whether the game is already up and we are just unwilling to face up to it?

Well, if you have had any of these thoughts, I have good news for you... news to brighten your day... put a smile on your face! Japan Inc., the same very smart and very aggressive and very determined Japan Inc. I was talking about above a few moments ago, has a much different picture of America's future than you might have at the moment! No doubt you are fully aware that Japan Inc. is sending the very cream of its young managers and scientists to America for advanced study, especially at the world-famous Massachusetts Institute of Technology. And you probably already know that Japan Inc. is lavishly donating money to M.I.T. to smooth the way for these already experienced young managers and professionals.

And you may be thinking that all of this activity lets Japan go on doing what they have done best for a half-century... buy, license, borrow and share the latest American manufacturing technology. It is widely agreed here in America that they plan to go on taking our technology back to Japan and use it to outproduce America. After all, Japan is now producing, using and exporting most of the industrial robots in the Western World... even though the robots were first conceptualized, designed, perfected and produced right here in the United States!

But you are in for a surprise! Japanese companies are scrambling just as fast as they can to invest in new plants right here in America. Oh, they are smart all right. Smart enough to know that the newest major industrial Boom in the world is already starting to gather steam right here in America! They are sending their best and brightest to schools in America because they want their managers to make friends with the future business and technology leaders in the United States... where Japanese companies now plan to invest heavily and enjoy most of their growth and profits during 1988 through 1995!

What is it that Japan Inc. knows that most U.S. business executives and investors do not yet know and appreciate? It is simply this: Despite all of the rhetoric in America about too much of our money being invested in military research, and too little of our money being sunk into research for non-military use, the truth is that enormous quantities of that military research either has direct

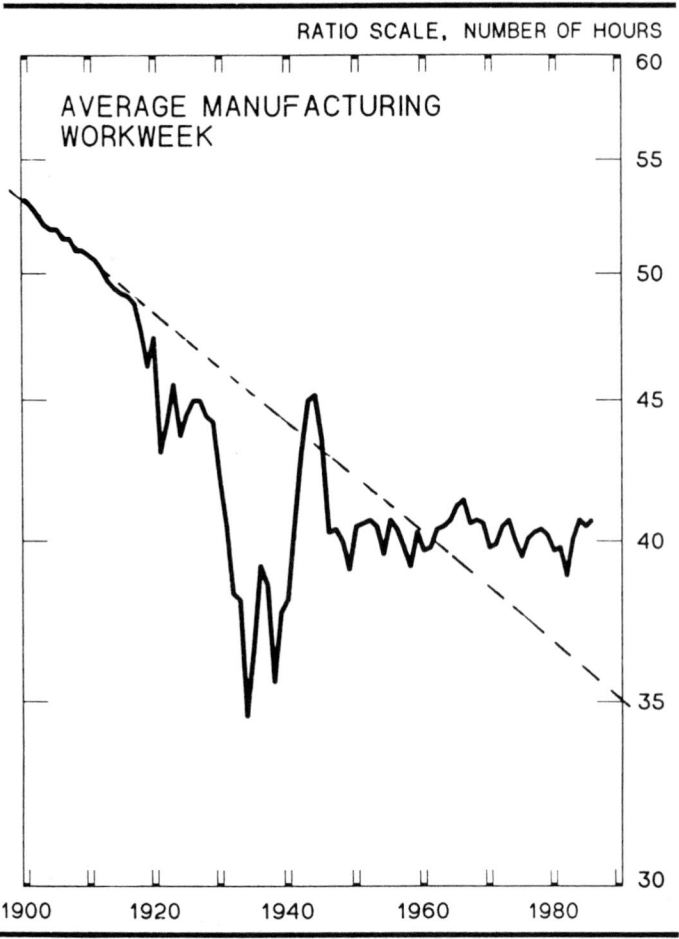

The new factories to be built in America will be so productive that they will allow large increases in output with only small increases in man / woman hours worked. It is our firm conviction that one important result will be a return to an historic trend that shows up here during the first thirty years of this century... and then came back for a while in the late 1940's.

application in U.S. private industry... or is giving birth indirectly to a whole new wave of new products, new ways of doing things, new tools and even whole new factory layouts and work-flow systems... all of which can be used, are about to be used and soon will dominate the non-military industrial world in the U.S.A.

The result of this new application of military research discoveries to civilian industry in America is nothing short of breath-taking. Once you make use of the technological breakthroughs by Pentagon research contractors to create new products for the U.S. civilian market... you have an America so very different from that of today that I believe by the year 1995 America will open up a gap in productivity and profit between us and the rest of the Free World (and the Communists too!). Thus the late-Twentieth Century will once again be called "The American Century," as it was after World Wars I and II! I am talking major innovations here! Computer aided management programs, industrial technological breakthroughs! I am talking of an America where one skilled worker and his managers can produce three, four, even five times as much as they do today... and all within seven years!

This is not the stuff of daydreams. It is hard reality. Already proven! In the past few years, The U.S. Air Force has poured hundreds of millions of dollars into its industrial technology modernization program (Tech-Mod). Two-thirds of the money was allocated to smaller subcontractors. (If they put in some of their own money they were allowed to earn up to 18% on their invested capital, and many did so!) Savings are incredible. The number of direct labor hours required to build an F-16 has been reduced from 110,000 to only 26,000... meaning every man-hour produces what four hours did a few years ago! The really exciting changes are coming in flexible manufacturing. Using computers to assist modern tools and new plant layouts, it is possible to produce one single part as cheaply as old methods turned out mass produced parts. The blank is taken from storage, then machined, inspected, repaired (if not perfect) and moved to the shipping area... all automatically. In an age when marketing is offering individuals products designed to their own tastes (instead of forcing them to accept look-alike products as in the old days of VW "Beetle" cars), such flexible low cost production will give U.S. industry a major advantage. Much of the Tech-Mod industrial technology is now being made available for license to any American manufacturer who wants to cut costs! Some will ignore it, and slowly fail. Others will grab it and run with it. One result will be a revitalization of American industry.

BEFORE 1989 IS OVER, AMERICAN-MADE AUTOMOBILES MAY BEGIN TO GRAB MARKET SHARE IN THE UNITED STATES BACK AWAY FROM CARS MADE IN JAPAN. *THIS SWITCH IN FORTUNES WILL BRING MULTI-BILLION-DOLLAR INVESTMENT IN BRAND NEW STATE OF*

THE ART AUTOMOBILE FACTORIES HERE IN THE UNITED STATES...

Wonderful, you may say. Or hard to believe, you might reply. But what I have just told you is based on trends of sales and pricing and production already well advanced. The truly remarkable fact about the above situation is that *the cars being made in Japan that are facing sales troubles are not all really Japanese cars. Some are being produced for the American "Big Three" and are being marketed in America under famous U.S. brand names.* Meanwhile, the "hot" cars selling at low prices, made in American plants and known for high-quality are very apt to be *JAPANESE brand names!* That is shocking. The truth is that Japan and America are now so intertwined that *separation is impossible!*

America depends on Japan for savings money to fund our Federal deficit and to buy our office buildings. But it cuts two ways. Japan knows that *it depends on us for a military shield!* And they look to us for research breakthroughs! You may wonder about this last part - about Japan depending on us for new ideas, new products and new marketing ideas. Don't! *In America, the buzzwords may be "Consensus Planning" and "Production Teams,"* as we strive to take from the Japanese culture and economy those things which we believe may benefit us the most. We may be asking ourselves how we can restructure our tax system to promote a higher level of savings... how we can instill in our students and our workers a pursuit of disciplined excellence that we see as the hallmark of Japan. *But meanwhile, in the NEW Japan that is coming into being at surprising speed, the desire is to become "more American!" Not entirely American, of course.* They still want to retain all that is good and useful and beautiful in Japanese society. *But at least they want to be more like Americans. They have an absolute hunger for things American - especially the educated, successful, young Japanese.*

They watch American television shows dubbed in Japanese. (Although a significant and growing number of Japanese now speak Engish.) *They see how we live.* The homes we live in. The yards with grass and trees. The driveways ending in two car garages. They see in our television shows how we get away on weekends to summer and winter homes *at the ocean, on the lake and in the mountains.* They see how we play golf and tennis and go hiking in the hills in the summer and skiing down the mountains in the winter. They see *on television in American shows* how we take one or more vacations a year... to "recharge our human batteries." *They see how we own and use motorboats, canoes, small family-style cruisers, luxury cabin cruisers and even yachts.* They see - and you had better brace yourself for this one - American movies and television shows set in the 1950's... and *they love the big cars* because these cars give them a sense of personal achievement, of success, of POWER that they do not get when they get into one of their smaller Japanese-made cars... *or when they pack like living sardines into the overcrowded commuter trains early each morning and late each night.*

So they are looking at themselves and taking stock of their lives... and of the futures they see looming up in front of them. Here is what they see (and it does not at all make them feel happy or satisfy them): *They see themselves living on an island nation no bigger than the state of California... but with six times the population of California.* They see themselves surrounded by water... *but not enjoying the sea* the way they would really like to. (About the only time most of them get on the water is when they crowd into a ferry boat for a short trip from one island to another.) They see beautiful mountains largely ignored and *unused.* They see rice paddies - hundreds of rice paddies - inside the city limits of Tokyo itself... with rice farmers being paid sixteen times the world price for rice by the Japanese Government, *while land for building is so scarce that they cannot even think of owning a home in the city.* They see hillside land left undeveloped in Tokyo because of a quaint old tradition that no one should build on land that can look down into the Imperial Palace or its GENEROUS grounds. They see Tokyo Bay... beckoning... inviting... with some *shallow areas near the shore that would permit a great deal of new dry land to be created at a low cost*, as they know was done in Boston (the now valuable Back Bay) and San Francisco in America. They see *open, rural land between the crowded BIG cities...* and they ask why new communication and transportation technology would not make it *practical to build suburbs there,* with American-style ranch homes, yards and garages! They look at their low-rise buildings with their cramped offices and their tiny apartments... *living spaces so small that problems are arising as Japan moves from a six-day work week to a five-day week "just like the Americans."* Wives are *complaining that their apartments are so crowded on the weekend with the mother and the one or two children all home from work and school that there is simply no room for their husbands. So the "men of the house" are being kicked out... forced to wander the streets until bedtime!*

And if they go to a movie it is apt to be an American film... and once again they see a lifestyle so different from their own that a *quiet anger grows inside of them!!*

And they are now asking questions that just a few years ago were unthinkable: "Why not use the new earthquake resistant buildings that have proven themselves in California... and go up twice as high with new buildings, so the *apartments can be made twice as large?* Why not use some of Japan's surplus savings to *build new sewer lines (and new modern roads) out into the countryside so that water and new communities can be built out there?* Why not change the laws that now tax farms inside the city at a pittance... so the owners will sell the land or *develop it?* Then end the Government subsidies on food and buy it *cheaply in America?*

This is just the beginning! Once the lid is off and thoughts start to flow, they really get warmed up! Why not, they ask, *make mortgage interest tax deductible and tax interest on savings...* so people will save less and put money into housing? Why not introduce creativity and *individual expression* into Japan's schools? Why not allow students to ask "WHY?" and "WHY NOT?" instead of just learning by fixed, unquestioning rote. *The shocker - not yet heard by most Americans - is that a new emerging CONSENSUS in Japan is carrying some of these proposed changes into LAW... and at the same time is accepting others into Japanese CUSTOM!* The biggest change in Japan is in its attitude about buying! A CONSUMER SOCIETY is springing to life in the newly-rich island nation on the rim of the Pacific.

The level of retail sales inside Japan has simply *exploded since late 1986...* after years of sales growth running far below that of Italy and the United States. (West Germany has not reformed its own miserly ways. The West Germans obviously do not enjoy shopping and buying.) *BUT A CONSUMER BOOM IS CLEARLY IN FULL SWING IN JAPAN. As a matter of fact, Japanese and American shoppers are now neck and neck... with the U.S. sales level now flat compared to the steeply rising level in Japan!*

When a young couple marries today it is almost automatic that they fly off to a honeymoon on American soil - often Hawaii. The bride is usually wearing an American-style diamond ring now... something new. *She and her husband stay at an American hotel.* They shop in American stores and when they get back home they spread their American purchases out for everyone to see. After much "oohing" and "aahing" the others find themselves asking *why they too should not have a taste of "The Good Life - American-Style." AFTER ALL - THEY CAN AFFORD IT. THE INCOME LEVEL OF THE JAPANESE IS NOW ON A PAR WITH THE AMERICANS... AN AMAZING FORTY-YEAR ACHIEVEMENT!* (This success story of capitalism and democracy is clearly tempting and tantalizing an old enemy of Japan... China!)

The Japanese discovery of an American lifestyle has come late for them. The rising yen (falling dollar) is making it hard for Japan to continue its export drive to the U.S., West Europe and other nations. The Japanese have swallowed about half the fall in the dollar. *They are deliberately keeping prices in the U.S. and elsewhere lower than they really ought to be.* This is forcing Japanese executives, bankers, and Government officials to huddle together and seek a new CONSENSUS on ways to keep the Boom going inside Japan.

Two separate but complementary answers have presented themselves to the Japanese. Both are now being tried. Both are succeeding!

FIRST - Japan is definitely moving to reshape itself more

in America's image. The work week is being shortened. Workers are being all but forced to take their vacation time... something new in workaholic Japan. Leisure activities are being developed. (The Japanese, ironically, are convinced that American leisure-time goods are superior to any others in the world... *and they insist on importing and buying such made in America products.)* It is a start. A modest one. But it is a start in redressing the trade imbalance. And leisure leads directly to the idea of "homes in the country." This one will really surprise you, I am sure: *The Japanese have gone mad for American-style "log cabins."* They are buying log cabin "kit" homes in the U.S. at such a rate that the U.S. Northwest lumber companies are having trouble keeping up with the demand. Shipload after shipload of cut and notched logs - pre-cut for log cabins - are *heading for Japan.* And these are not one-room cabins. *Many are full-sized log cabin style homes - "LUXURY LOG CABINS!"*

It is dawning on Japanese leaders that after four decades of working hard and saving their money (20% of their income!), they can now afford to relax at least a little bit... *and improve the QUALITY of life. Instead of sending cars to America, then keeping their dollars in America to buy T-Bonds and real estate - they are in a position to use the return on their real estate holdings and the interest from their U.S. bonds to buy American products and import those products back to Japan. In short, they are reversing the flow of recent years. And what a change this is going to be!*

Japan is still determined to set high-quality standards for their products. But now they are increasingly *making these products in the lowest-cost nation in the world. They see the United States as an ideal place to manufacture.* We have millions of acres of low-cost open land available for brand new, modern factories. We have superb communication, transportation and distribution (warehouse etc.) facilities in place... not just to service the United States and Canada, but to export to Europe. Goods made in America have a much easier time of getting into nations in West Europe than do goods made in Japan, Taiwan, South Korea or Hong Kong, since West Europe has a trade surplus with us and dares not refuse low-priced QUALITY products from Japanese-owned U.S. factories. *Japan is already exporting television sets MADE IN THE U.S. to Europe...* and will soon begin shipping some of these sets to Japan!

The Japanese yen has risen from 250 to the dollar three years ago to around 125 yen to the dollar of late. *Not so many months ago it was widely assumed in Japan and the West that a 125 yen dollar would cause a recession in The Land of the Rising Sun. It would mean the end of Japan's export-driven economic growth.* As it turned out, those predictions were correct only so far as they went. The growth of Japanese exports came to a screeching halt, then went into reverse. Japanese-made goods piled up on docks in America and Europe. Orders were cut back, then cancelled. But the recession so many people had worried about never came. The Japanese looked hard at their own way of life... their deprived condition. Then they looked at the unsold goods. And they said to themselves: *"What are we sitting here for... when we could be out buying those goods for ourselves?"* And so buy they did... and buy they are doing. After forty years of "doing without" and denying themselves even simple pleasures and possessions, Japanese citizens feel they are entitled to own a few of the products they now make so well. Automobiles, for example. Japanese automobile purchases are now climbing fast. *The huge Japanese middle class has saved so much money for so long that they can afford to raise the national standard of living.* Gifts for mothers and fathers who have worked so hard and taken so little for themselves. Gifts for the young! Many families in Japan, crowded into tiny living quarters, have been restricted to one or at the most two children. That means Japan is a nation where there are twice as many or even four times as many grandparents as there are grandchildren. And now, for the first time, it is socially acceptable in Japan for affluent grandparents to spoil their grandchildren.

Now a remarkable thing is happening in Japan. After a full quarter of zero growth (April thru June, 1987) *Japan pulled out of its stall and zoomed upward again. The growth number for the next quarter was 8.4%, annual rate.*

That was fast growth. It took Japan back to a growth level that was normal in the early 1970's... but it certainly has not been normal during the past decade. There was one other quarter of similar growth - October thru December, 1984. *But that growth was export led and was fueled by a then strong dollar (weak yen).* THE SIGNIFICANCE OF THIS QUARTER OF GROWTH IN JAPAN CAUSED ALMOST ENTIRELY BY DOMESTIC DEMAND HAS LARGELY BEEN OVERLOOKED BY THE AMERICAN FINANCIAL MEDIA AND BY WALL STREET. I continue to hear dire predictions of a crash in Japan... one that will pull America down in its wake. (This is a new phenomenon. It has long been taken for granted that America is the center of the financial universe, and that economic events in America set the tone for the rest of the free world. *Now it is widely recognized that Tokyo is the place to look for tomorrow's trends, as they develop!)*

The surprisingly strong domestic sales have had one result that exceeds even the fondest hopes of Japanese Government planners, Tokyo bankers and Japanese businessmen. They have restored the profitability of many Japanese companies. Where only operating losses - red ink - had forced hundreds of Japanese corporations to speculate in stocks and real estate, in the hopes of showing financial profits and covering up operating losses - *now the operating profits themselves are back. As a result there is much less interest in and concern about the Japanese stock market and real estate market. This has come just at the right time. The Japanese Government and Tokyo bankers had became alarmed at the way real estate and stocks had been soaring... mostly on a wave of buying driven by speculators. The basic idea in Japanese financial circles is that money is to be invested for real growth, not speculation. Japan Inc. does not really approve of real estate nearly doubling in price in a year, as happened during 1987 in Tokyo. They want any money available for real estate investment in Japan to go into bricks, steel, cement, construction costs... then into sewers and roads to open up the thinly populated regions between cities.*

Considerable pressure is being brought by the Powers-That-Be in Japan to cool down speculation in real estate and stocks. A resurgent level of operating profit makes it easier for Japanese companies to go along with banking and Government officials. Incidentally, do not take lightly the intention of the National Government of Japan to stop the rise in real estate prices and curb Japan's stock market. *Japan has been a democracy since General MacArthur made them one in 1945. And for thirty years the Liberal Democrats have enjoyed a majority in Parliament. This party, which is pro-business and conservative, caters to the huge middle class in Japan. It is sensitive to the fact that rising real estate prices are denying a significant number of taxpaying voters an opportunity to buy a home. Polls show more and more Japanese, as a result, now call themselves lower-middle class. No politician in a democracy wants to see polls showing people growing unhappy. That way lies unemployment in the next election.* There is a problem.

Rising domestic sales and growing corporate profits provide important solutions to this problem. You can expect the Government to press hard for a continuation of this brand new domestic sales growth.

Not only are Japanese customers now buying more of the goods produced in Japan, they are also importing more. Some products are being manufactured in Taiwan and Korea. But more goods are coming into Japan from the United States, Canada and West Europe than ever before. Japan Inc. is increasingly living up to promises it has been making to Western Governments at economic summits and G-7 meetings. To an extent many Japanese themselves did not believe possible, it is becoming a consumer as well as a producer nation.

Twenty Japanese-owned companies are already importing products from their U.S. plants to supply the Japanese market. For example, Honda-manufactured Goldwing motorcycles made in the United States are intended specifically for sale to Japanese consumers. *This will become increasingly common in 1988 to '89. Few people in America have as yet fully grasped this fact. Many Congressmen in particular, are still mentally in the "old days" - when it made sense to bash Japan. Today Japan is an ally and a partner. It is moving to honor its pledges to import more from and export less to the United States.*

That still leaves quite a large pool of money in Japan. The average Japanese family has a $50,000 nest egg tucked away. (In part this is seen as necessary because the Social Security Program in Japan is inadequate and must be supplemented from private savings.)

The cash surplus already in place continues to grow. Even with the increased consumer buying going on there is still considerable savings. Some of this is now being borrowed to expand that part of Japanese business serving either the consumer market or the fast growing new service industry... including a thriving but still young and small travel industry. (And America is their favorite vacation spot!)

Some of Japan's surplus continues to find its way into real estate and stocks. *But there is no great rush now to pull money out of bank accounts just to "climb aboard" speculative bull markets. The same holds true for gold.* The Japanese investors who responded to heavy gold promotions in 1986 and early 1987 have now seen the value of their gold holdings decline. *In just a couple of recent months, gold fell 20% in price and value inside Japan.* In the same two months Japanese holders of U.S. bonds saw the value of their holdings go down so fast that it will take their income from bonds in the next two years just to offset this capital loss. So it is understandable that the Japanese are now less anxious to buy U.S. T-bonds. The yield may be high in dollars. But the market value has fallen in yen. (I expect U.S. interest rates to fall sharply, driving up the price of the bonds in both dollars and yen. *That would make current holders of U.S. bonds in Japan happier. But it would also make them even less interested in buying new bonds, with their lower yields!)*

So Japan has to face the question of what to do with its surplus money. One prospect that seems increasingly attractive is *direct investment in U.S. plants and equipment. America bought $50 billion more from Japan in 1987 than America sold to Japan.* (The U.S. is not selling as much to Japan as it could.) Despite a lot of talk in the U.S. Congress about how the Japanese market is closed to foreign producers, the truth is that Japan's vast business and Government bureaucracy is actively seeking U.S. products to buy. Many companies and the Japanese Government itself are actually setting aside money for the sole purpose of BUYING AMERICAN. *But it is hard to buy products from a nation - the United States - which is making almost zero effort to sell to the large and rich Japanese market.* Japanese companies go to great trouble to learn the U.S. market well before launching products here. And they do everything they can to make products "right" for the U.S. market. Take appliances, for example. *Japanese appliances are often small. Refrigerators are tiny by U.S. standards. The average Japanese family lives in small rooms.* But when they set out to sell in America, the Japanese deliberately create whole new lines of products scaled to the taste of American buyers. *American companies make no such effort to scale U.S. products down to appeal to Japanese buyers.* It is usually "take it or leave it." The Japanese often leave it! (So would we if the shoe were on the other foot!) Other nations have been more aggressive and more successful in selling goods to Japan. In three years, while the U.S. dollar was falling from 250 yen to half that level, *three other nations which peg their currencies closely to the dollar have penetrated the Japanese market significantly. Taiwan has increased its sales to Japan by 115%. South Korea has expanded exports to Japan by 80%. Hongkong has boosted sales to Japan by 81%. (The U.S. exports to Japan, by way of contrast, are up only 14%.)*

The truth is that most American businessmen continue to regard Japan as an alien land... as distant and remote as if it were on the moon. Japan, by way of contrast, feels itself as having grown *close* to America. Some companies in Japan are now selling so much of their output in America that they think of themselves as being *every bit as much American as Japanese.* Take Sony, for example. Having decided to spend $2 billion to buy the CBS record division, Chairman Akio Morita seriously considered moving his company's headquarters to New York City. *Not the North American headquarters... but THE headquarters!* Would Sony then be an American company owned mostly by Japanese investors? The distinction may soon begin to blur, at least around the edges. THE FEELING IS TAKING HOLD IN JAPAN THAT THE ONLY WAY TO GET SOME KIND OF BALANCE IN TRADE RELATIONS BETWEEN THE UNITED STATES OF AMERICA AND JAPAN IS TO SEND MONEY AND EXECUTIVES TO AMERICA... *TO OPEN FACTORIES AND, USING JAPANESE*

PRODUCTION TECHNIQUES, QUALITY STAND-ARDS AND PRODUCT KNOW-HOW, CREATE GOODS THAT CAN BE MARKETED SUCCESS-FULLY BACK IN JAPAN. The American market share won by the Japanese is too valuable for them to give up now. But they know they will lose it to tariffs or protectionism if they do not import more and export less. Since their pockets are bulging with surplus money, *they have decided to do the job themselves. Japan Inc. is creating in the United States a new export-oriented manufacturing industry. It is using American land and American factories... many of them brand new, built for Japan Inc. It is installing as much American-made machinery as it can find to fit the requirements. The new plants are hiring American workers and mostly American executives. They are buying services and raw materials from American companies, and - to the greatest extent possible consistent with high quality and low prices - they are buying component parts from American factories. If necessary, Japan Inc. is even creating those component manufacturers in the United States!*

The pattern has already been established in the automobile industry. Now it is spreading to other fields. Japan Inc. is manufacturing television sets in America and exporting them to Japan. Where necessary, they are using special tools and dies to produce products preferred by Japanese consumers... in terms of *size and performance.*

So far, Japan Inc. accounts for a mere 7% of the world's

direct foreign investment. By way of contrast, *American companies own 36% of foreign-owned plants and property,* the British own 18%, the West Germans 8% and the Dutch 8.5%. But Japan is now moving up fast. The Japanese already own some $10 billion in manufacturing facilities in North America. Some 600 Japanese companies already operate in the United States. *And forty American states have opened Tokyo offices to lure additional billions in plant and equipment investments to the U.S.* It is my opinion that this direct Japanese investment will force American companies to expand and modernize their own U.S. plants just to *keep pace...* force-feeding a capital investment Boom such as the United States has not seen in peacetime since the thirty-year-long period of intense economic growth in the late 1800's. Interestingly enough, the main target of this Japanese-led Boom in state of the art factories will not really be Japan itself. *Despite all you hear from Washington, Japan now imports goods equal to 6.5% of its GNP - not that far below the 9.2% of GNP imported by the United States. No, the real target of these new Japanese-owned and Japanese-inspired American owned factories will be the good old U.S.A. itself! America! The products of Japanese factories now being gobbled up by eager Japanese consumers must be replaced in the American marketplace by goods manufactured in the United States. That is what the race is all about.* And it will not be easy! South Korea has also staked out the American market. South Korea, where workers learned the Japanese work ethic during some forty years as a

Japanese colony and where owner-executives learned all about American *competitive capitalism* during thirty-eight years of American military and economic support... Japan and America taught Korea too well. Korea is now exporting products to the U.S. and Japan. Despite waves of strikes in 1987, the Korean economy is remarkably "together." There is intense jealousy about the *Korean Economic Miracle* inside communist North Korea. And some people worry that North Korea will try to disrupt the 1988 Summer Olympics, scheduled mostly for South Korea. The super-productive South Korean factories will be moving to tear new chunks out of the U.S. market, like a shark attacking a victim. Japan-bashing has no place in the America of today *which needs Japanese help in developing America's own domestic manufacturing potential.*

While Wall Street prepares for recession and inflation, *decisions being made in Tokyo* - thousands of miles away - now build pressures for a far different future in the United States. Look at these facts and you will agree that *A BOOM WITH ZERO INFLATION OR DEFLATION IS NOW VIRTUALLY ASSURED FOR AMERICA:*

RICOH COMPANY has bought a factory in Tustin, California. It will manufacture its own copiers and laser printers in the 270,000 square foot plant. Ricoh will also expand its Santana, California toner plant on America's East Coast - all to serve its U.S. customers from American production facilities. *The intent is to keep prices as low as possible, avoiding the effects of a higher yen. It is deflationary!*

MAZDA MOTOR CORPORATION is turning over to the Ford Motor Company its own superior techniques for the manufacturing of parts. Mazda seeks *cost reductions,* to help make its cars made in America by Ford even *less expensive.* It hopes to seek a *price advantage* in the U.S. auto market - a *deflationary move.* It is expected that the techniques will produce *important savings* for Mazda!

NISSAN MOTOR COMPANY will double the output of its Tennessee plant to 400,000 units. It will expand its engine factory output there to 300,000 units. Nissan will begin producing four-cylinder and six-cylinder engines at the plant. Some of these engines will be sold to Ford. The primary intent is to replace Nissan imports from Japan with American-manufactured cars and engines. With the yen having gone up 100%, this will lower Nissan's costs here. It can then slash imports, keep its prices down and aim at a solid share of the increasingly price competitive American market.

JAPAN SYNTHETIC RUBBER COMPANY will engage in a joint venture with Shell Oil in Houston, Texas. It will manufacture energy-saving auto tires in a brand new plant. This will be the first Japanese rubber-maker to set up U.S. production facilities. The capacity of the new Texas facility will be 30,000 tons a year. Again, *the goal is low U.S. prices.*

NIPPON KOKAN STEEL - Japan's second largest steel maker - which paid $292 million for a 50% interest in National Steel in 1984, is now buying out the other half of this U.S. steel producer. The move is designed to assist Nippon Steel in serving from U.S. facilities the steel needs of new Japanese-owned auto plants in America. Since Nippon introduced new capital and management techniques, National Steel has moved back into the black ink. *Once more, the intent here is to replace costly imports from Japan with lower priced American-made steel. DEFLATIONARY!*

MATSUSHITA ELECTRIC INDUSTRIAL COMPANY said, when the yen rose to nearly 125 yen to the dollar, it would begin importing color televisions into Japan from its now lower-cost American production facilities in mid-1988. Director Tadakazu Yamamoto said: *"There is no doubt it will pay off for us to make these sets in America."*

FURUKAWA ELECTRIC COMPANY is building a factory in Georgia to produce high-grade cables for electronic equipment. The new plant will open by June. Director Junnosuke Furukawa said his company is shifting production to the U.S. partly to beat the rising yen and partly to follow the company's customers. The company believes its U.S. factory will give it a distinct cost advantage over other firms that import from Japan or Europe.

HITACHI METALS INC. will start up production of

aluminium wheels at its new plant in St. Mary's, Ohio, later this year. Hitachi sees its *low-cost U.S. plant as being able to win business* from both American-owned and Japanese-owned auto plants in the United States.

DAIDO STEEL COMPANY may take a different route to get into the U.S. market. It is studying proposals to license its expertise in producing high-quality, low-cost alloy steel parts to its U.S. counterpart - Copper Weld Steel. This would permit faster gains in winning U.S. business away from imports!

TOYOTA MOTOR CORPORATION'S imports of auto parts from the United States and other nations into Japan has jumped 35% to $600 million in the past year. *TOYOTA plans to increase foreign sourcing (in America, etc.) by another 17% in 1988... and is working hard to buy as much of that as possible from plants in the U.S.* In an age of a high yen, American-supplied auto parts give them major cost savings, helping them sell cars cheaper to the Booming domestic auto market inside Japan!

MITSUBISHI METAL AMERICA is opening a plant in Columbus, Indiana - joining a second Japanese company (ENKEI AMERICA) in that city. And Columbus Mayor, Robert Stewart, travels to Japan regularly, seeking still more firms looking for places where they will be welcome in the United States. He is not waiting for American companies to invest in new plants!

THERE IS PLENTY OF INTEREST IN JAPAN AS THE TREND TOWARDS LOCATING FACTORIES INSIDE THE UNITED STATES PICKS UP SPEED.

Increasingly, American managers are finding that the "just in time" inventory system used so effectively in Japan does not always transfer to the United States. Japan is a crowded little island nation. No city... no factory... is too far away from any customer. It is possible in Japan to manufacture parts just before they are needed. But Japanese executives at corporate headquarters in Tokyo hear a steady stream of complaints from managers of their U.S. operations. The worst complaints come from American factories that merely assemble parts made in Japan. Even overlooking the higher cost of these imported parts, there is still the inconvenience of planning American production using parts somewhere on the high seas. SO THE PRESSURE GROWS FOR AMERICAN PARTS MANUFACTURING FACIL-ITIES, CLOSE TO ASSEMBLY PLANTS IN THE U.S. *Japan is swimming in yen. So there is no problem financing such new U.S. factories...* or of their carrying larger inventories of manufactured parts than have lately been seen as normal for plants in the U.S. or Japan. Some U.S.-owned producers are being told to slow down their production lines and close down plants to work off inventory - at the same time that Japanese executives are opening new plants and expanding their planned inventory inside the United States. That is one reason Wall Street is so confused by numbers they are now feeding into their computers. The econometric models inside those computers do not comprehend the significance of the numbers. Most brokerage houses, banks, colleges and private forecasters are using what I now believe to be out of date and irrelevent models. These models assume that when production reaches current capacity levels, *prices tend to rise sharply*. The Fed then squeezes money growth. And *a recession occurs*. That was true in the 1970's. It was less true in the early and mid-1980's. It is not true today.

JAPANESE COMPANIES PREFER NOT TO RAISE THEIR U.S. PRICES BECAUSE OF A RISING YEN. INSTEAD THEY ARE HANGING ON TO THEIR U.S. MARKET SHARE, OFTEN AT VERY LOW PROFIT, AS THEY HURRY TO BUILD FACTORIES IN THE U.S.

Once the Japanese factories are up and running, they bid aggressively for as much business as they can win. They use all of their skills in cutting costs and keeping quality levels high. They foresake short-term profit, just as they are accustomed to doing in Japan, in order to win long-term market share and customer loyalty.

The Japanese pay no attention to forecasts of short, shallow dips in U.S. consumer purchases... even predictions of an American recession. When Japanese companies look at the U.S., they see a nation with thirty times the arable land of their own country... 170 times as much iron ore... nearly double the population... 1,300 times as much oil... and more than 300 times as much coal. *They scratch their heads and wonder as they hear Americans worry about the economic future of the U.S.* The Japanese see America as the number one world economic power for as far ahead as one can see... and they think American politicians and professors and authors who say otherwise are unwise. *Seen from Japan, America is a Land of Plenty... a New Promised Land inviting new investments in plants and equipment.* Japanese executives see America as ideally located to serve the Western European common market. They know that America sells less to Europe than it buys from Europe... while Japan sells MORE to Western Europe than it buys there. The result is unhappiness all around. America politicians want Western Europe to buy more American goods. And Western Europe wants to wipe out a surplus of exports from Japan.

The new domestic buying Boom inside Japan takes the pressure off Japanese businessmen. They can now build factories in the United States, and sell products from these American plants to Western Europe... as well as to the American domestic market. This will help balance trade on all sides... while making money too.

As a matter of fact, Japanese companies now see their American plants as becoming world-class competitors to parent operations inside Japan itself. That explains why 44% of today's overseas Japanese investment now pours into the United States! And such foreign investment by Japanese firms is now expanding at 69% per year.

AMERICAN HONDA MOTOR COMPANY is a good example of what I mean. The strong yen now makes cars produced in Ohio cheaper than autos made in Japan. So Honda America will now EXPORT TO JAPAN FROM AMERICA a new small car made exclusively in America. It is the 2,000 cc Honda Accord Coupe. Some 3,000 are scheduled to be shipped to Japan in the first year. As the construction of a second Honda plant in Ohio increases American Honda production capacity from 360,000 to 510,000 cars, these EXPORTS TO JAPAN will expand to 70,000 cars a year. In addition, Honda will be able to ship cars from its American factories direct to Western Europe. At the same time, imports from Japan to the U.S. will be cut back! HONDA U.S. WILL BECOME AN *AMERICAN* CAR COMPANY. Right now, American Honda has teams at work in Ohio designing a future all-U.S. Honda car... a uniquely American product.

Japanese manufacturing companies are aware of growing plans by American big business to "batten down the hatches" and prepare for a U.S. recession. But the Japanese also know that it is precisely attitudes such as this which have caused U.S. big business to chop off 1,400,000 employees since the 1974 recession. Meanwhile, some 41,000 new American manufacturing companies have been formed - many of them by former big business executives. These new companies have created almost as many new jobs as were cut back by U.S. big business. Some 160,000 of these new American jobs have been created by 600 Japanese firms that have already located operations in the U.S. IT CAN BE SEEN THAT JAPAN IS FAR FROM DOMINATING AMERICAN INDUSTRIAL EXPANSION. BUT IT IS A FACT THAT JAPANESE INVESTMENT IN AMERICA IS FORCING ADDITIONAL CAPITAL INVESTMENT BY AMERICAN COMPANIES, AS THEY SCRAMBLE TO SURVIVE AND HOLD MARKET SHARE IN AN INCREASINGLY COMPETITIVE MARKETPLACE. Forty-two percent of U.S. industrial output already takes place in companies with 250 or fewer employees. Current trends will bring that share up to and over 50% by 1990. This is a fact largely overlooked on Wall Street. Yet it points to small, special situation companies taking over much growth in the United States... possibly for good! A MAJOR FACTOR IN THE DECISION BY JAPANESE COMPANIES TO PARTICIPATE IN THIS NEW EXPANSION OF AMERICAN INDUSTRIAL CAPACITY IS SIMPLY *A NEED TO FUND FUTURE JAPANESE PENSIONS!*

The Japanese have limited births sharply in recent decades. The result is a surplus of doting grandparents. Many Japanese couples marry late and have only a single child. But in just a few years, this will create a situation that Japan fears. Forty percent of Japan's population will be collecting pensions in just a dozen years... a much higher ratio of retired persons than we have in the U.S.

The Japanese have saved for their Golden Years. But there will not be enough workers in Japan to make use of these savings. Thus the early Twenty-First Century looms in a frightening way to Japanese citizens now aged fifty to sixty-five... the very age group which has control of most business investment decisions made in Japan today. This power-generation sees investment in America as being potentially the safest, in terms of what they perceive to be a looming Soviet threat from across the waters in Vietnam. They also see it as being the most *sensible in terms of cost.* Unlike Japan itself and much of free Asia, the U.S. is seen as a nation of *virtually limitless land on which to build factories.* And with the yen now so high, this land looks *cheap* to them!

One reason Japanese companies will consider placing factories in rural areas is that new advances in semi-automated manufacturing techniques have *sharply reduced the number of workers needed in modern operations.* One Japanese manufacturer of VHS units for example, has managed to trim the number of workers needed in its operation from forty down to just four! As the trend towards investment in America accelerates, this kind of cost-cutting technology and computer-assisted management will increasingly show up in the factories built for Japanese firms in the U.S. All of these factors - including the increase in American industrial capacity at a time when U.S. consumer demand is apparently cooling down - point to flat or slightly declining product prices in America. As a matter of fact, the Japanese investment in

America - which jumped to an estimated $5.9 billion in 1987 - is probably already impacting American producer prices. Taken as a whole, the last two years have seen ZERO growth in U.S. wholesale prices. But more important, recent DECLINES IN PRICES have offset earlier gains. Those American manufacturers who have been dreaming of soft times, and who thought the "falling dollar" would result in a rapidly-rising level of prices on Japanese imports, now have another think coming. *The Japanese are increasingly setting up plants here to take advantage themselves of the lower U.S. dollar.* They are turning themselves inside-out to produce goods of high quality at the lowest possible prices... taking a long-term view of growth and profit. THE JAPANESE ARE BRINGING TO LIFE IN AMERICA THE SUPPLY-SIDE CONCEPTS FIRST PROPOSED IN 1980 BY THEN-CANDIDATE RONALD REAGAN... PERCEPTS IGNORED BY AMERICAN "INTERNATIONAL" CORPORATIONS IN THEIR HASTE TO "OUTSOURCE" PARTS AND PRODUCTS OVERSEAS. The label "Made in America" will soon be moving all over the world in ships and planes, as American-made goods begin to dominate foreign trade. This will impact America's trade balance to a degree hardly anyone in the U.S. Congress or on Wall Street suspects! This is not "MAYBE" or "MIGHT BE." I am talking *"IS NOW HAPPENING."* *The investment Boom conceived, planned and directed from Tokyo is already rolling across the U.S.A.!* Proof that this investment Boom is for real comes in the growing number of Japanese regional banks that are setting up offices in America. These banks - such as Hachijuni, Gunma, Ashikaga, Tokyo Tamin, Daishi, Juroku, Iyo, Kiyo, Senshu, Fukui, Suruga, Joyo and Osaka - feel they must open operations in America in order to serve their Japanese industrial customers now locating in the United States. These new American branches now form a conduit, through which hundreds of billions of Japanese yen can flow smoothly into factories, machines, parts, payrolls, inventories and accounts receivable at the new Japanese-owned American operations.

AS THIS JAPANESE MONEY AND JAPANESE INDUSTRIAL TECHNOLOGY FLOWS INTO AMERICA, THE LONG OUTFLOW OF JOBS REVERSES AND TURNS INTO A NEW INDUSTRIAL BOOM. One thing Wall Street seems to forget in its concentration on a build-up of business inventories in America is that these new plants are now building inventory to handle growing orders from inside America. Even if consumer orders should slip, there is available in America a ready market worth $100 billion. These are the orders that have been filled by imports from abroad. Now as new U.S. factories - some owned by Japanese companies and others built by Americans to match Japanese competition - come on stream, these orders can be filled in America. IF THERE IS A RECESSION IN TERMS OF AMERICAN CONSUMER DEMAND, THERE IS NOW EVERY REASON TO BELIEVE THAT THIS *RECESSION CAN BE EXPORTED... IN*

Adrian Van Eck

THE SENSE THAT ORDERS TO OVERSEAS PLANTS CAN BE CUT. That seems only fair, since in recent years America has been exporting its consumer Boom, by filling orders from foreign sources. *Japan itself is now forcing this changed outlook!*

CHAPTER TWENTY

These Will Be *Our* Years!

I have my teeth into a big strategic concept. In fact, the word big does not do it justice. This concept is huge. And so far as I know too few people in the entire Free World have taken the time to stand back, stare at it and recognize it for what it really is... an awesome opportunity to protect and preserve the money you have during a coming time of great and rapid change.

And it also tends to confirm my expectations that the real American Boom and the real American bull market has only now begun to get moving! When both of them really get rolling... the Boom forced by companies applying modern ultra-high technology to the production of goods and services and the bull market in Amex and over-the-counter growth stocks leading the way in the American Boom... you will see that by contrast America in 1981 to

'87 was actually in a sluggish recovery and a mostly Blue Chip stock market!!

I think it is important that you take the time to digest what I am going to tell you in the next couple of minutes. You know, today's high-speed computers allow Wall Street firms to learn and discount earnings reports and estimates so quickly that it is really quite difficult to stay ahead of *short-term* developments. In order to protect your personal and business investments, you really have to see major new strategic concepts unfolding in their earliest possible stages. Only the human mind is able to sense such massively important concepts at this early stage. Computers just do not have enough data available to project out the inevitable unfolding of coming events. And a computer has not yet been built that features a kind of instinctive sixth sense. (I say thank heavens for that... since I have always said in complete modesty that it is a highly developed sixth sense that accounts for my rather consistently accurate forecasts!)

I rely on instincts to spot the truly big concepts for you... the ones that can swing the market, the economy, the nation, even the whole world onto a new path. But then I do my homework, as you well know! The rest, however, is up to you!!

America faced a situation much like that of today 120 years ago. Right after the Civil War, America faced an island nation with seemingly overpowering economic and financial advantages. It was not Japan in 1867. It was England, on the other side of the world. It is hard to believe today, after a half-century of Fabian Socialism in England. But in those days the British had the machines, the money and the determination to dominate the entire world. There were many in England (and in America) who saw no future for the U.S.A. in the late 1800's except as just another planet in orbit around the English sun. And most said we would be a minor planet to boot!

But then a strange thing happened. Americans in search of fame and fortune created, developed and marketed a whole string of inventions that changed the world as it was then known. These inventions allowed one man to do as much work as five and even six men had done just a handful of years earlier. Think of that! Five and six-fold increases in productivity!

It is popular today in some circles to yearn for a return to what we imagine to be the old fashioned days of the gold standard. It is believed by many in Washington and around the U.S. that the economy after the Civil War was based almost entirely on circulating gold coins, thus keeping down inflation. It is, of course, true that in the Post Civil War period there was no inflation. In fact, prices fell by an average of 1% a year for thirty years... a total decline of 30% in thirty years. That is *deflation,* pure and simple. But it was not the gold standard that prevented inflation. And I can prove that. Listen to the way the gold standard really worked: No one was anxious to carry a bag full of gold coins around with them. Why invite a robber to knock you on the head and take your money away? So folks in those days did the sensible thing. They took gold coins that came into their possession to a bank and deposited them. Then they wrote out checks against their deposit. And they put the checks in the mail. Eventually the checks were cleared and paid. And the wheels of commerce and industry turned.

Meanwhile, the gold stayed in the bank vaults. It was held by the banks as their reserves. To the degree that this gold limited the ability of depositors to write checks, it certainly was true that the gold standard prevented runaway growth in the money supply.

But as you remember from Economics I, there is more to money than just the physical supply of gold or even checks. There is a thing called velocity. And what is velocity? It is the speed with which money turns over... meaning the speed of one depositor spending it and getting it into the hands of another depositor. So long as communication was by horseback, it was not possible to speed up payments. The telegraph, the railroad and steam boats allowed an incredible speed-up in velocity.

All at once in the 1800's, major changes simply exploded across the world economy. Life in the United States, England and Europe was ripped loose from its age-old customs and thrust ahead with breath-taking speed. All at once it was possible to telegraph money thousands of miles. Then goods were loaded onto steamboats, transported great distances at low cost, reloaded onto railroad trains... and shipped to cities remote from where the shipment had begun. The sudden speed-up in velocity had the same effect as a 50% or even 100% increase in the money supply. There were many who expected inflation to result. (It may come as a shock to you, but in the 1800's many economists were already monetarists. If you should get your hands on a crumbling, long out-of-print old copy of a book called "An Investigation into the Causes of the Great Fall in Prices" By Arthur Crump (published by Greenwood Press of New York), you will find on page five the following statement: "That an increase of the quantity of money raises prices and a dimunition lowers them is the most elementary proposition in the world of currency.")

But even money growth does not tell the whole story! And therein lies a tale that will make you money and preserve the money you have, if you will let it!

In the very old book I quoted a moment ago, the economist / author went on to say: "The proposition (that money supply determines prices) is true only when other things are the same." He added: "A greater change had been taking place during the several years previous to the great fall in prices in 'other things'" - that is in the circumstances generally affecting the operation of supply and demand - "than had perhaps ever been witnessed before. I refer, of course, to the improved means of production, improved machinery and improved means of communication." Does not that sound exactly like the kind of America I am talking about today? How can it be that so many self-styled "experts" today have forgotten this link between prices and productivity? Is it possible that each generation - or at least each century - must discover all over again the simple truths that were accepted as common sense thirty-five to one hundred twenty-five years earlier? It does seem so!

Computer-assisted management techniques and technology will now permit some parts of U.S. industry to slash labor costs by as much as 75%... wiping out the "cheap labor" advantage enjoyed by Asia and Latin America.

When you have up to a 300% increase in selected manufacturing productivity in a period of time as short as seven years (as I now foresee for certain American factory operations in 1988 to '95), then you cannot get inflation.

How can I be so very sure of that fact? Because I have ample historical proof, that is why. Think on this for a moment. America and the world went into the 1800's with a style of living not that far removed from the days of the Roman Republic! Most people lived on farms. Roads were poor, and in bad weather they were closed entirely. Communication was by mail, and the mail moved by horse or wind-powered boat. Business and banking were primitive by the standards of 1987... but were really not a great deal different from those of 50 B.C.

But think for a moment on the changes that took place in the 1800's, especially in the generation right after the U.S. Civil War. A brand new process of making steel faster and cheaper appeared on the scene. Bold and aggressive men like Andrew Carnegie (an immigrant who had only gone to the second grade) used the new process to make steel rails, barbed wire and other low cost products that opened up the American West.

Thousands and thousands of Civil War veterans homesteaded the newly opened western lands. In a few short years, these new American farmers were flooding the world with new supplies of foodstuffs. The railroads brought their wheat and corn to the Mississippi River. Steamboats carried them to the sea and then to Europe. As if this was not enough, Americans invented new machines to greatly speed up the planting and harvesting of crops. I checked back into the U.S. Treasury Department's "Annual Report and Statement of the Chief of the Bureau of Statistics on Foreign Commerce and Navigation of the United States." (U.S. Government Printing Office, 1891.) Some of the numbers in that old report now make very interesting reading, and back up forecasts of the changes I see coming soon.

Take the eight years from 1872 to '80 as just one example.

That time period opened with America running a serious trade deficit with Great Britain. We imported $17,633,231 worth of goods from them. But they bought only $2,743,494 from us. That sounds so familiar, does it not... when you think about today's trade gap with the island nation of Japan (which produces and sells worldwide today in much the same manner that the British did in 1872).

But take note of this: By 1880, just eight years later, America had closed that huge trade gap and actually was running a surplus in its trade with Great Britain: We imported $10,314,139 from the British and exported $10,856,579 in goods to the British!

This swing in trade changed the nature of the United States permanently. It also had a big impact on England. Prices for British products such as wheat fell about 40%. (Number Two Spring Wheat arriving from the Chicago market fell from $1.10 to 76.5¢ a bushel. Later it fell to 67¢. The British farms were not as efficient as ours. We could produce wheat and ship it to their market for less than it cost them to grow it. Similar results fell on the Germans, the French, the Italians and the Belgians.)

And America's surging productivity impacted a number of other economic activities as well. The London price of prime beef fell 18%. Pork tumbled 22%. American cheese slid in price from 13¢ to 10¢. Even hops were affected. The German Hop-Growers Association reported that the world supply of hops (93,310 tons) was in excess of world consumption, leaving an annual surplus of 10,000 pounds. This glut drove prices down sharply.

The same trend held in manufacturing. America brought modern steel mills into production... and grabbed market share from European mills still using the old-fashioned Bessemer process. This new low cost capacity from American mills pulled the price of steel down from $58 to $39.50 a ton! And the same thing held true in copper. New American mines and low cost smelters drove the world price of copper down from 25¢ to 9.5¢.

No amount of increased circulation of money could prevent deflation, given such enormous increases in American productivity. We were suddenly the envy of the world. *To put it another way, everyone hated us.* But we did not care! Andrew Carnegie, the poor immigrant boy, made $400 million! Thomas Edison invented the generator. Electric power transformed U.S. industry. Two other men who had known poverty (Henry Ford and John D. Rockefeller) put the U.S. in autos... and gas in the automobiles. Each became not a millionaire but a billionaire! It was a time of growth never seen anywhere in the world before or since. (Government regulation stifled this change and growth in the late 1800's.) President Ronald Reagan's most lasting legacy may be that he has pushed Congress into slashing away a good part of the regulatory crust that had formed and hardened on the U.S. economy over the past 80 years. Once again the competitive, capitalist urge of American businessmen is responding to opportunities the way they used to after the Civil War. The United States of America, the rest of the world will learn again, is not the richest country in the world by accident. We are all descended from immigrants. From all four corners of the globe, people with get up and go got up and came to America. As a result, Americans spawned by such ambitious folks tend to push, prod, create, manage and drive ourselves and others.

Inflation is apt to show up during major wars, when men and money are diverted from production. Deflation comes when the men come back home and start to produce surplus goods and services again.

In the 1920's and 1950's prices actually fell, as surges in productivity caused gluts in the market. Similar gluts are at work in world markets today. Lots of economists are aware that such gluts depress prices. Yet for some strange reason, few understand how this leads to DEFLATION. Hardly anyone seems to recall that the U.S. economy leaped ahead during earlier times of glut, as businessmen sought ways to cut costs and increase profits.

The standard of living of American families rose 40% during the 1950's. During the 1970's, the standard of living fell, despite "raises" each year. That is because with zero inflation, it is necessary to increase productivity to create real growth. This forces businessmen to start looking for ways to expand productivity! As the process takes hold again, America will catch up to and pass Japan!!

There are clear signs that important changes are already beginning in America's manufacturing sector. General Electric has announced it is bringing production of its big-screen television sets back from Japan. It will spend twenty million dollars to modernize a Bloomington, Indiana plant and will produce 500,000 television sets a year at that facility. Other similar moves are coming!

Automated factories are springing up all over America. As a result, production is being pulled back from Japan. The new computer-assisted management techniques and equipment lets one worker produce as much as three or four or more, making low wages less relevant. Any company or investor who fails to recognize what is going on now will be hurt in 1988 to '95. And those who join in and profit will benefit. *These will be America's years!* Prepare yourself!

Adrian Van Eck

CHAPTER TWENTY-ONE

America The Low-Cost Producer!

Now the tide is turning. Some of this has to do with the cheaper dollar. And some of it clearly has to do with the very rapid change in attitude going on now in the executive offices of American companies across this broad land. Finally it is dawning on some bosses that there is more money to be made by manufacturing goods here in the U.S. - using new computer-assisted management and machines - than there is in importing more expensive foreign goods. And that simple realization is bringing about a new willingness to modernize American plants, win work-rule concessions from American workers and aggressively take back a bigger share of our own U.S. market. Once this switch proceeds a little bit further, the U.S. GNP growth number can and I say will rise to 5% a year. (Do not expect the stock market to sit around and wait for this to happen. The market is itself a forecaster. It looks ahead and sees things not visible to the naked eye... sort of like a ship's radar on a sea covered with thick fog!)

And I will tell you something else the market is now recognizing: All of those fears put forth a generation ago by pessimistic scientists are not worth the paper they were printed on at the time. You remember the ones I mean... where a group of experts got together and warned that the whole world was using up its resources so fast that in just a few more decades everything would be gone... all the oil and iron ore and copper and fresh water and wood and even food! And then the world population would be reduced to fighting over the scraps that remained. It was seen as inevitable that a nuclear war would result... with the survivors, if any, reduced to living like cavemen and women. (It always amazes me just how eagerly the public absorbs such Gloom and Doom predictions.) Within a few years of its publication, that gloomy forecast was being treated as the final, ultimate word on limits to growth. Well, I hate to upset anyone who thrives on such negative predictions. (That is a fib. I get a kick out of upsetting people who allow themselves to be scared to death by end-of-the-economic-world worries.)

Two very big announcements have rocked the world of science, technology, business and investment! Together they make it plain that the future is now ready to open like a new flower.

First off, take the matter of energy. Sweden has announced it had struck gas at 20,000 feet in a well drilled through solid granite. This is the first time anyone has hit gas in an area not underlain by sedimentary rock, marking the bottom of an ancient sea. The tests performed on the gas showed it did not come from plant or animal remains. This tends to confirm a radical theory that methane gas is formed deep in the Earth and rises towards the surface. The implication: Potential drilling sites are multiplied many times over and possible world-wide reserves may be virtually *endless!*

Then there is the matter of a gigantic breakthrough in superconductors. Two American scientists caught every other researcher in the world off guard when they revealed their discovery of a ceramic mixture that permits superconductivity to take place a much higher temperatures than had ever been dreamed possible. Ceramic material usually blocks electrons, but a slight variation turns it into a conduct with almost zero resistance. Do you know what that means? Much of the electricity generated in the world is now lost during transmission. And it is difficult to store for later use. A superconductor material that can function near room temperature (now seen as a possibility as American and

Japanese researchers catch short naps and then rush back to work around the clock) would allow power plants to send electricity long distances at very low cost. It would allow batteries to hold ten times the power of current batteries. And it will permit the development of shoebox sized computers that will do the work of big main-frame units. Another plus: Fusion power is suddenly seen as a practical possibility, opening up an endless source of power to create electricity without nuclear waste!! Private business is at work already to capture this breakthrough and hurry it into the marketplace! What we have at hand now is the raw material of a massive technological revolution!

CHAPTER TWENTY-TWO

Truly A Time To Get Richer! *(And Keep Your Wealth)*

In the United States, the Government itself has a very limited role in creating money. The Mint (which is under the Treasury Department) produces pennies, nickels, dimes, quarters, half-dollars and silver dollars. It also makes the new gold coins, which are legal tender even though their face values are far below the current value of their gold content.

The Federal Reserve System prints the paper money. But when you add up all of the coins and the paper money, you still only account for a small fraction of the total amount of money in the United States. By far the bulk of money is actually created when a private bank loans money to an individual, a company or even the Government. Now it is true that the Fed can shrink the money supply almost at will. It can do so by selling T-Bonds from its own inventory. Whoever buys the bonds pays for them with a check. When that check is cleared by the Fed, the money is pulled out of a private bank. That bank must then cut its loans - either calling in loans or saying no to someone they might loan to, because they no longer have the money. But the process does not work as well in reverse. The Fed can pump reserves out into the banking system by buying T-Bonds... either from the Treasury or from a bank or private investor. In due course, the money the Fed creates to buy the bond is deposited in a bank account. If it buys from a bank, the money goes directly to a bank and it has extra reserves available to loan. If it buys from the Treasury, the Government spends the new money, perhaps sending it to a defense contract or paying a Federal employee. They, in turn, deposit it in their bank account and now the new money is in a bank, available to loan out. But it does not follow that the bank will in fact loan out their new reserves. They do not have to do so. And when you get the Fed breathing hard on the back of their neck (as it is now) demanding that they continue to build up their reserves so as to give them a bigger cushion against possible defaults by Latin American debtors, then you can get a slow-down in the loaning out of fresh reserves. When you also get bankers themselves determined to make as much profit as they can - choosing to make fewer but sounder loans to avoid losses and slow pay borrowers - then you also get a slow-down in the creation of new loans by the banks. And since it is precisely these loans by banks that turn reserves into circulating money in America, the whole situation now is gearing down... working to reduce the rate at which money is created. (President Eisenhower was very much aware of this ability of the Government to cut money growth back... but not to force its rapid acceleration. His favorite way of demonstrating this fact was to hand one end of a string to a visitor to the Oval Office. He would ask them to tug on the string. When they did they could exert real force. "Good," he would then say. "Now push on the string!" When they tried that nothing happened. The string went limp, then sagged. Pushing on the string had no force to cause action. "There," he would say, "now you see the limitations to what can be done.")

So the next time you hear someone tell you - at a seminar or a convention or just in a conversation - that we are headed for double-digit inflation in America just because the Fed has allowed bank reserves to build up, you confront them with Ike's common-sense logic and ask them: "How do you push on a string... and make something happen?" Money loose? Not really. Is it tight? Tighter than most people believe at the moment.

What is next? In 1982 I said in advance that a 4% drop in interest rates was coming as banks shut off deadbeats. Strict loan policies lower bank rates!

The banks, as you know, are under tremendous pressure today to lower the international rate of interest charged on foreign loans. Nations as far removed from each other as Peru and the Philippines say they simply cannot afford to pay the current high rates. And remember this: Most of the Third World is being charged a very high real rate of interest. To get the real rate of interest, you subtract inflation from the interest rate. Back in the late 1970's, when so many of the foreign loans were written, inflation in commodities - the number one export of many developing countries - was high. Even if they had to pay high interest rates, the *real* rate was quite low. (There were times when inflation was so high it equalled or was greater than the interest rate. This meant the real rate was at or near zero.) But in recent months, everything has gone into reverse for Third World nations. Commodities prices have gone down, not up. Yet the interest they are required to pay is still high by traditional standards. Now you have a case where the rate of deflation must be added to (not subtracted from) the interest rate. And the result is a real interest rate that can be well over 10% a year. That can break the back of even healthy borrowers, let alone lesser developed countries! But if the banks lower rates for LDC's, can they refuse to do so for U.S. farmers, who are suffering as much or more from high *real* interest rates? And what about the U.S. consumer?

Can banks go on charging interest rates on bank credit cards at a rate more than 12% *over* inflation? Can banks justify mortgage rates as high as they are with inflation so low? And can even the mighty United States of America afford to pay such high interest rates on a Federal debt now over two trillion dollars? In every case above my answer is and must be absolutely not!

The inflation rate I visualize for the next eight years can only justify and support banks paying 3% on checking and passbook savings accounts! When banks can buy or rent money at 3% a year, a lot of other numbers will fall back into old fashioned molds. Short-term T-Bills will pay no more than 3%. It is possible they will fall as low as 2.5%. Probably this sounds low to you. When I compare it to interest rates over the past ten years, it sounds low to me too. But I feel the last ten years are not the proper guide to the future. You have to take a broader look backwards in order to correctly see what is now ahead of us. Go back to the late 1800's. Go to the early part of the 1900's. Look at the 1920's, 1930's, 1940's, 1950's and 1960's. In each and every case you will see that the norm for interest rates is far below current levels. And you can go much further back than that. To the thriving business communities in Holland and England in the early 1500's... or all the way back to the days recorded in the Old Testament. Still you find interest rates well below those of today! In some periods the rates were even lower. (In my lifetime and perhaps in yours, short-term Treasury Bills paid only 1% interest... and they sold readily!) But I do feel that the historic norm has centered on the numbers 3% and 5%... with savers earning 3% on their money and borrowers paying 5% to banks. There is a small range above and below those two numbers that must be considered normal as well. For example, not all that many years ago it was possible to get 4.5% mortgages, bringing home ownership into line with incomes of first-time buyers. Will we see numbers like these in the years immediately ahead? Yes! You can be sure of that! The power of the norm in finance is very strong. Whenever - as in the 1970's - money rates get away from this central 3% to 5% range, incredibly strong natural forces tug and pull them back to such natural levels. You have seen that process at work since the early 1980's. It is not over yet! It will continue to unfold in 1988 to '95.

CHAPTER TWENTY-THREE

Write-Downs Of Latin Loans.

When CITICORP set aside $3,000,000,000 (Three billion dollars!) against Latin American loans that may never be paid - taking a write-off - another of my forecasts began to turn into reality! Here is that forecast:

"The other day we picked up a newspaper and saw a quote from a major Money-Center banker who said he was absolutely shocked and stunned by Brazil's sudden announcement that it was 'postponing' any interest payments on that nation's one hundred billion plus debt. He said that the Brazilian announcement had come without any warning... right out of the blue. My gosh! Can you believe that? We can't! It is our decided opinion that any major banker who could reach the latter stages of Winter, 1987 and still make a statement like that is incompetent to hold any position above doorman at his bank's home office!

"Frankly, we think Brazil did us all a big favor by ending the game of fraud and hypocrisy that has marked the big banks and their loans to such countries as Brazil!

"It is time that we face up to the reality here. We are not at all worried about these loans pulling down the American banks or the world economy. And neither should you be! There are more serious problems than whether or not Brazil finally admits it is a deadbeat country and our banks stop loaning them good money (after bad) to pretend that interest payments are being made. The banks have been hoarding billions of dollars in bad debt reserves since the crisis first hit the fan in 1982. You will be amazed at just how little damage will be done to the bank's financial strength by this 'postponement of interest payments.' The banks will now start to do what has to be done, namely writing down the debt to Brazil. The next time you hear someone involved in the Brazilian debt crisis say that he is 'absolutely shocked and stunned'... and that the 'announcement came without any warning... RIGHT OUT OF THE BLUE'... it will be a statement by a Brazilian political and / or financial leader. Only this man will be telling the truth! He will be shocked to the very core of his being to discover that what he thought was a brilliant 'get tough' bargaining position with the American banks is instead, a foolish move leading directly to a DEAD END!

"We will not go so far as to say that Brazil was "set up" by the New York banks. But we have to tell you... we think that is a very real possibility! Some of the U.S. regional banks have tried to cancel short-term trade loans... and pull their money back out of Brazil. (The Brazilian Government responded by telling their own banks to freeze all U.S. money on deposit there... and to pay it directly to the Brazilian Treasury if American banks tried to pull it back out of the country. Wow! What cheek!)

"You know, it is on days like this that we most miss the 1950's, when Ike was in the White House and life was a lot simpler. A raging communist led mob had Vice President Richard Nixon trapped in the U.S. Embassy in a major Latin American country... and there were fears for his life. Ike never even hesitated. He picked up a White House telephone right away (his temper was a fearsome thing to behold) and he called the President of that country directly. 'I have told my boy Dick Nixon to get in a car and drive to the airport,' Ike said. 'If anything should happen to him... if even his car should blow a tire and he should have an accident... if he should be harmed by a mob... well, I think you should know that I have our entire fleet of long-range S.A.C. bombers out on their runways now warming up their engines!' That President got the message loud and clear. Within minutes, their army's tanks had blocked off all exits and entrances on the highway to the airport... soldiers with machine guns had pushed the mobs back two blocks from the Embassy... and truckloads of heavily-armed soldiers had taken up position in front of and behind our Vice President's car as he sped to the airport. *That is the kind of respect we used to get from Latin America!*

"WE HAVE BEEN GRIPING FOR MONTHS ABOUT THE WAY BRAZIL HAS BEEN GETTING A FREE RIDE IN THE EXPORT-TO-AMERICA GAME. They sell us anything they feel like selling to us. We are prime suckers. Shoes? You want shoes? The American banks loaned them money to import the most modern shoe machinery from Italy. Then Brazil virtually took over the U.S. market, putting American manufacturers out of the business of producing shoes. (Some of the Americans have foolishly given up their U.S. plants and have begun to put their label on shoes from Brazil, making them vulnerable to a shut-down of the Brazilian connection.) And shoes are only one item on a long list of imports from Brazil. They have until now enjoyed wide-open access to our huge free market. BUT IT IS A ONE-WAY STREET. When we tried to sell them our autos and our computers we have found big signs up saying 'KEEP OUT - AND THIS MEANS YOU NORTH AMERICANS!' They are determined to protect their own domestic market, even when their stuff is lower quality and costs much more than what we offer to them.

"When anyone complained in America Brazil just issued a

blanket threat: 'You better watch out or we will stop paying interest on our loans!'

"So cocky did Brazil get that during the 1986 Brazilian Presidential election campaign, the Brazilian Government went on a populist consumer goods buying frenzy to make its people happy. Japanese goods were bought by the shipload! All the money that had been earned selling things to America, money that was supposed to be paid to our banks in interest, was instead blown. In fact, that was not even enough for the politicians. They sold out the 1987 sugar crop on the Futures Market in Chicago. Then they used the money and sugar to bake sweets for the people of Brazil... and told the Futures Market it could not deliver the sugar. Brazen! Incredibly brazen!

"Then the time came to pay the money to the banks. And they said: 'We don't have any money. If you want your interest, you will have to loan us the money to pay you. And while you are at it, we want some new loans...'" (End quote.)

At first, American bankers were tough. The U.S. banks set aside billions in reserves for bad debts. *But then the banks split ranks. Many financially-strong regional U.S. banks wrote off 100% of their Brazilian loan exposure. But several of the big and weaker New York banks backed away from such firmness. And as we go to press, they are once again talking about loaning money to Brazil to cover interest. That would be a mistake.*

What does all this mean to America? It means that when all is said and done, the loans to Latin America will eventually have to be written down. By half at first, then by more later. Dollar by dollar the money will evaporate. That will be one more force bringing DEFLATION to American finance!

Adrian Van Eck

CHAPTER TWENTY-FOUR

The Survival Of The Fittest!

I would like to talk with you about the American economy as I see it unfolding during 1989, 1990 and beyond. You hear a lot of *bad* predictions for this period. Others tell you that prices will now climb right up in a straight line... and often you hear that this *inflation will come at the same time that the U.S. economy sinks fast into a new depression. They are wrong!* As a matter of fact, I think people who say this is 1929 all over again have little idea what they are talking about.

1929? I have actual bound pages of a top-ranked financial newspaper from those years. In 1929 American exports were falling. Factory orders were weak and getting worse. Business was feeble.

BUT, DEAR READER, *LOOK AT 1988. FACTORY ORDERS ARE UP. EXPORTS ARE UP. IN FACT, AMERICAN MINES AND FACTORIES ARE OPERATING AT THEIR HIGHEST RATE OF CAPACITY IN SEVERAL YEARS.* JAPAN INC. IS INVESTING IN NEW FACTORIES. THESE NEW PLANTS COULD DIVERT BILLIONS OF DOLLARS NOW GOING OUT OF THE COUNTRY FOR EXPORTS... DIVERT IT BACK INTO AMERICA. *A BOOM IS JUST STARTING.* IT WILL FEATURE LOW INFLATION AND LOW INTEREST RATES. AND MOST *INVESTORS WILL MISS IT.* THEY WILL REFUSE TO BELIEVE WHAT IS HAPPENING.

Since Watergate and Vietnam, America has developed a massive *inferiority complex.* For twenty years the United States has refused to believe in its own destiny. You have to go back a way to find a comparable period. *My choice is the late 1930's. America then was still wallowing in a terrible period of self-doubt.* Franklin Delano Roosevelt had it right when he told America that all we had to fear was fear itself. But try as he might, this man who had overcome crippling polio himself could not infuse his own optimism into the United States. *In fact, it was really World War II that snapped America out of its mood of self-pity, fear and even self-loathing.*

Japan has an unbreakable respect for the United States as a result of that war. It does not choose to challenge us again for the world's supremacy. So they are going by the old rule: "If you can't lick them, join them." They are "joining" us! Japan Inc. is now infusing into the U.S. domestic economy billions of dollars for the creation of brand new state of the art industrial plants.

Meanwhile, Japanese companies are working with almost forty State Governments in America as they search out places to *build new factories here.* These plants will produce for two markets. One is the U.S. market. *The goods they manufacture will replace products now being imported.* The other market is Japan and the rest of the world. *Japan Inc. believes the U.S. is ideally located to ship goods in all directions - to Asia, Latin America, Europe and Africa. They already have plants inside the U.S. operating successfully and profitably. And they see these first plants as merely "toe-in-the-water" ventures. Now comes the BIG WAVE of Japanese investment.*

WHAT WILL THIS MEAN TO YOU IN 1988 TO 1995?

Wall Street has forgotten what real investment is all about. Too often investment is confused with trading in pieces of paper.

Back in the late 1800's, American business was mostly run by the men who had founded and built their own companies... and who owned large chunks of their own corporate stock. Some, like Henry Ford, owned their companies outright. Others, such as John D. Rockefeller, owned enough stock to allow them to dominate and control their companies as if they still owned all of them. *To a man, they saw investment as meaning SPENDING MONEY NOW ON PLANTS AND EQUIPMENT TO MAKE EVEN MORE MONEY LATER ON! Rockefeller started with a little refinery in Ohio.* It looked like a still in a wooden shed. Year after year he invested in bigger and better facilities. He never lost the personal touch. He would drive his employees without mercy to reach the goals he set for himself... and for them. In the middle of the night he would suddenly appear at one of his refineries and taste the product as it flowed into tanks. *"Too much sulfur!," he yelled at a careless crew at 2 a.m. on one memorable night. He was ruthless to those who let him down and generous to those who did not.* STANDARD OIL became ever-more efficient.

Rockefeller and those like him saw unmet needs... new opportunities. They worked hard and sunk every penny they could earn back into modernizing and expanding their operations. Thanks to them, America attracted millions of new citizens from all over the world... people who wanted their children and their children's children to have a better life than they could find in "The Old Country." And thanks to such entrepreneurs the per-capita standard of living of Americans improved five-fold between the end of the Civil War and the Spanish-

American War... from 1865 to '98. (From Abe Lincoln to Teddy Roosevelt's charge up San Juan Hill!) Trouble is, many of today's executives know almost nothing about this era of real investment in factories and mines and oil wells and new transportation. Luckily for us, men like General Douglas MacArthur did know the truth about those days. He saw to it that businessmen and politicians in Japan and Korea learned these facts... and adopted the same kind of *investment for growth policies. Now the circle is coming round again. This time it is America that is about to get lessons in our own Nineteenth Century business practices.* In those days market share meant survival. New machinery... new power sources... could and often did make factories obsolete when they were still capable of turning out usable products. Competition drove managers to do things they did not want to do. *Adam Smith's "Invisible Hand" did work.* And it was, as Smith proclaimed, *The Survival of the Fittest! YOU ARE NOW ABOUT TO SEE AGAIN THE KIND OF ALL-OUT COMPETITION FOR U.S. MARKET SHARE THAT FORCES MANAGERS TO DO THINGS THEY DO NOT WANT TO DO. YOU WILL SEE MORE NEW FACTORIES IN MORE NEW LOCATIONS THAN YOU HAVE SEEN IN YOUR ENTIRE LIFETIME. BEFORE THIS NEW GROWTH ERA RUNS ITS COURSE, YOU WILL NOT EVEN RECOGNIZE AMERICA COMPARED TO THE U.S OF TODAY!*

Oh yes, I know about reports suggesting that America

must now cut its standard of living sharply for the rest of this century (the next twelve years) in order to get the Federal budget deficit and the U.S. trade deficit under control. I have even seen new predictions of higher U.S. interest rates ahead. These people should get their heads out of their computers and *talk to folks in the real world*. Purchasing agents, for example. They now say they are "extremely optimistic about the outlook." *I BEG YOU TO TAKE NOTE OF THE WORD THEY USED: EXTREMELY OPTIMISTIC.* Not mildly optimistic. Not luke-warm optimistic. Not just a little bit optimistic. Definitely not the phrase so popular in recent years - "cautiously optimistic." *No, I am talking EXTREMELY optimistic. And this just since the October 19, 1987, market drop!* What is more, the purchasing agents say *there are signs that prices are flattening out. I love it when people in the real world ignore experts who predict a depression in America... a depression with high inflation yet!*

For too long, Wall Street has been dominated by a clique who talk nonsense. They eat lunch at the same restaurants, swap gossip, tell each other what they are thinking... and all end up saying almost the same thing. (A couple of brokerage firms have *broken from the pack* and are issuing forecasts that I find bold and accurate.) All too many economists have it in their mind that when business picks up, so do interest rates. They cheer bad news, saying it is bullish for bonds. I feel sorry for them. *How hard it will be for them to explain... or even to understand... when business turns good, gets better... gets even better... and interest rates go down!* They think the world began back in 1973. History from 1865 to '98 is irrelevant, they say. *Irrelevant? When we are about to relive it again in America?*

The period after the Civil War was marked by gentle deflation. As I have said, deflation forces companies to invest in the most modern plants and equipment. Deflation makes cost cutting a *necessity.* Deflation suggests that factories with a high ratio of debt to output could go belly up. Deflation turns executive thinking to thoughts of *survival...* their own and that of their company. Inflation makes managers complacent. That is why so many American factories grew *inefficient* during the long years on inflation... 1967 through 1981.

The Reagan Administration called its economic program "supply-side." *That is a good name. But we did not see a supply-side Boom in the U.S. during the mid-1980's. Quite the contrary. A large number of factories shut down.* Some are idle... still rusting away (or in mothballs). The supply-side of the equation was ignored and starved. Factories were moved to Mexico, Canada, Brazil, Korea, Taiwan, Japan, Hong Kong, Singapore and West Europe. But soon many new factories will be built in America. *Now you will see at last the supply-side "revolution" promised by Reaganomics seven years ago.* Corporations can now keep two dollars out of every three they earn. *That is a tremendous incentive to invest in new plants and equipment, even without an investment tax credit!* (Remember, there was no tax credit during Ike's eight years (1953 to '60). Yet investment in plants and equipment was *very* strong. Inflation ran about 1% a year. Interest rates were very low. Profits were high. *Real income growth was strong.* And stocks tripled!) And there is another incentive too. It is the certain knowledge that *only the fittest survive!*

CHAPTER TWENTY-FIVE

The Kondratieff Cycle.

Stalin threw the man who thought up the Kondratieff Cycle into Siberia. I now wonder how many of the folks who fool-around with this theory would back away from it if told that they would be "sent away" if and *when their nonsensical writings were exposed by the passage of time?* This theory cannot stand the application of common-sense.

The Kondratieff Cycle purports to show a BUSINESS CYCLE. *What it really shows is a PRICE CYCLE.* I agree with its 1980-date for the start of a new period of DEFLATION. But no DEPRESSION began then. Nor will one start in the next several years. DEFLATION, in history, has often forced businessmen to invest in modern plants and equipment to get their costs down, keep market share and survive. *BY FAR THE GREATEST BOOM in all U.S. history came during the long period of DEFLATION after the Civil War.* Kondratieff shows that as a long depression. Nonsense! Electricity, the telephone, the railroads to the West, steel mills and even the auto came in that period. America's standard of living grew 400% while prices were slipping an average of 1% a year. *Prepare yourself for a great Superboom with low interest rates. But inflation is doomed!*

Adrian Van Eck

CHAPTER TWENTY-SIX

Sound The General Alarm!

SOUND THE GENERAL ALARM! THE TWO YEAR RECESSION IN U.S. HOME BUILDING MAY HAVE HIT ITS BOTTOM. THE TWENTY-FOUR MONTH DECLINE WENT UNNOTICED FOR TWENTY-THREE MONTHS. ONLY IN EARLY 1988 DID IT CAPTURE WALL STREET'S ATTENTION, AS NEW HOUSING STARTS TUMBLED 16.2% FOR THE WORST SINGLE MONTH DECLINE IN THREE YEARS.

Ironically, this decline caused many people in Government, real estate and finance to act as if a major housing recession may have just begun. They tried to tie it to the October 19th stock market debacle.

They were wrong, wrong, wrong! The decline that had just been announced was possibly the *climax* of a two year "silent crash" in housing that began in January, 1986. During these two years new housing starts fell a third, from around two million units to a annual rate of 1.37 million units.

I have been pointing this decline out for several months... and warning each month that housing permits were staying ahead of and below new housing starts... suggesting each month that a lower LOW lay ahead. *But now permits have hit rock bottom... bedrock, or close to it.* They are at about the same level as new starts. That suggests to me that starts may be - and I believe are - groping for their own bottom. *Next comes the upturn!* Most people will be as shocked by the housing recovery as they were by the discovery that December, 1987, housing starts were all the way back down to levels not seen since the 1982 recession - five years earlier! That is because most people have not seen what I have seen and reported... *the much-anticipated recession may be partly over. It was hidden away inside the so-called recovery of 1983 to '86.* It showed up in different industries and in different places at different times... sort of like a rolling artillery barrage. Thus it went unseen by observers on a national level... who keep their eyes stuck up against their computer terminals... and never look out their windows to see what was going on in the real world! Autos for example, have been hurting. *And housing has been weak and getting weaker. Builders and real estate agents avoided the worst possible scenario (falling incomes) by concentrating on big, upscale housing.* That happens to be the one part of the housing market I think will be in *very serious trouble a year from now.* Major changes will come as the housing market now *shifts gears.* A much different mix of home building and home sales lie just ahead. So if you own one or more homes, finance real estate, sell it, develop it, manage it or are planning to invest in it... *listen up!*

There will be other rolling adjustments in the U.S. economy. The total pattern will be so confusing it will threaten to blow the fuses on computers used by most forecasters. Their "econometric models" are designed with the *false notion* that the 1970's were normal, and they keep looking for clues that the 1970's are coming back... complete with INFLATION! I have seen forecasts by real estate organizations of real estate inflation above 6% a year compounded, running on until the end of the next decade... which is to say, until the end of the century. (That would double real estate prices in twelve years.) I see absolutely no evidence of the kind of buying pressures or real estate shortages that would allow such a presumption. It is clearly based on the usual "establishment" predictions of continued declines in the U.S. dollar, steady increases in the prices of imported goods... plus a U.S. recession leading to wide-open money creation at the Fed and $300 billion to $400 billion a year

Federal deficits. Since I agree with none of these scary predictions, it should come as no surprise that *I scoff at the forecast of real estate inflation.* I THINK THE U.S. REAL ESTATE INDUSTRY WILL BE HARD-PRESSED TO HOLD PRICES CLOSE TO WHERE THEY ARE, ON THE AVERAGE, NATIONWIDE, BETWEEN NOW AND 1995. WHEN I SAY "HOLD THEM CLOSE TO WHERE THEY ARE," I MEAN *KEEP THEM FROM DECLINING 10% OR MORE,* ON THE AVERAGE FROM COAST TO COAST. (THAT AVERAGE COULD MASK WIDE VARIATIONS, WITH 20% DECLINES IN SOME KINDS OF PROPERTY IN SOME MARKETS AND ACTUAL *PRICE INCREASES* IN THE SAME OR DIFFERENT KINDS OF PROPERTY IN OTHER AREAS.) I will not digress here into the reasons for the threat of DEFLATION. My intent is to assure you that *DEFLATION, once loosed in society, can strike real estate too. It is not immune as so many real estate people now believe.*

If you do not believe that flat (zero gain) or minus 1% a year cost of living numbers can change the whole real estate industry, you are in for the same kind of culture shock that hit Wall Street brokerage firms on October 19, 1987. That, as you know, was the day *a whole generation of brokers and customers discovered that stock prices could go down as well as up.* In the same fashion, we have a generation of real estate professionals and home owners who often refuse to believe or even to discuss the notion that real estate prices can go down as well as up. *They can!*

If you are a student of American real estate history, you know that in each and every year in which long Booms in real estate prices turned into pricing downturns, a few tell-tale signs appeared. First, a backlog of unsold property began to build up on the market. Then prices turned flat. Both of those clues are already present now in the previously "hot" real estate markets on both the east and west coasts. Where just a year or two ago would-be buyers fought on front lawns, ripping up and holding "for sale" signs to stake a claim to a piece of property, now there is nearly a full-year's supply of homes for sale... all hanging over the market. As a result, buyers are turning shy... saying "we would like to look at more homes before we decide anything." Prices are soft. And when a deal is closed, it often falls through because the buyer cannot move his or her old home. After a while, panic sets in. People who desperately have to sell *do so* at whatever price they can get, even if they have to chop 10% off their first asking price.   Brokers and banks, wanting to preserve property values in neighborhoods and whole communities, *do all they can to hold prices up.* And the better the schools are... the better the city or town's reputation is... the better their chances are of *maintaining prices.* But still I am talking about zero gains in prices - A FLAT TREND! And that, I am quite convinced, is the best you can hope for in the next few years in such recently "hot" markets as Boston, New York, Northern

New Jersey and Washington D.C. in the East and both Los Angeles and San Francisco in the West. *SO WHERE THEN DO I SEE A HOUSING TURNABOUT TAKING ROOT IN 1988... AND WHY?*

Let me take the why first. The why is interest rates. At the National Association of Home Builders they have been predicting that 1988 will end with thirty-year fixed-rate mortgages at around 12%.

You are getting this 12% number or something close to it from a lot of sources. The Home Builders Association is a prestige outfit. Their word counts for a lot. There are not many people in the industry who would dare stick their neck out and take exception to a forecast by such a highly regarded organization. I would love to be able to say that I agree with the Association. I am not a contrarian. And I am not anti-establishment. When I agree with them, I say so loud and clear and then I praise their judgement. But this time I respectfully have to disagree. For you see, there is not the slightest chance that thirty-year mortgage money will be going for 12% by the end of 1988. Or 11%. Or 10%. Or 9%. I am not prepared to argue at this time with anyone who sees the rate for late 1988 at 7.5%. Because there are factors present now in the mortgage market that muddy the waters. But my own view is that *a thirty-year rate closer to 7% would be more in harmony with inflation, the supply of money and the demand for money!* American consumers are paying down some of their debt. These payments flow into banks and credit unions and finance companies and move right into the nationwide flow of money available for new investments. Meanwhile, the bloom is definitely off the rose in the junk bond business. Highly leveraged buy-outs are, in many cases, proving to be a trap for unwary speculators. Some of the worst losses are being suffered by Savings & Loans that should have been loaning money to real estate buyers... but instead bought the high yielding junk bonds seeking bigger returns. *Their setbacks are forcing other S&L's back into the housing market.*

THE NEW TAX LAWS MAKE THE DEDUCTION FOR INTEREST ON MORTGAGES LESS VALUABLE BY FAR THAN IT WAS IN 1980. And the glut of empty apartments in multiple housing units (the worst unrented ratio in twenty years) has kept rents from rising even as fast as moderate inflation in the past year. So you are not likely to see the kind of speculative home buying (for inflationary profit expectations) that you were seeing in 1983, 1984, 1985 and early 1986. I AM LOOKING AHEAD NOW TO THE MOST SENSIBLE, SOBER, RATIONAL AND PRACTICAL HOUSING MARKET IN QUITE A LONG TIME. *A real estate market such as I see ahead can yield solid returns.* What is more, so long as you are aware of what is coming - which is to say so long as you are willing to clamp your lips shut, *stay silent when almost everyone you know says that higher rates and bad times are coming - then you can pretty much count on making money and increasing your wealth in*

1988 to '95!

BUT YOU MUST REMEMBER: THESE COMING YEARS VERY DEFINITELY WILL NOT BE A CONTINUATION OR A REPLAY OF THE PAST TWO YEARS.

We have passed a juncture... a place where major roads cross. The real estate market had options available at that juncture. Now it has made its choice. It has *turned onto a new path... heading in a new direction.* What invariably happens at such a turn-off is that most of the "crowd" does not see or sense what is happening. They are too busy chatting about their own little private worlds to notice what is going on in the larger world outside. So they miss that turn-off. *They keep right on going straight ahead and eventually they will be stopped cold by roadblocks.* For they are moving along on a dead end road... a highway to nowhere... and when they reach the end, with their excess inventory of over-priced luxury homes in areas being impacted by the $33 billion cut in defense spending and thousands of layoffs in the financial, banking and legal fields... they will lose money. The cities and suburbs that have been "hot" places to build, buy, finance and sell homes and stores and offices are turning cold. A combination of anti-growth forces, over-building and too high prices are all going to catch up with them at once! The key to protecting yourself and making money is to *latch onto new factory placements.*

THERE IS LITTLE MYSTERY AS TO WHERE THE NEW *INDUSTRIAL BOOM* WILL COME IN AMERICA. IT IS HAPPENING ALREADY. *The key word is rural.* Some of the factories are being located in *rural states* themselves. Others are being spotted in *rural counties inside industrial states.* The picture here in New England is a microcosm of the national scene. Traffic in and immediately around bigger cities is so bad that getting to work and getting home from work is now taking too large a portion of the average person's day. Plus it is exacting a terrible emotional drain. People who moved to the suburbs - but still work in cities - find commuting burdensome. *Years ago, industry began to move to the suburbs to reach out for and attract workers.* It was then believed this would solve the problem. *Instead it made things worse.* People often live in one suburb but commute to another. So instead of one traffic surge into the city each morning and out of the city each night, we have multiple traffic surges that criss-cross in each direction, block each other's path and raise the level of anger and frustration. This, of course, is what leads to the ANTI-GROWTH movement that was born in California and has rapidly spread to major East Coast urban areas, including even FAST-GROWTH FLORIDA!

THE SOLUTION? Growth is moving away from cities... towards rural areas. And it is now leaping wider and faster. In Massachusetts growth has already jumped to open farm country in the central part of the state. It has pushed out southeastward towards Cape Cod. *And now it is leaping right over New Hampshire to land in Southern Maine.* As usual, it is upsetting some impacted locals and exciting others. But the trend is now too powerful to stop. The same thing is happening around every major city in America. The old idea of growth inside a beltway is being changed. Instead of marking a barrier to growth, the beltways are springboards - setting off and marking the start of the new frontiers of growth. Remember this: in the past twenty years much of America's marketing distrubution system has moved its headquarters and warehouses out to beltways... the better to circumnavigate and distribute to cities and their suburbs. Now these distribution centers have discovered themselves to be not on the outer fringes of markets but rather in the CENTER of new, evolving markets. They can easily reach and service customers in a band running one hour's driving time out and away from the beltways. The same is true of the workers who moved out to those beltways to get away from crowded city conditions. They can also commute a full hour in the other direction... and can often travel much further in terms of miles in that hour going away from cities than they have been able to do in driving for one hour into cities. But history suggests very strongly that housing will follow the new factories... with exurbia being the place where the housing boom of the 1990's will take shape.

Always bear in mind that the new factories are quite unlike those of the past. They are loaded with semi-automated, expensive equipment. Owners and managers will seek out educated and highly motivated workers. So states with reputations for good school systems and low-cost building sites are attracting attention from those who will be placing the factories. *DO NOT OVERLOOK THE COMEBACK POTENTIAL OF TEXAS IN THIS SCHEME OF THINGS! And one more thing: Wherever you are, get ready to buy BARGAINS when others fail to sense the above! Keep your debt low and your cash ready!!*

A Post Script:

Volcker And Greenspan.

If you are worried about Alan Greenspan, please don't be.

For several months I watched Paul Volcker twist and turn in a kind of personal agony. It was painful to watch. It must have been even more painful for him to live through.

First it was Donald Regan. To start with, Donald Regan liked to control people. A fact I began pointing out in August of 1985. He discovered Volcker was beyond his control and he tried to break the Fed Chairman. One effort was to propose that the Fed should come under the control of the Treasury. When that idea got nowhere he let it be known that he personally would make an ideal Fed Chairman. If there was s single positive result of the Iran / Contra mess, it was ending the possibility of Donald Regan becoming Fed Chairman.

So Volcker was free of Donald Regan. He still had the

curse of being called a "Carter man" by the populists in the White House. One by one as they sent new members to the Fed Board of Governors, he absorbed them... so that most of them now think, act and sound like him. He got the regional Fed banks to name Presidents who also think, sound and act like him. They have five of the twelve seats on the Federal Reserve Board Open Market Committee on a rotating basis - with Volcker clone E. Gerald Corrigan (President of the New York Fed) holding his seat "ex officio" on a regular basis. So the Board now reflects Volcker's ideas and will for years to come.

Volcker told the White House that the President would have to ask him to stay personally, if indeed the President wanted him to stay. This would have enhanced his status. The President balked... I think unwisely. So Volcker - a poor man after thirty-five years of devoted public service - was free of the burdens of the Fed. More power to him. (He was free to make millions in the private sector.)

Gold rose on the news. It need not have. Alan Greenspan will carry on similar policies with - if anything - even greater effort on boosting U.S. growth, raising productivity and ending inflation through stepped-up new capital investment! ALL OF THIS ASSURES LOW-INFLATION AND STRONGER-THAN-EXPECTED GROWTH!

Adrian Van Eck, America's Premier Economic Forecaster Since 1979, Says:

NOW HERE COMES A NEW SEVEN-YEAR SUPERBOOM, WITH AMERICA AGAIN INVESTING IN NEW PLANTS AND EQUIPMENT...

AND WITH THE DOW CROSSING 4000!

Adrian Van Eck

THE FINANCIAL RESEARCH CENTER
MONEY-FORECAST LETTER

Announcing:

If this guide helps you realize that it is possible to see ahead in the economy with quite remarkable accuracy, you may well ask how you can build on this guide's foundation. *The answer can be found on page 331.*

There you will find an offer for Adrian Van Eck's remarkable 32-page monthly Letter: *The Financial Research Center Money-Forecast Letter.*

This basic Letter, like this guide, is simple and so easy to read that no special education or training is needed to share Adrian Van Eck's insights into coming trends. He says it is all the result of actions and reactions by people and their money, both public and private. *For nine consecutive years he has forecast the future with an accuracy that astounds his readers.* Now you can try his basic Money-Forecast Letter! (See order form, facing.)

Pin your check to this order form and mail today to:
The Financial Research Center, Inc.,
Subscription Department,
5 Tripp Street, Framingham, MA 01701.

THE FINANCIAL RESEARCH CENTER
MONEY-FORECAST LETTER

Yes! Please enter my subscription today for Adrian's 32-page *basic* monthly Letter... **The FRC Money-Forecast Letter.** *My check is enclosed for the term I prefer: $152 (U.S.) for one year or $254 (U.S.) for two years.* I understand I get a pro-rata money-back guarantee.

Name (please print): _____

Address: _____

City: _____ State: _____ Zip: _____

AG/MF-101

Adrian Van Eck

GROUP RATES

A Way To Roll Your Costs Back To 1963:
ANNOUNCING SPECIAL GROUP SUBSCRIPTION RATES FOR
THE FRC MONEY-FORECAST LETTER ($51 per year each).

From time to time readers have asked us if there was perhaps a way they could get together in groups, at an office or a club or in an association, *and take several subscriptions together at one time, at a reduced rate.*

The idea has intrigued us. Just recently we did some cost analysis and came up with a set of rules and prices for such GROUP SUBSCRIPTIONS. We telephoned some of the people who had earlier expressed an interest in the idea and their response was very positive. So we have decided to try it for one year as an experiment. If it works out okay for all those concerned, *we will make it permanent.*

WE MUST INSIST ON A MINIMUM OF SIX PEOPLE IN A GROUP. FOR NOW WE WILL SET A MAXIMUM OF 100 PER GROUP, BUT THAT LIMIT MAY BE LIFTED LATER ON, AFTER WE GET EXPERIENCE WITH THE PLAN. *THE PRICE PER GROUP MEMBER WILL BE $51 (U.S.) PER YEAR. THE MINIMUM GROUP CHARGE IS THUS $306. One of these six orders can be your renewal or new subscription. The others can be anyone you choose to invite to join you in this money-saving group.*

We will mail the individual subscriptions to *individual homes or offices,* as you request. But we must have *one order from one person or company at one time.* If it is possible, we would prefer that you gather the $51 payments from the other five or more group members and lump the fee into a single check made payable to The FRC Money-Forecast Letter. We will refund pro-rata payments on request. But if a cancellation drops the number of group members below a total of six, we would have to cancel your group and refund all monies due pro-rata to the group.

Your Guide To Personal Wealth

Group Order Form:

Mail the form below today to:
The Financial Research Center, Inc.,
Subscription Department,
5 Tripp Street, Framingham, MA 01701.

Yes! Please enter my group subscription order for six or more individuals, *according to the rules set forth in your letter* for... **The FRC Money-Forecast Letter.** *Our annual payment is enclosed at the rate of $51 (U.S.) per member* - a minimum of $306 (U.S.) for a minimum of six group members.

If you continue this program in a year, send the renewal bill for the group to me at the address below. We can at that time, if we decide to stay on as a group subscriber, add or subtract names... *so long as we maintain a minimum group of six members.* I understand I get a pro-rata money-back guarantee.

Name (please print):

Address:

City: State: Zip:

AG/MF-GS1

Please print the names and addresses of the other five or more members. We will mail individual Letters to homes or offices, as you request. Please use an extra sheet of paper.

Adrian Van Eck

THE FINANCIAL RESEARCH CENTER INVESTMENT-PLANNING LETTER

A timely offer for our 16-page affiliated Investment-Planning Letter;

One year at $76 (U.S.)
Two years at $127 (U.S.)

Adrian Van Eck began publishing a supplementary Investment-Planning Letter in September, 1985, at a point we felt would prove to be a major market bottom. (It was!) It was designed for those investor / subscribers who wanted *guidance in applying the forecasts in our basic monthly Letter.*

Adrian's Investment-Planning Letter was practically alone, when the Dow was 1450 and falling, in predicting that the Dow would turn up explosively in late 1985... and reach 2000 by the end of 1986. (He was off by only five trading days!) In December of 1986, Adrian scoffed at the bearish forecasts so popular then and flat-out said the Dow would break out of the 1900 range and surge upward to record highs in early 1987. Sure enough the Dow exploded upward 800 points! That made Wall Street drop its guard. Everyone was sure the Dow would soar over 3000 by the end of 1988 - and then collapse. Again Adrian was almost alone. He warned that a TIME-OUT was coming.

Adrian said - when the market was right at its peak of 2700 - that the Dow would test 2000 before going up to 4000. Wall Street laughed at him - until the Dow fell 1000 points. Then everyone else announced a bear market had arrived. Not Adrian. He said that the market had simply corrected the first leg upward in a prolonged (thirteen-year) bull market. He predicts a peak of 4000 or higher by 1995. He also promises a giant bull market in *bonds!*

TO FIND OUT WHEN THIS WILL OCCUR, TAKE ADVANTAGE OF ADRIAN'S OFFER!

(See order form, over.)

Adrian Van Eck

Pin your check to this order form and mail today to:
The Financial Research Center, Inc.,
Subscription Department,
5 Tripp Street, Framingham, MA 01701.

THE FINANCIAL RESEARCH CENTER
INVESTMENT-PLANNING LETTER

Yes! Please enter my subscription today for your affiliated supplementary monthly Letter... **The FRC Investment-Planning Letter.** *My check is enclosed for the term I prefer: $76 (U.S.) for one year or $127 (U.S.) for two years.* I understand I get a pro-rata money-back guarantee.

Name (please print):

Address:

City: State: Zip:

AG/IP-101

Group Order Form:

Mail the form below today to:
The Financial Research Center, Inc.,
Subscription Department,
5 Tripp Street, Framingham, MA 01701.

Yes! Please enter my group subscription order for six or more individuals, *according to the rules set forth in your letter* for... **The FRC Investment-Planning Letter**. *Our annual payment is enclosed at the rate of $25.50 (U.S.) per member* - a minimum of $153 (U.S.) for a minimum of six group members.

If you continue this program in a year, send the renewal bill for the group to me at the address below. We can at that time, if we decide to stay on as a group subscriber, add or subtract names... *so long as we maintain a minimum group of six members*. I understand I get a pro-rata money-back guarantee.

Name (please print): _____

Address: _____

City: _____ State: _____ Zip: _____

AG/IP-GS1

Please print the names and addresses of the other five or more members. We will mail individual Letters to homes or offices, as you request. Please use an extra sheet of paper.

Adrian Van Eck

THE FINANCIAL RESEARCH CENTER
REAL ESTATE LETTER

ATTENTION: INVESTORS, BANKERS, BROKERS, MANAGERS, DEVELOPERS, CORPORATE PLANNERS, RENTERS, BUILDERS AND PROFESSIONAL ARCHITECTS.

You are cordially invited to become a subscriber to our 16-page monthly mini-Letter for those who buy, sell, finance, design, organize, produce or use real estate!

The editors of the Financial Research Center Federal Letter warned us months ago that "tax reform" was going to turn *real estate investing* upside-down in the United States of America.

Thus forewarned, we began to prepare our clients for the day when *everyone connected with real estate* in any of the capacities above would be asking each other WHAT IS GOING ON? WHERE? *...WHAT DOES IT MEAN FOR AMERICAN REAL ESTATE FOR 1988... 1989... 1990 AND BEYOND?* It has become obvious that changes are taking place in American real estate of such a magnitude and of such a *speed and duration,* that not a single man or woman connected with real estate in any way can hope to escape involvement. *Nothing like this complete turning upside-down of real estate has happened before in America in such a short time span!*

We decided to publish a Letter on real estate for one very simple reason: When we started our serious research on the subject *we sent several hundreds of dollars to subscribe to all the Letters we could find dealing with real estate.* NOT ONE OF THEM - NO MATTER WHAT THE PRICE - COULD ANSWER THE QUESTIONS WE HAD ABOUT REAL ESTATE FOR THIS YEAR, NEXT YEAR AND THE YEARS AFTER THAT.

We decided that if such a Letter did not exist, then we would research it... shape it... write it... edit it... publish it. *We were able... because of our size and the number of subscribers we knew we would attract at once after our announcement to keep our price down to a rock-bottom $76 (U.S.) a year.*

When you subscribe you will see why we now predict the *biggest* single year of building and selling single-family homes in U.S. history... *even bigger than the Boom years after World War Two,* when the G.I.'s came home and wanted a place of their own in the suburbs. *You will see why commercial real estate* (with tax shelters ended) *will revert back to the positive cash-flow INCOME investments* they used to be in the "Old Days" - changing all rules fast! You will see which areas will be hot... and which will be cold... (Some *surprises* here!)

(See order form, over.)

Pin your check to this order form and mail today to:
The Financial Research Center, Inc.,
Subscription Department,
5 Tripp Street, Framingham, MA 01701.

THE FINANCIAL RESEARCH CENTER
REAL ESTATE LETTER

Yes! Please enter my subscription today for your 16-page supplementary monthly mini-Letter... **The FRC Real Estate Letter.** *My check is enclosed for the term I prefer: $76 (U.S.) for one year or $127 (U.S.) for two years.* I understand I get a pro-rata money-back guarantee.

Name (please print): _____

Address: _____

City: _____ State: _____ Zip: _____

AG/RE-101

Your Guide To Personal Wealth

Group Order Form:

Mail the form below today to:
The Financial Research Center, Inc.,
Subscription Department,
5 Tripp Street, Framingham, MA 01701.

Yes! Please enter my group subscription order for six or more individuals, *according to the rules set forth in your letter* for... **The FRC Real Estate Letter.** *Our annual payment is enclosed at the rate of $25.50 (U.S.) per member* - a minimum of $153 (U.S.) for a minimum of six group members.

If you continue this program in a year, send the renewal bill for the group to me at the address below. We can at that time, if we decide to stay on as a group subscriber, add or subtract names... *so long as we maintain a minimum group of six members.* I understand I get a pro-rata money-back guarantee.

Name (please print):

Address:

City: State: Zip:

AG/RE-GS1

Please print the names and addresses of the other five or more members. We will mail individual Letters to homes or offices, as you request. Please use an extra sheet of paper.

Adrian Van Eck

THE FINANCIAL RESEARCH CENTER
FEDERAL LETTER

Special Announcement!

A FEW YEARS AGO, WHEN ALMOST NO ONE BELIEVED THE REAGAN ADMINISTRATION WAS REALLY SERIOUS ABOUT TAX REFORM, WE SAW THAT THEY WERE... AND WE FLAT-OUT PREDICTED THEY WOULD GET A MAJOR "TAX REFORM" BILL THROUGH CONGRESS. WHEN MAJOR INTEREST SURFACED IN OUR PREDICTIONS, WE BEGAN PUBLISHING A "FEDERAL TAX LETTER." FOR TWO YEARS WE CORRECTLY AND ACCURATELY PREDICTED WHAT WAS COMING IN "TAX REFORM." *Now most of the nation is finally digesting the Tax Reform Law and coming to realize that we were right all along* - in the guise of reform it stripped away deductions and would bring tax increases to corporations and upper-middle income businessmen and investors.

But where does America go from here? We see tremendous pressures being brought on the next President *to go along with new taxes.* Not an income tax... but any one of several other choices. Meanwhile, pressures from the deficit are going to bring unexpected and often unwanted budget cuts. (Yet at the same time, Congress is thinking up *new* ways to spend money!) It is impossible to ignore either the income or outgo side of the federal budget.

To look ahead for you and help you find the safest path through coming months, we have broadened our service. We now cover Federal spending, Federal taxes and Federal legislation affecting most of our clients, such as the 1988 Trade Bill. Our new name - THE FEDERAL LETTER - is intended to reflect this broader and more intense approach to your understanding the Federal government's impact on the economy... and on your personal profits and income - both before and after taxes!

(See order form, over.)

Adrian Van Eck

Pin your check to this order form and mail today to:
The Financial Research Center, Inc.,
Subscription Department,
5 Tripp Street, Framingham, MA 01701.

THE FINANCIAL RESEARCH CENTER
FEDERAL LETTER

Yes! Please enter my subscription today for your 16-page supplementary monthly mini-Letter... **The FRC Federal Letter.** *My check is enclosed for the term I prefer: $76 (U.S.) for one year or $127 (U.S.) for two years.* I understand I get a pro-rata money-back guarantee.

Name (please print): _____

Address: _____

City: _____ State: _____ Zip: _____

AG/F-101

Your Guide To Personal Wealth

Group Order Form:

Mail the form below today to:
The Financial Research Center, Inc.,
Subscription Department,
5 Tripp Street, Framingham, MA 01701.

Yes! Please enter my group subscription order for six or more individuals, *according to the rules set forth in your letter* for... **The FRC Federal Letter**. *Our annual payment is enclosed at the rate of $25.50 (U.S.) per member* - a minimum of $153 (U.S.) for a minimum of six group members.

If you continue this program in a year, send the renewal bill for the group to me at the address below. We can at that time, if we decide to stay on as a group subscriber, add or subtract names... *so long as we maintain a minimum group of six members*. I understand I get a pro-rata money-back guarantee.

Name (please print): _____

Address: _____

City: _____ State: _____ Zip: _____

AG/F-GS1

Please print the names and addresses of the other five or more members. We will mail individual Letters to homes or offices, as you request. Please use an extra sheet of paper.

Adrian Van Eck

THE NEW-JAPAN LETTER

When Federal Reserve Board Chairman Paul Volcker warned recently that America was on the verge of losing control of its own destiny, he was simply pointing out a truth that has been obvious to a lot of businessmen and investors for some months now!

Until the United States develops enough Puritan self-denial and self-discipline to keep spending inside the limits imposed by American earning and saving power, we have no choice but to go to Japan, hat in hand, and beg them either to invest in American property or loan us money. We have counted on Japan to buy some 40% of our new Treasury Bonds!

What is more, until American industry gears up with new computer-controlled factories and produces more of the product we need and want right here in the U.S.A., we must and will continue to import tens of billions of dollars worth of Japanese goods each year.

That means Japan Inc. - the nation we defeated in 1945 and occupied under General Douglas MacArthur - is now able to make key decisions concerning our business and finance. To a degree that the America of 1950 would have thought absolutely impossible, Japan has come much too close to being able to treat America as a virtual colony!

And if all of the above is not enough reason for you to be fully aware of fast-breaking new trends and developments, the rapid growth of American and Canadian holdings of foreign stocks - through new sector mutual funds and other means - makes it imperative that you know what is happening... and what is coming! The stock market in Japan has grown ten times as fast and gone ten times as high as the American market since 1949. This is attracting American investors. But is that wise? When we could not find answers to our own questions, we decided to investigate the subject in depth. And we asked businessmen and investors if they would like to share what we found; the response was strong and positive. So we are publishing a 16-page monthly Letter - THE NEW-JAPAN LETTER.

(See order form, over.)

Adrian Van Eck

Pin your check to this order form and mail today to:
The New-Japan Letter,
Subscription Department,
2 Tripp Street, Framingham, MA 01701.

THE NEW-JAPAN LETTER

Yes! Please enter my subscription today for your new 16-page monthly mini-Letter... **The New-Japan Letter.** *My separate check is enclosed for the term I prefer: $76 (U.S.) for one year or $127 (U.S.) for two years.* I understand I get a pro-rata money-back guarantee.

Name (please print): _____

Address: _____

City: _____ State: _____ Zip: _____

AG/NJ-101

Your Guide To Personal Wealth

Group Order Form:

Mail the form below today to:
The New-Japan Letter,
Subscription Department,
2 Tripp Street, Framingham, MA 01701.

Yes! Please enter my group subscription order for six or more individuals, *according to the rules set forth in your letter* for... **The New-Japan Letter.** *Our annual payment is enclosed at the rate of $25.50 (U.S.) per member* - a minimum of $153 (U.S.) for a minimum of six group members.

If you continue this program in a year, send the renewal bill for the group to me at the address below. We can at that time, if we decide to stay on as a group subscriber, add or subtract names... *so long as we maintain a minimum group of six members.* I understand I get a pro-rata money-back guarantee.

Name (please print): _____

Address: _____

City: _____ State: _____ Zip: _____

AG/NJ-GS1

Please print the names and addresses of the other five or more members. We will mail individual Letters to homes or offices, as you request. Please use an extra sheet of paper.

Adrian Van Eck

THE FINANCIAL RESEARCH CENTER
SPECIAL SITUATIONS LETTER

THE EDITOR OF THE FRC SPECIAL SITUATIONS LETTER, *HAVING DONE FAR BETTER THAN EITHER THE DOW JONES INDUSTRIAL AVERAGE OR THE AVERAGE FOR OTC STOCKS IN HIS FIRST TWO YEARS,* HAS NOW OUTDONE HIMSELF, IN ADRIAN'S OPINION. AFTER WEEKS OF SEARCHING, SIFTING AND EXAMINING OTC STOCKS WITH STRONG POTENTIAL, *HE HAS COME UP WITH A STOCK - IN HIS NEW MONTHLY REPORT - THAT BRINGS ADRIAN'S OWN FORECASTS VIVIDLY TO LIFE. WE URGE YOU TO SEND FOR OUR SPECIAL SITUATIONS LETTER TODAY... AND GET OUR LATEST REPORT FREE OF EXTRA COST AS YOUR COMPLIMENTARY GET-ACQUAINTED BONUS.*

In March, 1986, we proudly announced our new Special Situations Letter. And we installed as Executive Editor a gifted and sensitive veteran of service as editor at a very large and very important New York City investment advisory publishing firm. *Then we told you how pleased we were to report that he had gotten so that he could take seriously Adrian Van Eck's own, shall we say eccentric, way of looking at the economy.* (His very first stock selection rose 150% in ten months.)

Now our Special Situations editor has pleased Adrian mightily again. He has come up with a very low-priced stock that sure does look to us like it is on its way to being a real winner. He is featuring this little-known but well-run and importantly-backed SPECIAL SITUATION in a report that you will receive when you subscribe. We think this low-priced stock can triple.

(See order form, over.)

Adrian Van Eck

Pin your check to this order form and mail today to:
The Financial Research Center, Inc.,
Subscription Department,
5 Tripp Street, Framingham, MA 01701.

THE FINANCIAL RESEARCH CENTER
SPECIAL SITUATIONS LETTER

Yes! Please enter my subscription today for your monthly Letter... **The FRC Special Situations Letter.** *My check is enclosed for the term I prefer: $304 (U.S.) for one year or $508 (U.S.) for two years.* Please rush me as a complimentary get-acquainted bonus, your report featuring a low-priced stock that you believe could triple. I understand I get a pro-rata money-back guarantee.

Name (please print): _____

Address: _____

City: _____ State: _____ Zip: _____

AG/SS-101